THE HUMANISTIC TRADITION

THIRD EDITION

6

The Global Village of the Twentieth Century

THE HUMANISTIC TRADITION

THIRD EDITION

6 The Global Village of the Twentieth Century

Gloria K. Fiero

McGraw Hill

New York St. Louis San Francisco Auckland Bogotá Caracas
Lisbon London Madrid Mexico City Milan Montreal New Delhi
San Juan Singapore Sydney Tokyo Toronto

McGraw-Hill

A Division of The **McGraw·Hill** *Companies*

THE HUMANISTIC TRADITION, BOOK 6

Copyright © 1998 by The McGraw-Hill Companies, Inc.
Previous editions © 1995, 1992 by William C. Brown Communications, Inc.
All rights reserved. Except as permitted under the United States Copyright Act
of 1976, no part of this publication may be reproduced or distributed in any
form or by any means, or stored in a data base or retrieval system, without
the prior written permission of the publisher.

Permissions Acknowledgments appear on page 168,
and on this page by reference.

Library of Congress Catalog Card Number: 97–071266

ISBN 0–697–34073–2

Editorial Director *Phillip Butcher*
Senior Sponsoring Editor *Cynthia Ward*
Director of Marketing *Margaret Metz*
National Sales Manager *Jerry Arni*

This book was designed and produced by
CALMANN & KING LTD
71 Great Russell Street, London WC1B 3BN

Editor *Ursula Payne*
Designer *Karen Osborne*
Cover Designer *Karen Stafford*
Timeline Designer *Richard Foenander*
Picture Researcher *Carrie Haines*
Maps by Oxford Illustrators Ltd.

Developmental Editing by M. J. Kelly for McGraw-Hill

Typeset by Fakenham Photosetting, Norfolk
Printed in Hong Kong

10 9 8 7 6 5 4 3 2 1

http://www.mhhe.com

Front cover
Main image: Marisol Escobar, detail of *Women and Dog*, 1964. Wood, plaster, synthetic
polymer, and miscellaneous items, full assemblage 72¼ × 73 × 30¹⁵⁄₁₆ in. Collection of
the Whitney Museum of American Art, New York. Purchase, with funds from the Friends
of the Whitney Museum of American Art (64.17 a–g). Photo: Robert E. Mates, N.J.
© Marisol Escobar/DACS, London VAGA, New York 1997.
Insets: (top) Marie-Louise-Elisabeth Vigée-Lebrun, detail of *Marie Antoinette*,
1788. Oil on Canvas, full image 12 ft. 1½ in. × 6 ft. 3½ in. Musée de Versailles.
Giraudon/Art Resource, New York.
(center) Charles-Henri-Joseph Cordier, detail of *African in Algerian Costume*,
ca. 1856–1857. Bronze and onyx, complete sculpture 37¾ × 26 × 14 in.
Musée d'Orsay, Paris. Photo: © R.M.N., Paris.
(bottom) Toshusai Sharaku, *Bust Portrait of the Actor Segawa Tomisaburo as
Yadorigi, the Wife of Ogishi Kurando*, 1794–1795. Woodblock print, 14½ × 9¼ in.
Photograph © 1997, The Art Institute of Chicago, All Rights Reserved.
Clarence Buckingham Collection, 1928.1056.

Frontispiece
Niki de Saint Phalle, *Black Venus*, 1965–1967. Painted polyester, 110 × 35 × 24 in.
Collection of the Whitney Museum of American Art, New York.
Gift of the Howard and Jean Lipman Foundation, Inc. 68.73.
Photograph copyright © 1997 Whitney Museum of American Art.
Photography by Sandak, Inc./Division of Macmillan Publishing Company.
© ADAGP, Paris and DACS, London 1997.

Series Contents

Book 6
Contents

35 The Quest for Meaning   70

PART II

The Postmodern Turn   97

36 Identity and Liberation   99

MUSIC LISTENING SELECTIONS

MAPS

Preface

"It's the most curious thing I ever saw in all my life!"exclaimed Lewis Carroll's Alice in Wonderland, as she watched the Cheshire Cat slowly disappear, leaving only the outline of a broad smile. "I've often seen a cat without a grin, but a grin without a cat!" A student who encounters an ancient Greek epic, a Yoruba mask, or a Mozart opera—lacking any context for these works—might be equally baffled. It may be helpful, therefore, to begin by explaining how the artifacts (the "grin") of the humanistic tradition relate to the larger and more elusive phenomenon (the "cat") of human culture.

The Humanistic Tradition and the Humanities

In its broadest sense, the term *humanistic tradition* refers to humankind's cultural legacy—the sum total of the significant ideas and achievements handed down from generation to generation. This tradition is the product of responses to conditions that have confronted all people throughout history. Since the beginnings of life on earth, human beings have tried to ensure their own survival by achieving harmony with nature. They have attempted to come to terms with the inevitable realities of disease and death. They have endeavored to establish ways of living collectively and communally. And they have persisted in the desire to understand themselves and their place in the universe. In response to these ever-present and universal challenges—*survival, communality,* and *self-knowledge*—human beings have created and transmitted the tools of science and technology, social and cultural institutions, religious and philosophic systems, and various forms of personal expression, the sum total of which we call culture.

Even the most ambitious survey cannot assess all manifestations of the humanistic tradition. This book therefore focuses on the creative legacy referred to collectively as *the humanities*: literature, philosophy, history (in its literary dimension), architecture, the visual arts (including photography and film), music, and dance. Selected examples from each of these disciplines constitute our *primary sources*. Primary sources (that is, works original to the age that produced them) provide first-hand evidence of human inventiveness and ingenuity. The primary sources in this text have been chosen on the basis of their authority, their beauty, and their enduring value. They are, simply stated, the great works of their time and, in some cases, of all time. Universal in their appeal, they have been transmitted from generation to generation. Such works are, as well, the landmark examples of a specific time and place: They offer insight into the ideas and values of the society in which they were produced. The drawings of Leonardo da Vinci, for example, reveal a passionate determination to understand the operations and functions of nature. And while Leonardo's talents far exceeded those of the average individual of his time, his achievements may be viewed as a mirror of the robust curiosity that characterized his time and place—the age of the Renaissance in Italy. *The Humanistic Tradition* surveys such landmark works, but joins "the grin" to "the cat" by examining them within their political, economic, and social contexts.

The Humanistic Tradition explores a living legacy. History confirms that the humanities are integral forms of a given culture's values, ambitions, and beliefs. Poetry, painting, philosophy, and music are not, generally speaking, products of unstructured leisure or indulgent individuality; rather, they are tangible expressions of the human quest for the good (one might even say the "complete") life. Throughout history, these forms of expression have served the domains of the sacred, the ceremonial, and the communal. And even in the waning days of the twentieth century, as many time-honored traditions have come under assault, the arts retain their power to awaken our imagination in the quest for survival, communality, and self-knowledge.

The Scope of the Humanistic Tradition

The humanistic tradition is not the exclusive achievement of any one geographic region, race, or class of human beings. For that reason, this text assumes a global and multicultural rather than exclusively Western perspective. At the same time, Western contributions are emphasized, first, because the audience for these books is predominantly Western, but also because in recent centuries the West has exercised a dominant influence on the course and substance of global history. Clearly, the humanistic tradition belongs to all of humankind, and the best way to understand the Western contribution to that tradition is to examine it in the arena of world culture.

As a survey, *The Humanistic Tradition* cannot provide an exhaustive analysis of our creative legacy. The critical reader will discover many gaps. Some aspects of culture that receive extended examination in traditional Western humanities surveys have been pared down to make room for the too often neglected contributions of Islam, Africa, and Asia. This book is necessarily selective—it omits many major figures and treats others only briefly. Primary sources are arranged, for the most part, chronologically, but they are presented as manifestations of *the informing ideas of the age* in which they were produced. The intent is to examine the evidence of the humanistic tradition thematically and topically, rather than to compile a series of mini-histories of the individual arts.

Studying the Humanistic Tradition

To study the creative record is to engage in a dialogue with the past, one that brings us face to face with the values of our ancestors, and, ultimately, with our own. This dialogue is (or should be) a source of personal revelation and delight; like Alice in Wonderland, our strange, new encounters will be enriched according to the degree of curiosity and patience we bring to them. Just as lasting friendships with special people are cultivated by extended familiarity, so our appreciation of a painting, a play, or a symphony depends on close attention and repeated contact. There are no shortcuts to the study of the humanistic tradition, but there are some techniques that may be helpful. It should be useful, for instance, to approach each primary source from the triple perspective of its *text*, its *context*, and its *subtext*.

The Text: The *text* of any primary source refers to its *medium* (that is, what it is made of), its *form* (its outward shape), and its *content* (the subject it describes). All literature, for example, whether intended to be spoken or read, depends on the medium of words—the American poet Robert Frost once defined literature as "performance in words." Literary form varies according to the manner in which words are arranged. So poetry, which shares with music and dance rhythmic organization, may be distinguished from prose, which normally lacks regular rhythmic pattern. The main purpose of prose is to convey information, to narrate, and to describe; poetry, by its freedom from conventional patterns of grammar, provides unique opportunities for the expression of intense emotions. Philosophy (the search for truth through reasoned analysis) and history (the record of the past) make use of prose to analyze and communicate ideas and information. In literature, as in most kinds of expression, content and form are usually interrelated. The subject matter or the form of a literary work determines its *genre*. For instance, a long narrative poem recounting the adventures of a hero constitutes an *epic*, while a formal, dignified speech in praise of a person or thing constitutes a *eulogy*.

The visual arts—painting, sculpture, architecture, and photography—employ a wide variety of media, such as wood, clay, colored pigments, marble, granite, steel, and (more recently) plastic, neon, film, and computers. The form or outward shape of a work of art depends on the manner in which the artist manipulates the formal elements of color, line, texture, and space. Unlike words, these formal elements lack denotative meaning. The artist may manipulate form to describe and interpret the visible world (as in such genres as portraiture and landscape painting); to generate fantastic and imaginative kinds of imagery; or to create imagery that is nonrepresentational—without identifiable subject matter. In general, however, the visual arts are spatial, that is, they operate and are apprehended in space.

The medium of music is sound. Like literature, music is durational: It unfolds over the period of time in which it occurs. The formal elements of music are melody, rhythm, harmony, and tone color—elements that also characterize the oral life of literature. As with the visual arts, the formal elements of music are without symbolic content, but while literature, painting, and sculpture may imitate or describe nature, music is almost always nonrepresentational—it rarely has meaning beyond the sound itself. For that reason, music is the most difficult of the arts to describe in words. It is also (in the view of some) the most affective of the arts. Dance, the artform that makes the human body itself a medium of expression, resembles music in that it is temporal and performance-oriented. Like music, dance exploits rhythm as a formal tool, but, like painting and sculpture, it unfolds in space as well as time.

In analyzing the text of a work of literature, art, or music, we ask how its formal elements contribute to its meaning and affective power. We examine the ways in which the artist manipulates medium and form to achieve a characteristic manner of execution and expression that we call *style*. And we try to determine the extent to which a style reflects the personal vision of the artist and the larger vision of his or her time and place. Comparing the styles of various artworks from a single era, we may discover that they share certain defining features and characteristics. Similarities (both formal and stylistic) between, for instance, golden age Greek temples and Greek tragedies, between Chinese lyric poems and landscape paintings, and between postmodern fiction and pop sculpture, prompt us to seek the unifying moral and aesthetic values of the cultures in which they were produced.

The Context: We use the word *context* to describe the historical and cultural environment. To determine the context, we ask: In what time and place did the artifact originate? How did it function within the society in which it was created? Was the purpose of the piece decorative, didactic, magical, propagandistic? Did it serve the religious or political needs of the community? Sometimes our answers to these questions are mere guesses. Nevertheless, understanding the function of an artifact often serves to clarify the nature of its form (and vice versa). For instance, much of the literature produced prior to the fifteenth century was spoken or sung rather than read; for that reason, such literature tends to feature repetition and rhyme, devices that facilitate memorization. We can assume that literary works embellished with frequent repetitions, such as the *Epic of Gilgamesh* and the Hebrew Bible, were products of an oral tradition. Determining the original function of an artwork also permits us to assess its significance in its own time and place: The paintings on the walls of Paleolithic caves, which are among the most compelling animal illustrations in the history of world art, are not "artworks" in the modern sense of the term but, rather, magical signs that accompanied hunting rituals, the performance of which was essential to the survival of the community. Understanding the relationship between text and context is one of the principal concerns of any inquiry into the humanistic tradition.

The Subtext: The *subtext* of the literary or artistic object refers to its secondary and implied meanings. The subtext embraces the emotional or intellectual messages embedded in, or implied by, a work of art. The epic poems of the ancient Greeks, for instance, which glorify prowess and physical courage in battle, suggest that such virtues are exclusively male. The state portraits of the seventeenth-century French ruler Louis XIV carry the subtext of unassailable and absolute power. In our own century, Andy Warhol's serial adaptations of soup cans and Coca-Cola bottles offer wry commentary on the supermarket mentality of postmodern American culture. Identifying the implicit message of an artwork helps us to determine the values and customs of the age in which it was produced and to assess those values against others.

Beyond *The Humanistic Tradition*

This book offers only small, enticing samples from an enormous cultural buffet. To dine more fully, students are encouraged to go beyond the sampling presented at this table; and for the most sumptuous feasting, nothing can substitute for first-hand experience. Students, therefore, should make every effort to supplement this book with visits to art museums and galleries, concert halls, theaters, and libraries. *The Humanistic Tradition* is designed for students who may or may not be able to read music, but who surely are able to cultivate an appreciation of music in performance. The clefs that appear in the text refer to the forty-five Music Listening Selections found on two accompanying cassettes,

available from the publishers. Lists of suggestions for further reading are included at the end of each chapter, while a selected general bibliography of humanities resources appears at the end of each book.

The Third Edition

On the threshold of the new millennium, this third edition of *The Humanistic Tradition* brings increased attention to the theme of global cross-cultural encounter and, in particular, to the interaction of the West with the cultures of Islam, East Asia, and Africa. In this connection, literary selections by Ibn Battuta, Shen Fu, Iqbal, and other non-Western writers have been added. New Western readings include selections from the works of Hernán Cortés, Jonathan Swift, Mary Shelley, Ralph Waldo Emerson, Alice Walker, Malcolm X, and Seamus Heaney. Japanese theater, the transatlantic slave trade, Islamic literature, and contemporary computer art are among the topics that receive expanded treatment in this edition.

The third edition also features two new study aids, both of which are designed to facilitate an appreciation of the arts in relation to their time and place: *Science and Technology Boxes*, which appear throughout the chapters, list key scientific and technological developments that have directly or indirectly affected the history of culture. *Locator Maps* (keyed to the map that appears on p. xii) assist readers in linking specific cultural events with the geographic region in which they occurred. This edition also expands on the number of color illustrations and large color maps, renumbers the Readings by book, and updates the Suggestions for Reading and Selected General Bibliography. Finally, in the transcription of the Chinese language, the older Wade-Giles system has been replaced by the more modern Hanyu Pinyin.

A Note to Instructors

The key to successful classroom use of *The Humanistic Tradition* is *selectivity*. Although students may be assigned to read whole chapters that focus on a topic or theme, as well as complete works that supplement the abridged readings, the classroom should be the stage for a selective treatment of a single example or a set of examples. The organization of this textbook is designed to emphasize themes that cut across geographic boundaries—themes whose universal significance prompts students to evaluate and compare rather than simply memorize and repeat lists of names and places. In an effort to assist readers in achieving global cultural literacy, every effort has been made to resist isolating (or "ghettoizing") individual cultures and to avoid the inevitable biases we bring to our evaluation of relatively unfamiliar cultures.

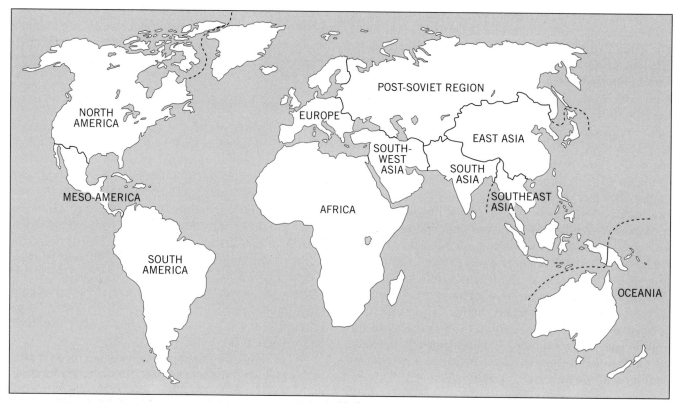

Keymap Indicating Areas Shown as White Highlights on the Locator Maps.

Acknowledgments

Writing *The Humanistic Tradition* has been an exercise in humility. Without the assistance of learned friends and colleagues, assembling a book of this breadth would have been an impossible task. James H. Dormon read all parts of the manuscript and made extensive and substantive editorial suggestions; as his colleague, best friend, and wife, I am most deeply indebted to him. I owe thanks to the following faculty members of the University of Southwestern Louisiana: for literature, Allen David Barry, Darrell Bourque, C. Harry Bruder, John W. Fiero, Emilio F. Garcia, Doris Meriwether, and Patricia K. Rickels; for history, Ora-Wes S. Cady, John Moore, Bradley Pollack, and Thomas D. Schoonover; for philosophy, Steve Giambrone and Robert T. Kirkpatrick; for geography, Tim Reilly; for the sciences, Mark Konikoff and John R. Meriwether; and for music, James Burke and Robert F. Schmalz.

The following readers and viewers generously shared their insights in matters of content and style: Michael K. Aakhus (University of Southern Indiana), Vaughan B. Baker (University of Southwestern Louisiana), Katherine Charlton (Mt. San Antonio Community College), Bessie Chronaki (Central Piedmont Community College), Debora A. Drehen (Florida Community College—Jacksonville), Paula Drewek (Macomb Community College), William C. Gentry (Henderson State University), Kenneth Ganza (Colby College), Ellen Hofman (Highline Community College), Burton Raffel (University of Southwestern Louisiana), Frank La Rosa (San Diego City College), George Rogers (Stonehill College), Douglas P. Sjoquist (Lansing Community College), Howard V. Starks (Southeastern Oklahoma State University), Ann Wakefield (Academy of the Sacred Heart—Grand Coteau), Sylvia White (Florida Community College—Jacksonville), and Audrey Wilson (Florida State University).

In the preparation of the third edition, I have benefited from the suggestions and comments generously offered by numerous readers, only some of whom are listed below. Rodney D. Boyd (Collin County Community College), Arnold Bradford (Northern Virginia Community College), Patricia L. Brace (Southwest State University), Orville V. Clark (University of Wisconsin—Green Bay), Carolyn Copeland (Bethune Cookman), Susan Cornett (St. Petersburg Junior College—Tarpon Center), Anthony M. Coyne (University of North Carolina), Kenneth Ganza (Colby College), Margaret Hasselman (Virginia Polytechnic Institute and State University), Victor Hébert (Fayetteville State University), Ellen Hofmann (Highline Community College), Enid Housty (Hampton University), Mabel Khawaja (Hampton University), James W. Mock (University of Central Oklahoma), Lewis Parkhill (East Central University), Joseph G. Rahme (University of Michigan—

Flint), David Simmons (Brevard Community College), J. Paul De Vierville (St. Phillip's College), Bertha L. Wise (Oklahoma City Community College), and Jon Young (Fayetteville State University). My gratitude goes to Julia Girouard, who provided research assistance for the third edition, and to Professor Timothy Reilly, who kindly helped with the Locator Keymap. I am indebted to Darrell Bourque for his thoughtful assistance on

materials related to AIDS and for his insights on the subject of postmodernism, and to Robert A. Wiggs, who shared with me invaluable information for chapter 37 concerning structural systems and the topology of space.

The burden of preparing the third edition has been lightened by the assistance of M. J. Kelly, Developmental Editor, and by the editorial vigilance of Ursula Payne at Calmann & King.

SUPPLEMENTS FOR THE INSTRUCTOR AND THE STUDENT

A number of useful supplements are available to instructors and students using *The Humanistic Tradition*. Please contact your sales representative or call 1-800-338-3987 to obtain these resources, or to ask for further details.

Audiocassettes
Two ninety-minute audiocassettes containing a total of forty-five musical selections have been designed exclusively for use with *The Humanistic Tradition*. Cassette One corresponds to the music listening selections discussed in books 1–3 and Cassette Two contains the music in books 4–6. Each selection on the cassettes is discussed in the text and includes a voice introduction for easier location. Instructors may obtain copies of the cassettes for classroom use by calling 1-800-338-3987. Individual cassettes may be purchased separately; however, upon the request of instructors who place book orders, Cassette One or Two can be packaged with any of the six texts, so that students may use the musical examples *along with* the text.

Slide Sets
A set of fifty book-specific slides is available to qualified adopters of *The Humanistic Tradition*. These slides have been especially selected to include many of the less well-known images in the books, and they will be a useful complement to your present slide resources. A larger set of two hundred book-specific slides is available for purchase. For more information, contact your McGraw-Hill representative.

Instructor's Resource Manual
The Instructor's Resource Manual is designed to assist instructors as they plan and prepare for classes. Course outlines and sample syllabuses for both semester and quarter systems are included. The chapter summaries emphasize key themes and topics that give focus to the primary source readings. The study questions for each chapter may be removed and copied as handouts for student discussion or written assignments. A Test Item File follows each chapter along with a correlation list that directs instructors to the appropriate music examples, slides, transparencies, and software sections of the other supplements. A list of suggested videotapes, recordings, videodiscs, CD-ROMs, and their suppliers is included.

MicroTest III
The questions in the Test Item File are available on MicroTest III, a powerful but easy-to-use test generating program. MicroTest is available for DOS, Windows, and Macintosh personal computers. With MicroTest, an instructor can easily select the questions from the Test Item File and print a test

and answer key. You can customize questions, headings, and instructions and add or import questions of your own.

Humanities Transparencies
A set of seventy-one acetate transparencies is available with *The Humanistic Tradition*. These show examples of art concepts, architectural styles, art media, maps, musical notation, musical styles, and musical elements.

Culture 3.0 CD-ROM
Culture 3.0 CD-ROM is a unique Macintosh reference tool that emphasizes the interaction of varied disciplines. It contains 40 historical maps, 120 signature melodies, 50,000 hypertext links, and 170 essays on topics ranging from Greek gods and goddesses to the Cold War. Thirty-two CultureGrids are arranged chronologically from the biblical era to the twentieth century, organizing people, places, and events by country, discipline, and generation. (*Culture 2.0* is also available in a seven-disk set for Mac and IBM.)

Student Study Guides, Volumes 1 and 2
Written by Gloria K. Fiero, two new Student Study Guides are now available to help students gain a better understanding of subjects found in *The Humanistic Tradition*. Volume 1 accompanies books 1–3 and Volume 2 accompanies books 4–6. Each chapter contains: a Chapter Objective; a Chapter Outline; Key Terms, Names, and Dates; Vocabulary Building; Multiple Choice Questions; and Essay Questions. Many chapters also contain a Visual/Spatial Exercise and Bonus Material. At the end of each Part, Synthesis material helps students draw together ideas from a set of chapters.

The Art Historian CD-ROM, Volumes 1 and 2
This flexible two-volume series on dual platform (Mac and Windows) CD-ROMs is designed to supplement introductory level art history education. Volume 1 covers ancient and medieval art, and Volume 2 covers Renaissance to modern art. The images included on the CD were gathered from over three hundred museums, galleries, and private collections throughout the world, and the text and test questions were written by current scholars from universities across the United States. With *The Art Historian*, students may listen to multimedia presentations, review full-color high-resolution images, and test their knowledge with flashcards and essay questions. *The Art Historian* is flexible, allowing students to take notes, compare two images on the screen at the same time, and create personalized collections of images for study and review. With *The Art Historian*, we place the power of multimedia *and* art at your fingertips.

	To 1900	1905	1915	1925	1935
WORLD EVENTS	Planck: quantum theory Wright Brothers: air flight Edison: moving pictures	Einstein: special theory of relativity Ford: motorcar Wireless radio	— WORLD WAR I — 8 million die Russian Revolution 1917 Nationalist Revolution in China 1911	The Great Depression Heisenberg: principle of uncertainty	WORLD Stalin becomes Soviet dictat 1930 Nazi revolution in Germany Hitler becomes chancello 1933 Gandhi: decolonization of India
LITERATURE AND PHILOSOPHY	Freud: *Interpretation of Dreams*; *Totem and Taboo*; *Civilization and Its Discontents*	*Futurist Manifesto* IMAGISTS Pound: poems from *Personae* *Imagist Manifesto* 1913 Frost: "The Road Not Taken"	Lenin: *The State and Revolution* Joyce: *Ulysses* Proust: *Remembrance of Things Past* Kafka: *Metamorphosis*; *The Trial* WORLD WAR I POETRY AND PROSE Owen; Yeats; Remarque: *All Quiet on the Western Front*	Woolf: "A Room of One's Own" Hitler: *Mein Kampf* Tagore: "The Man Had No Useful Work" e.e. cummings: "she being Brand" O'Neill: *Mourning Becomes Electra* Stanislavsky: method acting Eliot: "Love Song of J. Alfred Prufrock"; "The Waste Land"	Wright: *Native Son*; *Ethics of Living Jim Crow* Wittgenstein: linguistic philosophy Camus: *The Stranger* Huxley: *Brave New World* ISLAMIC POETRY Anwar and Iqbal HARLEM RENAISSAN Hughes: "Theme English B" Brooks: "We Rea Cool"
VISUAL ARTS AND ARCHITECTURE	CUBISM Picasso: *Les Demoiselles d'Avignon* Braque: *Still Life on a Table* Méliès: *A Trip to the Moon* Porter: *The Great Train Robbery*	FAUVISM Matisse: *The Dance* ABSTRACTION IN SCULPTURE Brancusi: *Bird in Space*	FUTURISM Balla: *Street Light* Boccioni: *Unique Forms of Continuity in Space* Duchamp: *Nude Descending a Staircase* EXPRESSIONISM Munch: *The Scream* Kirchner: *Street, Berlin* NONOBJECTIVE ART Kandinsky: *Painting No. 198* Malevich: *White on White* Mondrian: *Composition in Red, Yellow, Blue, and Black* CONSTRUCTIVISM Popova: Set design for *Le Cocu magnifique* Griffith: *Birth of a Nation* Wright: Robie House	METAPHYSICAL ART de Chirico: *Nostalgia of the Infinite* FANTASY Chagall: *I and the Village* DADA MOVEMENT Duchamp: *L.H.O.O.Q* Höch: *Cut with the Kitchen Knife* Ernst: *Two Ambiguous Figures* Grosz: *Fit for Active Service* SURREALISM Breton: *Surrealist Manifesto* Miró: *Person Throwing a Stone* Klee: *Fish Magic* Magritte: *False Mirror* Dali: *Persistence of Memory* Kahlo: *Broken Column* O'Keeffe: *Cow's Skull* Oppenheim: *Object* Buñuel: *Un Chien Andalou* Eisenstein: *Battleship Potemkin* Gropius: Bauhaus Le Corbusier: *Towards a New Architecture*; Villa Savoye	HARLEM RENAISSA Lawrence: *The Migration of th Negro* Picasso: *Guernica* REGIONAL REALISM Benton: *City Activitie* Hopper: *Nighthawks* MEXICAN MURALISTS Rivera Orozco FILM AND PHOTOGRAPHY Riefenstahl: *Triumph of the Will* Lange: *Migrant Moth* Wright: Kaufmann House
MUSIC AND DANCE	Strauss: *Salome* Ragtime	Schoenberg: *Pierrot Lunaire* Stravinsky: *Rite of Spring* Modern dance Nijinsky; Graham Handy: "St. Louis Blues"	Bartók: *Bluebeard's Castle* Berg: *Wozzeck*; *Lulu* Jazz Armstrong and Hardin: "Hotter Than That"	Prokofiev: symphonies, suites Gershwin: *Rhapsody in Blue*	Shostakovich Dunhar Primus Cage invents prepared piano: 4' 33"; aleatory

AR II ├─────── COLD WAR (U.S. vs former U.S.S.R) ──────────────────────────────── Berlin Wall Falls

1 million die in | Berlin Wall erected | Vietnam War | | | Persian Gulf War
Holocaust | Sputnik | | | Energy crisis | Collapse of
tomic bomb | First earth | First lunar landing | | | Communist rule in
eveloped 1945 | satellite launched | 1969 | | Chaos Theory | former U.S.S.R.
| 1957 |
| Color TV; digital computers; | NOW founded | | Home computers; robotic technology; the internet
| microchip invented | Mao Zedong: | Gay Rights Movement: | | Tienanmen
Communist | | Cultural Revolution | The Stonewall Riots | | Square
Revolution in | Civil Rights | Malcolm X assassinated | | NASA discovers evidence
China | Movement | Martin Luther King assassinated | | of life on Mars 1996

EXISTENTIALISM | Friedan: *Feminine* | DECONSTRUCTIONISM: | | Szymborska:
Sartre: *Being and Nothingness* | *Mystique* | Derrida, Foucault, | | "The Terrorist,
de Beauvoir: *The Second Sex* | | Rorty | | He Watches"
ung: | Malamud: "A Summer's Reading" | | |
sychological | BLACK HUMOR NOVELS | | SCIENCE FICTION | Calvino: *If on a Winter's*
spects of | Vonnegut | | LeGuin: *Left Hand of* | *Night a Traveler*
he Mother | Heller: *Catch-22* | | *Darkness*
rchetype | BLACK REVOLUTION | | Clarke and Kubrick:
Skinner: *Walden Two* | Ellison: *Invisible Man* | | *2001: A Space*
Orwell: *1984* | Baldwin: "Stranger in | | *Odyssey* | | Oates: "Ace"
Bradbury: *Fahrenheit 451* the Village" | | Walker: "Elethia"
| Fanon: *Black Skin* | | | Kushner: *Angels*
| | | | *in America*
Miller: *Death* | Beckett: *Waiting for Godot* | |
of a Salesman | | | MAGIC REALISM
Neruda: "United | | | Marquez
Fruit Co." | | | Allende: "Two Words" POSTMODERNISM:
| Wiesel: *Night* | Achebe: "Dead Men's Path" | | Ashbery: "Paradoxes and
| | Snyder: "Smokey the Bear Sutra" | | Oxymorons"
WORLD WAR II POETRY | | | | Paz: "To Talk"
Jarrell: "Ball Turret Gunner" | | Feminist poetry | | Heaney: "Squarings:
Shuson: World War II *haikus* | | Sexton, Plath, Sanchez, Rich | | Lightenings"

ABSTRACT EXPRESSIONISM | POP ART | MINIMALISM | NEW EXPRESSIONISM
Pollock: *Convergence* | Warhol: *Marilyn* | Judd: *Untitled* | Baselitz
de Kooning: *Woman* | Johns: *Painted Bronze* | Noguchi: *Cube* | Salle: *Yellow Bread*
Kline: *New York, N.Y.* | Oldenburg: *Soft Toilet* | Stella: shaped canvases | CAMP ART
Rothko: *Untitled* | Lichtenstein: *M-Maybe* | NEW REALISM | Morimura
Frankenthaler: *Interior Landscape* | ASSEMBLAGE | Estes: *Helene's Florist* | CYBERART
| HAPPENINGS | Rauschenberg, Chamberlain, | Close: *Self-Portrait* | Paik: *Megatron*
| Kaprow: *Fluids* | Nevelson | Hanson: *Tourists* | Iwai: *Prano*
Smith: *Cubi* series | Performance Art | | TOTAL ART | SOCIAL CONSCIENCE ART
Calder: mobiles | Klein: | OP ART | Smithson: *Spiral Jetty* | Abakanowicz: *Crowd 1*
Giacometti: *City Square* | *Anthropometry* | Riley: *Current* | Christos: *Running Fence* | Yanagi: *World Flag Ant Farm*
| | Vasarely | | Azaceta: *Coke Heads VIII*
Miller: *Buchenwald* | | Chryssa | | Feng Mengbo: *Video End*
| | | | *Game Series*
Bergman: | Segal: *Bus Riders* | | | AIDS ART
Seventh Seal | Kienholz: *State* | FEMINIST ART | Chicago: SOCIAL CONSCIENCE FILM | General Idea:
| *Hospital* | Marisol: *Women and Dog* | *Dinner* *Raise the Red Lantern* | *One Day of AZT...*
| | Saint-Phalle: *Black Venus* | *Party* *The Story of Qui Ju*
| | | *Schindler's List* | PHOTOGRAPHY
| | | AFRICAN-AMERICAN ART | Sherman: studio photos
| | | Colescott: *Les Demoiselles* | Mapplethorpe: *Lisa Lyon*
| | | *d'Alabama* | Kruger: "Your Body is a
| | | Saar: *Liberation of Aunt Jemima* | Battleground"
Mies and Johnson: Seagram Building | Johnson: Sony Building |
Saarinen: TWA Terminal | | | | Pei: Louvre Pyramid
Wright: Guggenheim Museum | | Moore: Piazza d'Italia | | Gehry: Weisman Museum

---

Cunningham: | Rock music: Little | The Beatles | Marley: reggae | West Coast acid rock | McLean: *Etunytude*
Summerspace | Richard; Elvis; Haley | | | Dylan: folk rock
eningrad" Symphony | | Ligeti: *Atmospheres* | | Taaffe Zwilich | Toru Takemitsu
nces of Haiti | Britten: *War Requiem* | | | Webber: rock musicals
rican Dance | *Musique concrète* | | Penderecki: *Threnody* |
| | | | MINIMALISM
| Stockhausen: electronic music | | | Glass: *Einstein on the* | Corigliano: Symphony
| Babbitt: *Ensembles for Synthesizer* | | | *Beach; Satyagraha* | No. I; *Ghosts of*
Jazz: Park; Gillespie; Davis | | | Reich; Adams; Gorecki | *Versailles*

PART

I

THE TRIUMPH OF
MODERNISM

Since the birth of civilization, no age has broken with tradition more radically or more self-consciously than the twentieth century. In part, this break represents the willful rejection of former values. The modernist break with the past also registers the revolutionary effects of science and technology on all aspects of life. Electronic technology has transformed the planet earth into what Canadian sociologist Marshall McLuhan has called a "global village." In the global village of the twentieth century, communication between geographically remote parts of the world is almost instantaneous, and every new development—technological, ecological, political, and intellectual—potentially affects every villager. Social and geographic mobility, receptivity to change, and a self-conscious quest for the new, the different, and even the outrageous are the hallmarks of this largely secular and materialistic world community.

The metaphoric "shrinking" of the planet actually began at the end of the nineteenth century, with the invention of the telephone (1876), wireless telegraphy (1891), and the internal combustion engine (1897), which made possible the first automobiles. By 1903, the airplane joined the string of enterprises that ushered in an era of rapid travel and communication. Such technology was as revolutionary for the twentieth century as metallurgy was for the fourth millennium B.C.E.

(opposite) Pablo Picasso, detail of *Guernica*, 1937. Oil on canvas, whole painting 11 ft. 5½ in. × 25 ft. 5¾ in. Prado, Madrid. Museo Nacional Centro de Arte Reina Sofía, Madrid. Photo: Oronoz, Madrid. © Succession Picasso/DACS 1997.

However, while metallurgy ushered in the birth of civilization, modern technology (machine guns, poison gas, and nuclear power) gave civilization the tools for self-destruction.

The end of the nineteenth century was a time of relative peace and optimistic faith in technological progress and human productivity. Throughout the world, however, sharp contrasts existed between rich and poor, between democratic and totalitarian ideologies, and between technologically backward and technologically advanced nations. As the powerful nations jockeyed for political and economic primacy, and as Europe and the United States continued to build their industrial and military might, few anticipated the possibility of armed conflict. In 1914, that possibility became a reality in the outbreak of the first of two world wars. The "Great War," the first total war in European history, ended forever the so-called age of innocence. And by the end of World War II, in 1945, nothing would ever seem certain again.

The modern era—roughly the first half of the twentieth century—has yielded a rich diversity of ideas and art styles. These are addressed thematically: Chapter 32, "The Modernist Assault," surveys the arts of the first decades of the twentieth century, especially as they reflect revolutionary changes in technology and new perceptions of time, space, and motion introduced by the science of atomic physics. Imagist poetry, abstract and nonrepresentational art, international-style architecture, and atonal music all demonstrate the modernist's quest to "make it new." Chapter 33, "The Freudian Revolution," takes as its subject the nature and influence of the works of Sigmund Freud, whose investigations into the subconscious life struck at the very heart of Western rationalism. This chapter links the theories of the founder of psychoanalysis to stream of consciousness fiction, and to expressionism and surrealism in literature, music, painting, sculpture, and film. "Total War, Totalitarianism, and the Arts," chapter 34, examines the brutal impact of the two wars that rocked the world between 1914 and 1945. It reviews some of this century's most poignant responses to modern warfare in poetry, fiction, painting, photography, film, and music. More briefly, it deals with the ways in which the arts were affected by the Russian Revolution, the horrors of the Holocaust, and the totalitarianism of Soviet Russia and Nazi Germany. Chapter 35, "The Quest for Meaning," explores the conditions of alienation and anxiety as they appeared in response to World War I (as in T. S. Eliot's "Love Song of J. Alfred Prufrock") and after World War II at mid-century. While it reviews the dominant postwar intellectual and artistic movements in the West—existentialism, theater of the absurd drama, and abstract expressionism—it also considers some non-Western efforts to come to terms with modernism's assault on traditional values.

32
The Modernist Assault

The New Physics

At the turn of the nineteenth century, atomic physicists advanced a model of the universe that altered the model Isaac Newton had provided two centuries earlier. Newton's universe had operated according to smoothly functioning mechanical laws that generally corresponded with the world of sense perception. Modern physicists, however, discovered that at the physical extremities of nature—in the microcosmic realm of atomic particles and in the macrocosmic world of outer space—Newton's laws did not apply. The laws that, in fact, governed these systems only became clear when physicists succeeded in measuring the speed of light as it moved through space. In 1900, the German physicist Max Planck (1858–1947) discovered that light was a form of radiant energy that traveled through space in *quanta*, that is, separate and discontinuous bundles of atomic particles—the fundamental units of matter. Following this and other ground-breaking discoveries in quantum physics (as the field came to be called), another German physicist, Albert Einstein (1879–1955), explained the intrinsic relationship between matter and energy. Energy, argued Einstein, is itself matter multiplied by the speed of light squared, a relationship expressed by the formula $E = mc^2$.

In 1905, Einstein also produced his *special theory of relativity*, a radically new approach to the concepts of time, space, and motion. While Newton had held that an object preserved the same properties whether at rest or in motion, Einstein theorized that as an object approached the speed of light, its mass increased and its motion slowed. Time and space, according to Einstein, were not separate coordinates (as physicists had heretofore conceived) but, rather, indivisible and reciprocal entities. Einstein's discoveries indicated that the universe was shapeless and subject to constant change and, further, that the positions of atomic particles and their velocity might not be calculable with any certainty. In 1920 the research of the German physicist Werner Heisenberg (1901–1976) confirmed Einstein's theory:

Heisenberg's *principle of uncertainty* stated that since the very act of measuring subatomic phenomena would alter those phenomena, the position and the velocity of a particle could not be measured simultaneously with any accuracy. Thus, at the onset of the twentieth century, modern physics had replaced the absolute and rationalist model of the universe with one that seemed chaotic and uncertain.

The practical and the theoretical implications of quantum physics and relativity were immense. Jet propulsion, radar technology, and computer electronics were only three of the numerous long-range consequences of atomic physics. The new science gave humankind greater insight into the operations of nature, but it also provided a gloomier view of the cosmos. In contrast with the optimistic (if mechanical) view of nature provided by Enlightenment cosmology and nineteenth-century technology, modern physics described a universe whose operations violated the inexorable sequence of cause and effect. While Newtonian physics encouraged human control of nature, modern science pictured an indifferent cosmos whose basic components—atomic particles—were inaccessible to both the human eye and the camera (and hence beyond the realm of the senses). Moreover, the operations of that cosmos seemed to lie beyond predictability or control.

The new physics, dependent mainly on mathematical theory, became increasingly remote from the average person's understanding. Atomic fission, the splitting of atomic particles (accomplished only after 1920), and the atomic bomb itself (first tested in 1945) confirmed the validity of Einstein's formula, $E = mc^2$. But it also paved the way for the atomic age, an age that carried with it the possibility of total annihilation. And even if the planet did escape atomic destruction, its demise, in the long run, was inevitable; for, according to the new physics, substance and energy were diffusing inexorably into darkness. As one writer explained, "The sun is slowly but surely burning out, the stars are dying embers, and everywhere in the cosmos heat is turning to cold, matter is dissolving into radiation, and energy is

1900	Max Planck (German) announces his quantum theory
1903	Henry Ford (American) introduces the Model A automobile
1905	Albert Einstein (German) announces his special theory of relativity
1910	Bertrand Russell and Alfred North Whitehead (British) publish their *Principia Mathematica*, a systematic effort to base mathematics in logic
1913	Niels Bohr (Danish) applies quantum theory to atomic structure
1916	Einstein announces his general theory of relativity

being dissipated into empty space."* Though the final curtain was not predicted to fall for billions of years, the portents were ominous.

As Einstein challenged the established way of viewing the external world, the Austrian physician Sigmund Freud was proposing a new and equally revolutionary way of perceiving the internal, or subconscious, world of the human being (see chapter 33). And, as if to confirm Freud's darkest insights, in 1914 Europe embarked on the first of two wars, both of which used the potentially liberating tools of the new science to annihilate human life. World War I, more devastating than any previously fought on this planet, compounded the prevailing mood of insecurity and convinced many that the death of culture was at hand.

Early Twentieth-Century Poetry

The literature of the early twentieth century mirrored the somber mood of uncertainty. Unlike the romantics of the nineteenth century, early modern poets found in nature neither a source of ecstasy nor a means of personal redemption. Their poetry did not characterize human beings as heroic or inspired; rather, it described an indifferent cosmos, whose inhabitants might be insecure, questioning, and even perverse. While early twentieth-century poetry was less optimistic than romantic poetry, it was also less effusive and self-indulgent. Indeed, its lyric strains were frequently as discordant as those of early modern music and modern art.

The Imagists

Poets of the early twentieth century cultivated a language of expression that was as conceptual and abstract as that of modern physics. Like the nineteenth-century symbolist poets (see chapter 31), early twentieth-century poets rejected self-indulgent sentiment and sought a more concentrated style, one that involved

paring down the subject in order to capture its intrinsic or essential qualities—a process called **abstraction**. They rejected fixed meter and rhyme and wrote instead in a style of free verse that became notorious for its abrupt and discontinuous juxtaposition of lean and sparse images. Appropriately, these poets called themselves *imagists*. Led by the Americans Ezra Pound (1885–1972), Amy Lowell (1874–1925), and Hilda Doolittle (1886–1961), who signed her poems simply "H.D.," the imagists took as their goal the search for verbal compression, concentration, and economy of expression.

The American expatriate Ezra Pound was one of the most influential of the imagist poets. By the age of twenty-three, Pound had abandoned his study of language and literature at American universities for a career in writing that led him to Europe, where he wandered from England to France and Italy. A poet, critic, and translator, Pound was thoroughly familiar with the literature of his contemporaries. But he cast his net wide: He studied the prose and poetry of ancient Greece and Rome, China and Japan, medieval France and Renaissance Italy—often reading the work of literature in its original language. As a student of Oriental calligraphy, he drew inspiration from the sparseness and immediacy of Chinese characters. He was particularly fascinated by the fact that the Chinese poetic line, which presented images without grammar or syntax, operated in the same intuitive manner that nature worked upon the human mind. It was this vitality that Pound wished to bring to poetry.

In Chinese and Japanese verse—especially in the Japanese poetic genre known as *haiku*—Pound found the key to his search for concentrated expression. The *haiku*, Japan's most popular light verse form from the seventeenth to the nineteenth century (see chapter 23), is a seventeen-syllable poem of three lines with five, seven, and five syllables each. *Haikus* consist of a few pictorial images that communicate a response to nature as it affects or intervenes in human experience. The power of the poem depends usually on the pairing of contrasting ideas or moods. In the following *haiku*, the nineteenth-century Japanese poet Issa takes as his subject spring rain:

> Rain on a spring day:
> to the grove is blown a letter
> someone threw away.*

Issa seizes on two contrasting images and juxtaposes them without logical connectives, thus recreating the effects of immediate experience. Pound sought similar effects in his *haiku*-like poems, two examples of which are found in the collection called *Personae*.

---

*Lincoln Barnett, *The Universe and Dr. Einstein*. New York: The New American Library, 1948, 102.

*Harold G. Henderson, *An Introduction to Haiku*. New York: Doubleday, 1958, 136.

READING 6.1
From Pound's *Personae*

"In a Station of the Metro"

The apparition of these faces in the crowd;
Petals on a wet, black bough.

"The Bathtub"

As a bathtub lined with white porcelain,
When the hot water gives out or goes tepid,
So is the slow cooling of our chivalrous passion,
O my much praised but-not-altogether-satisfactory lady.

◆

Pound imitated the *haiku*-style succession of images to evoke subtle, metaphoric relationships between things. He conceived what he called the "rhythmical arrangement of words" to produce an emotional "shape." In the *Imagist Manifesto* of 1913 and in various interviews, Pound outlined the cardinal points of the imagist doctrine: Poets should use "absolutely no word that does not contribute to the presentation"; they should employ free verse rhythms "in sequence of the musical phrase." Ultimately, Pound summoned his contemporaries to cast aside traditional modes of Western versemaking and to "make it new"—a dictum allegedly scrawled on the bathtub of an ancient Chinese emperor. "Day by day," wrote Pound, "make it new/cut underbrush/pile the logs/keep it growing." The injunction to "make it new" became the rallying cry of modernism.

The imagist search for an abstract language of expression, which, as we shall see, loosely paralleled the visual artist's quest for absolute form, stood at the beginning of the modernist revolution in poetry. It also opened the door to a more concealed and elusive style of poetry, one that drew freely on the cornucopia of world literature and history. The poems that Pound wrote after 1920, particularly the *Cantos* (the unfinished opus on which Pound labored for fifty-five years), challenge the reader with foreign language phrases, obscene jokes, and arcane literary and historical allusions. These poems contrast sharply with the terse precision and eloquent purity of Pound's early imagist efforts.

Frost and Lyric Poetry

Not all of Pound's contemporaries heeded the imagist doctrine. Robert Frost (1874–1963), the best known and one of the most popular of American poets, offered an alternative to the highly abstract style of the modernists. In contrast to the imagists, Frost embraced the older tradition of lyric poetry. He wrote in metered verse and jokingly compared the modernist use of free verse to playing tennis without a net. Frost avoided dense allusions and learned references. In plain speech he expressed deep affection for the natural landscape, yet he never shared the buoyant optimism of the romantics. He described American rural life as uncertain and enigmatic—at times, notably dark. Frost's "The Road Not Taken" (1916) is written in the rugged and direct language that became the hallmark of his mature style. The poem exalts a profound individualism as well as a sparseness of expression in line with the modernist injunction to "make it new."

READING 6.2
Frost's "The Road Not Taken"

Two roads diverged in a yellow wood,   1
And sorry I could not travel both
And be one traveler, long I stood
And looked down one as far as I could
To where it bent in the undergrowth;   5

Then took the other, as just as fair,
And having perhaps the better claim,
Because it was grassy and wanted wear,
Though as for that the passing there
Had worn them really about the same,   10

And both that morning equally lay
In leaves no step had trodden black.
Oh, I kept the first for another day!
Yet knowing how way leads on to way,
I doubted if I should ever come back.   15

I shall be telling this with a sigh
Somewhere ages and ages hence:
Two roads diverged in a wood, and I—
I took the one less traveled by,
And that has made all the difference.   20

◆

Early Twentieth-Century Art

As with modernist poetry, the art of the first decades of the twentieth century came to challenge all that preceded it. Liberated by the camera from the necessity of imitating nature, **avant-garde** painters and sculptors turned their backs on academic standards and the tyranny of representation. They pioneered an authentic, "stripped down" style that, much like imagist poetry, evoked rather than described experience. Like the imagists, visual artists tried to abstract the intrinsic qualities and essential meanings of their subject matter to arrive at a concentrated emotional experience. The language of pure form did not, however, rob art of its humanistic dimension; rather, it provided artists with a means by which to

Figure 32.1 Paul Cézanne, *The Large Bathers*, 1906. Oil on canvas, 6 ft. 10⅞ in. × 8 ft. 2¾ in. Philadelphia Museum of Art. Purchased with the W. P. Wilstach Fund. Photo: Graydon Wood, 1988 (W'37–1–1).

Figure 32.2 Pablo Picasso, *Les Demoiselles d'Avignon*, Paris, June–July 1907. Oil on canvas, 8 ft. × 7 ft. 8 in. The Museum of Modern Art, New York. Acquired through the Lillie P. Bliss Bequest. Photograph © 1997 The Museum of Modern Art, New York. © Succession Picasso/DACS 1997.

move beyond traditional ways of representing nature and to interpret the visual world in daring new ways.

Early modern artists probed the tools and techniques of formal expression more fully than any artists since the Renaissance. They challenged the role of art as illusion and broadened Western conceptions of the meaning and value of art. Exploring unconventional media, they created art that blurred the boundaries between painting and sculpture. And, like the imagists, they found inspiration in the arts of non-Western cultures; primitivism, abstraction, and experimentation were hallmarks of the modernist revolt against convention and tradition.

Picasso and the Birth of Cubism

The most influential artist of the twentieth century was the Spanish-born Pablo Picasso (1881–1973). During his ninety-two-year lifespan, Picasso worked in almost every major art style of the century, some of which he himself inaugurated. As a child, he showed an extraordinary gift for drawing, and by the age of twenty his precise and lyrical line style rivaled that of Raphael and Ingres. In 1903, the young painter left his native Spain to settle in Paris. There, in the bustling capital of the Western art world, he came under the influence of impressionist and postimpressionist painting, and took as his subjects café life, beggars, prostitutes, and circus folk. Much like the imagists, Picasso worked to refine form and color in the direction of concentrated expression, reducing the colors of his palette first to various shades of blue and then, after 1904, to tones of rose. By 1906, the artist began to abandon traditional Western modes of pictorial representation. Adopting the credo that art must be subversive—that it must defy all that is conventional, literal, and trite—he initiated a bold new style. That style was shaped by two major forces: Cézanne's paintings, which had been the focus of two major Paris exhibitions; and the arts of Africa, Iberia, and Oceania, examples of which were appearing regularly in Paris galleries and museums (see chapters 19 and 31). In Cézanne's canvases, with their flattened planes and arbitrary colors (Figure 32.1), Picasso recognized a rigorous new language of form that worked to define nature's underlying structure. And in African and Oceanic sculpture, he discovered the significance of art as fetish, that is, as the palpable embodiment of potent magical forces. Under Picasso's hand, the aesthetics of tribal art merged with the lessons of Cézanne to lay the groundwork for an audacious new style that would come to be called *cubism*.

The first astonishing product of Picasso's assault on tradition was *Les Demoiselles d'Avignon*, a large painting that features five nude women—the "ladies" of an Avignon brothel—in a curtained interior (Figure **32.2**).

Figure 32.3 Mindassa/Wumbu peoples, Janiform guardian figure for a reliquary (*Mbulu viti*), from Gabon. Wood, brass, and copper, 22¾ × 11⅜ × 3 in. Courtesy of New Orleans Museum of Art. Gitter Collection, 77.245.

In terms of subject matter, *Les Demoiselles*, begun early in 1907, drew on the long and respectable tradition of the female nude group, a subject often set in a landscape (see chapter 30). However, in the summer of 1907, as Picasso fell more deeply under the spell of tribal art, he reworked the canvas until it came to violate every shred of tradition. Indeed, *Les Demoiselles* made Manet's *Olympia* (see chapter 30) look comfortably old fashioned. The manner in which Picasso "made new" a traditional subject in Western art is worth examining: The figures in *Les Demoiselles* seem to have been taken apart and reassembled as if the artist were testing the physics of violent disjunction. Each figure is rendered not from a single vantage point but from multiple viewpoints, as if one's eye could travel freely in time and space. The

Figure 32.4 Pablo Picasso, *Man with a Violin*, 1911. Oil on canvas, 39½ × 29⅞ in.
Philadelphia Museum of Art. Louise and Walter Arensberg Collection. © Succession Picasso/DACS 1997.

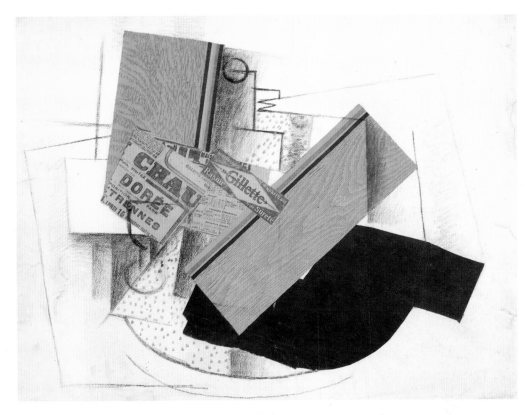

Figure 32.5 Georges Braque, *Still Life on a Table*, ca. 1914. Collage on paper, 18⅞ × 24⅖ in. Collection of Mr. and Mrs. Claude Lauren, Paris. Photo: Musée national d'art moderne, Centre Georges Pompidou, Paris.

body of the crouching female on the far right is seen from the back, while her face, savagely striated like the surface of an African mask or sculpture (Figure **32.3**), is seen from the front. The noses of the two central females appear in profile, while their eyes are frontal— a convention Picasso may have borrowed from ancient Egyptian frescoes. The relationship between the figures and the shallow space they occupy is equally disjunctive, a condition compounded by brutally fractured planes of color—brick reds and vivid blues—that resemble shards of glass. Picasso stripped his female subjects of all sensuous appeal and made them as forbidding as tribal fetish figures. In one disquieting stroke, he banished the alluring image of the female nude from the domain of Western art.

Les Demoiselles was the first step toward cubism, the style that came to challenge the principles of Renaissance painting as dramatically as Einstein's theory of relativity had challenged Newtonian physics. In the decade that followed *Les Demoiselles*, the comfortable, recognizable world of the senses disappeared beneath a scaffold of semitransparent planes and short, angular lines; ordinary objects were made to look as if they had exploded and been reassembled somewhat arbitrarily in bits and pieces (Figure **32.4**). With *analytic cubism*, as the style came to be called, a multiplicity of viewpoints replaced one-point perspective. The cubist image, conceived as if one were moving around, above, and below the subject and even perceiving it from within, appropriated the fourth dimension—time itself. As Picasso and his French colleague Georges Braque (1882–1963) collaborated in a search for an ever more pared down language of form, compositions became increasingly

abstract and colors became cool and controlled: Cubism came to offer a new formal language, one wholly unconcerned with narrative content. Years later, Picasso defended the viability of this new language: "The fact that for a long time cubism has not been understood . . . means nothing. I do not read English, an English book is a blank book to me. This does not mean that the English language does not exist."

Around 1912, a second phase of cubism, namely *synthetic cubism*, evolved. Picasso and Braque, who thought of themselves as space pioneers (much like the Wright brothers), began pasting mundane objects such as wine labels, playing cards, and scraps of newspaper onto the surface of the canvas—a technique known as **collage** (from the French *coller*, "to paste"). The result was a kind of art that was neither a painting nor a sculpture, but both at the same time. The two artists filled their canvases with puns, hidden messages, and subtle references to contemporary events; but the prevailing strategy in all of these artworks was to test the notion of art as illusion. In Braque's *Still Life on a Table* (Figure **32.5**), strips of imitation wood graining, a razor blade wrapper, and newspaper clippings serve the double function of "presenting" and "representing." Words and images wrenched out of context here play off one another like some cryptographic billboard. Prophetic of twentieth-century art in general, Braque would proclaim, "The subject is not the object of the painting, but a new unity, the lyricism that results from method."

In these same years, Picasso created the first assemblages—artworks that were built up, or pieced together, from miscellaneous three-dimensional objects. Like the

Figure 32.6 (above) Ceremonial mask, from Wobé or Grebo, Ivory Coast, late nineteenth century. Painted wood, feathers, and fibers, height 11 in. Musée de l'Homme, Paris. Photo: © R.M.N., Paris.

Figure 32.7 (below) Pablo Picasso, *Guitar*, Paris, winter 1912–1913. Construction of sheet metal and wire, 30½ × 13¾ × 7⅝ in. The Museum of Modern Art, New York. Gift of the artist. Photograph © 1997 The Museum of Modern Art, New York. © Succession Picasso/DACS 1997.

Figure 32.8 (below) Alexander Archipenko, *Woman Combing Her Hair*, 1915. Bronze, 13¾ × 3¼ × 3⅛ in., including base. The Museum of Modern Art, New York. Acquired through the Lillie P. Bliss Bequest. Photograph © 1997 The Museum of Modern Art, New York.

collage, the assemblage depended on the imaginative combination of found objects and materials, but the new procedure constituted a radical alternative to traditional techniques of carving in stone and modeling in clay or plaster. The art of assemblage drew inspiration from African and Oceanic traditions of combining natural materials (such as cowrie beads and raffia) for masks and costumes; it also took heed of the expressive simplifications that typify fetish figures, reliquaries, and other tribal artforms (Figure 32.6). Thus, Picasso's *Guitar* of 1912–1913 achieved its powerful effect by means of fragmented planes, deliberate spatial inversions (note the projecting soundhole), and the wedding of commonplace materials such as sheet metal and wire (Figure 32.7).

Within a decade, Western sculptors were employing the strategies of synthetic cubism in ways that reflected modern models of time and space. The Russian-born cubist Alexander Archipenko (1887–1964) fashioned the female form so that an area of negative space actually constitutes the head (Figure 32.8). Similar efforts at integrating space and mass characterize the monumental bronze sculptures of the British artist Henry Moore (1898–1986).

Figure 32.9 Giacomo Balla, *Street Light* (*Lampada—Studio di luce*), dated by the artist 1909.
Oil on canvas, 5 ft. 8¾ in. × 3 ft. 9¼ in. The Museum of Modern Art, New York. Hillman Periodicals Fund.
Photograph © 1997 The Museum of Modern Art, New York.

Futurism

The intimate relationship between modern science and modern art inspired the Italian movement called *futurism*. The Italian poet and iconoclast Filippo Tommaso Marinetti (1876–1944) issued a series of manifestoes that attacked museum art (and all forms of academic culture) and linked contemporary artistic expression to industry, technology, and urban life. Marinetti demanded an art of "burning violence" that would free Italy from its "fetid gangrene of professors, archeologists, antiquarians, and rhetoricians." "We declare," he wrote in his *Futurist Manifesto* of 1909, "that there can be no modern painting except from the starting point of an absolutely modern sensation. . . . A roaring motorcar is more beautiful than the winged *Victory of Samothrace*" (the famous Hellenistic sculpture illustrated in chapter 6).

The futurists were enthralled by the speed and dynamism of automobiles, airplanes, and other products of twentieth-century technology. In the painting *Street Light* (Figure **32.9**), the Italian futurist Giacomo Balla (1871–1958) pays homage to the electric Brunt Arc lamps that were installed in the streets of Rome during the first decade of the century. The witty Balla claimed that this painting, which shows modern electric light outshining moonlight, hailed the demise of romanticism in Western art. In sculpture Umberto Boccioni (1882–1916) tried to depict the sensation of motion in what is traditionally a static genre. Boccioni transformed the striding male figure into a series of dynamic, jagged planes that intersect space (Figure **32.10**). "One must *abolish in sculpture*, as in all the arts, the *traditionally exalted place of subject matter*," urged Boccioni in his 1912 *Technical Manifesto of Futurist Sculpture*. Persuaded by the futurist obsession with objects in motion and fascinated by new experiments in rapid-action photography, the French artist Marcel Duchamp (1887–1968) painted the controversial *Nude Descending a Staircase* (Figure **32.11**). Critics mockingly called the painting "an explosion in a shingle factory," yet it had a major impact on American artists when it was exhibited in the famous Armory Show held in New York City in 1914. Futurism did not last beyond the end of World War I, but its impact was felt in both the United States

Figure 32.10 Umberto Boccioni, *Unique Forms of Continuity in Space*, 1913. Bronze (cast 1931), 43⅞ × 34⅞ × 15¾ in. The Museum of Modern Art, New York. Acquired through the Lillie P. Bliss Bequest. Photograph © 1997 The Museum of Modern Art, New York.

and Russia, where futurist efforts to capture the sense of form in motion would coincide with the first developments in the technology of cinematography (discussed later in this chapter).

Matisse and Fauvism

While cubists and futurists were principally concerned with matters of space and motion, another group of modernists, led by the French artist Henri Matisse (1869–1954), made *color* the principal feature of their canvases. This group, named "fauves" (from the French *fauve*, "wild beast") by a critic who saw their work at the 1905 exhibition in Paris, employed flat, bright colors in the arbitrary manner of van Gogh and Gauguin. But whereas the latter had used color to evoke a mood or a decorative effect, the younger artists were concerned

1901	the first international radio broadcast is made by Guglielmo Marconi (Italian)
1903	Orville and Wilbur Wright (American) make the first successful airplane flight
1927	the first motion picture with synchronized sound (*The Jazz Singer*) is released
1927	Werner Heisenberg (German) announces his "uncertainty principle"

Figure 32.11 Marcel Duchamp, *Nude Descending a Staircase, #2*, 1912. Oil on canvas, 58 × 35 in. Philadelphia Museum of Art. Louise and Walter Arensberg Collection. © ADAGP, Paris and DACS, London 1997.

Figure 32.12 Henri Matisse, *Open Window, Collioure*, 1905. Oil on canvas, 21¾ × 18⅛ in. From the collection of Mrs. John Hay Whitney, New York. © Succession H. Matisse/DACS 1998.

with color only as it served pictorial structure; their style featured bold spontaneity and the direct and instinctive application of pigment. Critics who called these artists "wild beasts" were in fact responding to the use of color in ways that seemed both crude and savage. They attacked the art of the fauves as "color madness" and "the sport of a child." For Matisse, however, color was the font of pure and sensuous pleasure; like smell, color pervaded the senses subtly and directly (Figure **32.12**). In contrast with Picasso, who held that art was a weapon with which to jar the senses, Matisse sought "an art of balance, of purity and serenity, devoid of troubling or depressing subject matter . . . something like a good armchair in which to rest from physical fatigue."

Matisse was among the first to articulate the modernist scorn for representational art: "Exactitude is not truth," he insisted. In *Notes of a Painter*, published in 1908, he explained that colors and shapes were the equivalents of feelings rather than the counterparts of forms in nature. Gradually, Matisse moved in the direction of bold, schematic simplicity, fluid design, and extraordinary color sensuousness. A quintessential

Figure 32.13 Henri Matisse, *The Dance*, 1910. Decorative panel, oil on canvas, 8 ft. 6½ in. × 12 ft. 10 in. Hermitage Museum, St. Petersburg. © Succession H. Matisse/DACS 1998.

example of his facility for color abstraction is *The Dance* (Figure **32.13**). The painting's sinuous arabesques and unmodeled fields of color, which recall the style of classical Greek vase paintings, evoke a mood of restrained lyricism. At the same time, the painting captures the exhilaration of the primordial round—the traditional dance of almost all Mediterranean cultures.

Brancusi and Abstraction in Sculpture

Although cubists, futurists, and fauves pursued their individual directions, they all shared the credo of abstract art: the belief that the artist must evoke the essential and intrinsic qualities of the subject rather than describe its physical properties. In early modern sculpture, the guardian of this credo was Constantin Brancusi (1876–1957). Born in Romania and trained in Bucharest, Vienna, and Munich, Brancusi came to Paris in 1904. There, after a brief stay in Rodin's studio, he fell under the spell of ancient fertility figures and the tribal sculpture of Africa and Polynesia. Inspired by these objects, whose spiritual power lay in their visual immediacy and their truth to materials, Brancusi proceeded to create an art of radically simple, organic forms. While he began by closely observing the living object— whether human or animal—he progressively eliminated all naturalistic details until he arrived at a form that captured the essence of the subject. Like his good friend Ezra Pound, Brancusi achieved a concentrated expression in forms so elemental that they seem to speak a universal language. A case in point is *Bird in Space* (Figure **32.14**), of which Brancusi made over thirty versions in various sizes and materials. The sculpture is of no particular species of feathered creature, but captures perfectly the concept of "birdness." It is, as Brancusi explained, "the essence of flight." The slender form, curved like a feather, unites birdlike qualities of grace and poise with the dynamic sense of soaring levitation characteristic of mechanical flying machines, such as rockets and airplanes. Indeed, when Brancusi's bronze *Bird* first arrived in America, United States customs officials mistook it for a piece of industrial machinery.

Nonobjective Art

Between 1909 and 1914, three artists working independent of one another in different parts of Europe moved to purge art of all recognizable subject matter. The Russians Wasily Kandinsky (1866–1944) and Kasimir Malevich (1878–1935) and the Dutchman Piet Mondrian (1872–1944), pioneers of **nonobjective art**, had all come into contact with the principal art movements of the early twentieth century: cubism, futurism, and fauvism. They were also familiar with the postimpressionist

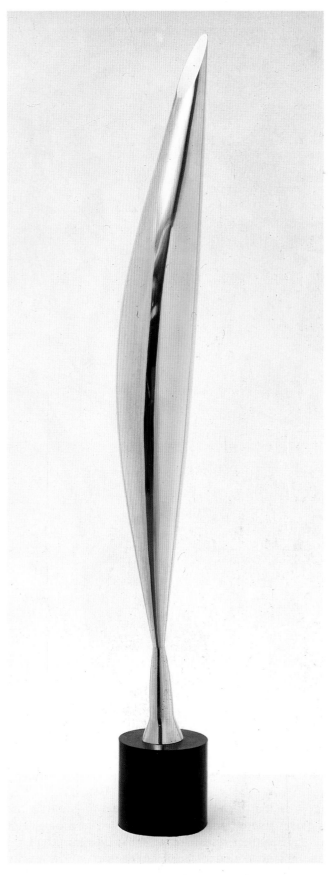

Figure 32.14 Constantin Brancusi, *Bird in Space*, ca. 1924. Polished bronze, height 4 ft. 1¾ in. Philadelphia Museum of Art. Louise and Walter Arensberg Collection. © ADAGP, Paris and DACS, London 1997.

Figure 32.15 Wasily Kandinsky, *Panel for Edwin R. Campbell No. 3*, 1914. Oil on canvas, 5 ft. 4 in. × 3 ft. ¼ in. The Museum of Modern Art, New York. Mrs. Simon Guggenheim Fund. Photograph © 1997 The Museum of Modern Art, New York.

and by Russian folk art. (He later confessed a debt as well to atomic theory and urged young artists to study the new physics.) While he filled his early paintings with intense and vibrant colors, he observed with some dismay that the subject matter in his canvases tended to "dissolve" into his colors. One evening, upon returning to his studio in Munich, Kandinsky experienced a "revelation" that led him to abandon pictorial subject matter. The incident is described in his *Reminiscences* of 1913:

> I saw an indescribably beautiful picture drenched with an inner glowing. At first I hesitated, then I rushed toward this mysterious picture, of which I saw nothing but forms and colors, and whose content was incomprehensible. Immediately I found the key to the puzzle: it was a picture I had painted, leaning against the wall, standing on its side. . . . Now I knew for certain that the [pictorial] object harmed my paintings.*

From this point on, Kandinsky began to assemble colors, lines, and shapes without regard to recognizable objects (Figure 32.15). He called his absolute paintings "improvisations" or "abstract compositions" and numbered them in series. In his engaging treatise *Concerning the Spiritual in Art* (1910), he described colors as potent

---

*"Reminiscences," in *Modern Artists on Art*, ed. Robert L. Herbert. Englewood Cliffs, N.J.: Prentice-Hall, 1964, 32.

Figure 32.16 Kasimir Malevich, *Suprematist Composition: White on White*, 1918. Oil on canvas, 31¼ × 31¼ in. The Museum of Modern Art, New York. Photograph © 1997 The Museum of Modern Art, New York.

premise that a painting was, first and foremost, a flat surface covered with colors assembled in a particular order. But their research into subjectless form had yet another goal: that of achieving an art whose purity would offer a spiritual remedy for the soullessness of modern life.

Kandinsky, whose career in art only began at the age of forty, was deeply influenced by both the fauves

Figure 32.17 Piet Mondrian, *Horizontal Tree*, 1911. Oil on canvas, 29⅝ × 43⅞ in. Munson-Williams-Proctor Institute, New York.

forces for evoking mood and insisted that "color can exercise enormous influence upon the body." Such insights anticipated modern research in chromotherapy, that is, the use of colors and colored light to affect body states. According to Kandinsky, painting was a spiritually liberating force akin to music—he himself was an amateur cellist and friend of many avant-garde composers. "Painting," he proclaimed, "is a thundering collision of different worlds, intended to create a new world."

Kandinsky's Russian contemporary Kasimir Malevich arrived at nonrepresentational art not by way of fauvism but through the influence of analytic cubism, a style that asserted the value of line over color. Seeking to "free art from the burden of the object" and to rediscover "pure feeling in creative art," Malevich created an austere style limited to the strict geometry of the square, the circle, and the rectangle (Figure **32.16**). Malevich called these shapes "suprematist elements" and his style *suprematism*. "To the suprematist," wrote Malevich, "the visual phenomena of the objective world are, in themselves, meaningless; the significant thing is feeling . . . quite apart from the environment in which it is called forth."* By restricting his art to the arrangement of ideal geometric shapes on the two-dimensional picture plane, Malevich replaced the world of appearance with a language of form as precise and exacting as that of modern physics.

The early works of the third pioneer of nonobjective art, Piet Mondrian, reveal this Dutch artist's keen sensitivity to his native countryside as well as his inclination to geometric order (Figure **32.17**). These landscapes also reflect his distant kinship to Jan Vermeer (see chapter 22), as well as his admiration for another of his countrymen, Vincent van Gogh (see chapter 31). As early as 1910, however, Mondrian began to strip his canvases of references to recognizable subject matter. He limited his visual vocabulary to "pure" forms: rectangles laid out on a grid of horizontal and vertical lines, the three primary colors (red, yellow, and blue), and three values—white, gray, and black (Figure **32.18**). The paring-down process achieved a compositional balance of geometric elements, an "equivalence of opposites" similar to the satisfying equilibrium of an algebraic equation. Although Mondrian would eventually migrate to America, in the Netherlands the movement he initiated was called simply *De Stijl* (The Style). Despite differences of opinion among its members—Mondrian resigned in 1925 in opposition to a colleague's use of diagonals—De Stijl was to have worldwide impact.

The disappearance of the object in early twentieth-century art is often mistakenly associated with the dehumanization of modern life. However, one of the great ironies of the birth of nonobjective art is its indebtedness to the mystical and transcendental philosophies that were current in the early modern era. One of the most influential of these was *theosophy*, a blend of Eastern and Western religions that emphasizes communion with nature by purely spiritual means. Mondrian, a member of the Dutch Theosophical Society, equated spiritual progress with geometric clarity. In his view, the

---

*"Suprematism," in *Modern Artists on Art*, 93.

Figure 32.18 Piet Mondrian, *Composition in Red, Yellow, Blue, and Black*, 1921. Oil on canvas, 23¼ × 23¼ in. Collection, Haags Gemeentemuseum, The Hague.

Figure 32.19 (below) Liubov Popova, Set design for Fernand Crommelynk, *Le Cocu magnifique*, State Institute of Theatrical Art, Moscow, 1922. Gouache on paper, 19½ × 27 in. State Trekiov Gallery, Moscow. Gift of George Custakis.

law of equivalence reflected "the true content of reality." "Not only science," wrote Mondrian, "but art also, shows us that reality, at first incomprehensible, gradually reveals itself by the mutual relations that are inherent in things. Pure science and pure art, disinterested and free, can lead the advance in the recognition of the laws which are based on these relationships."* The commitment to pure abstraction as the language of spirituality—a commitment central to the careers of Kandinsky, Malevich, and Mondrian—reflects the idealized humanism of modernists who perceived their art as a wellspring of harmony and order.

Russian Constructivism

While De Stijl had a formative influence on modern architecture, furniture design, and commercial advertising, the most utilitarian and (at the same time) utopian of the movements for "pure art" flourished in pre-revolutionary Russia. *Constructivism*, which had its roots in both futurism and the purist teachings of Malevich, advocated the application of geometric abstraction to all forms of social enterprise. Russian constructivists, who called themselves "artist-engineers," worked to improve the everyday lives of the masses by applying the new abstraction to the industrial arts, theater, film, typography, textile design, and architecture. Liubov Popova (1889–1924), one of the many talented female members of this movement, designed stage sets and costumes for the Russian theater (Figure **32.19**), thus putting into practice the constructivist motto "Art into production." Like other modernists, the constructivists worked to break down the barriers between fine and applied art, but unlike any other modern art movement, constructivism received official state sanction. The failure of the Russian Revolution (see chapter 34) would also bring about the demise of one of the most innovative episodes in modern art.

The Birth of Motion Pictures

It is no coincidence that the art of motion pictures was born at a time when artists and scientists were obsessed with matters of space and time. Thomas Edison was among the first to publicly project moving images on a screen in 1895; within a decade, motion pictures became a popular form of entertainment. In 1902 the French filmmaker George Méliès (1861–1938) completed a storytelling sequence called *A Trip to the Moon*. One year later, the American director Edwin S. Porter (1869–1941) produced his twelve-minute silent film, *The Great Train Robbery*, which showed the holdup, followed by the pursuit and capture, of the bandits. These

pioneer narrative films established the idiom for two of the most popular genres in twentieth-century American cinema—the science fiction film, which conjured up new worlds beyond planet earth, and the "western," which treated the myth of American frontier life.

Between 1908 and 1912, D. W. Griffith (1875–1948) introduced to film the use of multiple cameras and new techniques such as close-ups, fade-outs, and flashbacks, all of which expanded the visual potential of the motion picture medium. Griffith's three-hour-long silent film *The Birth of a Nation* (1915) was an epic account of the American Civil War and the Reconstruction that followed in the South. Unfortunately, despite the film's technical excellence, its negative portrayal of African-Americans contributed to creating an image of them as violent and ignorant savages. Until the late 1920s, all movies were silent—filmmakers used captions to designate the spoken word wherever appropriate. But well before the era of the "talkies," cinematographers began to use the camera not simply as a disinterested observer but as a medium for developing the emotional states of the characters. As such innovative techniques were refined, film was destined to become one of the major artforms of the twentieth century.

Early Twentieth-Century Architecture

While modern concepts of simultaneity and motion were realized in the technology of motion pictures, the revolution in visual abstraction found monumental expression in architecture. Early modern architects made energetic use of two new materials—structural steel and ferroconcrete—in combination with the cantilever principle of construction. The cantilever, a horizontal beam supported at only one end and projecting well beyond the point of support, had first appeared in the timber buildings of China (see chapter 14); but the manufacture of the structural steel cantilever ushered in a style whose austere simplicity had no precedents. That style was first inaugurated by Frank Lloyd Wright (1869–1959), the leading figure in the history of early modern architecture.

The Architecture of Wright

Frank Lloyd Wright, the first American architect of world significance, was the foremost student of the Chicago architect Louis Sullivan (see chapter 30). Wright's style combined the new technology of steel and glass with the aesthetic principles of Oriental architecture. Wright visited Japan when he was in his thirties and was impressed by the grace and purity of Japanese art. He especially admired the respect for natural materials and

Figure 32.20 Frank Lloyd Wright, Robie House, Chicago, Illinois, 1909. Brick, glass, natural rock. Photo: Wayne Andrews/Esto.

Figure 32.21 Frank Lloyd Wright, Falling Water, Kaufmann House, Bear Run, Pennsylvania, 1936–1939. Reinforced concrete, stone, masonry, steel-framed doors and windows, enclosed area 5,800 sq. ft. Photo: Hedrich-Blessing, courtesy Chicago Historical Society.

the sensitivity to the relationship between setting and structure that characterized traditional Japanese architecture (see chapter 14). In his earliest domestic commissions, Wright embraced the East Asian principle of horizontality, by which the building might hug the earth. He imitated the low, sweeping ceilings and roofs of Chinese and Japanese pavilions and pagodas. From the Japanese, whose interior walls often consist of movable screens, Wright also borrowed the idea of interconnecting interior and exterior space. At the same time, he used the structural steel frame and the cantilever technique to open up large areas of uninterrupted space; and he insisted that the exterior appearance of the structure clearly mirror all major divisions of interior space. Wright refined this formula in a series of innovative domestic homes in the American Midwest, pioneering the so-called Prairie School of architecture that lasted from roughly 1900 until World War I.

The classic creation of Wright's early career was the Robie House in Chicago, completed in 1909 (Figure **32.20**). Here, Wright made the fireplace the center of the residential interior. He crossed the long main axis of the house with counteraxes of low, cantilevered roofs that push out into space over terraces and verandas. He subordinated decorative details to the overall design of the house, allowing his materials—brick, glass, and natural rock—to assume major roles in establishing the unique character of the structure. The result was a style consisting of crisp, interlocking planes, contrasting textures, and interpenetrating solids and voids—a domestic home that was as abstract and dynamic as an analytic cubist painting. Wright's use of the cantilever and his integration of landscape and house reached new imaginative heights in Falling Water, the extraordinary residence he designed for Edgar J. Kaufmann at Bear Run, Pennsylvania, in 1936 (Figure **32.21**). Embracing a natural waterfall, the ferroconcrete and stone structure seems to grow organically out of the natural wooded setting, yet dominate that setting by its pristine equilibrium.

The Bauhaus and the International Style

Wright's brilliant synthesis of art and technology melded with the utopian vision of Russian constructivism to pave the way for the establishment of the *Bauhaus*, modernism's most influential school of architecture and applied art. Founded in 1919 by the German architect and visionary Walter Gropius (1883–1969), the Bauhaus pioneered an instructional program that reformed modern industrial society by fusing the technology of the machine age with the purest principles of functional design. Throughout its brief history (1919–1933), and despite its frequent relocation (from Weimar to Dessau, and finally Berlin), the Bauhaus advocated a

Figure 32.22 Walter Gropius, Workshop wing, Bauhaus Building, Dessau, Germany, 1925–1926. Steel and glass. Photograph courtesy The Museum of Modern Art, New York.

close relationship between function and formal design, whether in furniture, lighting fixtures, typography, photography, industrial products, or architecture. Bauhaus instructors had little regard for traditional academic styles; they eagerly endorsed the new synthetic materials of modern technology, a stark simplicity of design, and the standardization of parts for affordable, mass-produced merchandise, as well as for large-scale housing. Some of Europe's leading artists, including Kandinsky and Mondrian, taught at the Bauhaus. Like Gropius, these artists envisioned a new industrial society liberated by the principles of abstract design. When the Nazis closed down the school in 1933, many of its finest instructors, such as the photographer László Moholy-Nagy, architect and designer Marcel Breuer, and artist Joseph Albers, went to the United States, where they exercised tremendous influence on the development of modern American architecture and industrial art.

Under the direction of Gropius, the Bauhaus launched the *international style* in architecture, which brought to the marriage of structural steel, ferroconcrete, and sheet glass a formal precision and geometric austerity that resembled a Mondrian painting (see Figure 32.17). In the four-story glass building Gropius designed to serve as the Bauhaus craft shops in Dessau, unadorned curtain walls of glass (which meet uninterrupted at the corners of the structure) were freely suspended on structural steel cantilevers (Figure **32.22**). This fusion of functional space and minimal structure produced a purist style that paralleled the abstract trends in poetry, painting, and sculpture discussed earlier in this chapter.

The revolutionary Swiss architect and town planner Charles-Edouard Jeanneret (1887–1965), who called himself Le Corbusier (a pun on the word "raven"), was not directly affiliated with the Bauhaus, but he shared Gropius' fundamental concern for efficiency of design, standardization of building techniques, and promotion of low-cost housing. In 1923, Le Corbusier wrote the treatise *Towards a New Architecture*, in which he proposed that modern architectural principles should imitate the efficiency of the machine. "Machines," he predicted, "will lead to a new order both of work and of leisure." Just as form follows function in the design of airplanes, automobiles, and machinery in general, so it must in modern domestic architecture. Le Corbusier was fond of insisting that "the house is a machine for living." With apocalyptic fervor he urged,

> We must create the mass-production spirit.
> The spirit of constructing mass-production houses.
> The spirit of living in mass-production houses.
> The spirit of conceiving mass-production houses.
>
> If we eliminate from our hearts and minds all dead concepts in regard to the house, and look at the question from a critical and objective point of view, we shall arrive at the "House-Machine," the mass-production house, healthy (and morally so too) and beautiful in the same way that the working tools and instruments that accompany our existence are beautiful.*

In the Villa Savoye, a residence located outside of Paris at Poissy-sur-Seine, Le Corbusier put these revolutionary concepts to work (Figure **32.23**). The residence, now considered a "classic" of the international style, consists of simple and unadorned masses of ferroconcrete

*Le Corbusier, *Towards a New Architecture*, translated by Frederick Etchells. New York: Praeger, 1970, 12–13.

Figure 32.23 Le Corbusier, Villa Savoye, Poissy, France, 1928–1929. Ferroconcrete and glass. Photo: Charlotte Benton.

Figure 32.24 Le Corbusier, Apartment block in Marseilles, France, 1946–1952. Photo: © Lucien Hervé, Paris.

punctured by ribbon windows. It is raised above the ground on *pilotis*, pillars that free the ground area of the site. (Some modern architects have abused the *pilotis* principle to create parking space for automobiles.) The Villa Savoye features a number of favorite Le Corbusier devices, such as the roof garden, the open spatial plan that allows one to close off or open up space according to varying needs, and the free facade that consists of large areas of glass—so-called "curtain walls." Le Corbusier's genius for fitting form to function led, during the 1930s, to his creation of the first high-rise urban apartment buildings—structures that housed over a thousand people and consolidated facilities for shopping, recreation, and child care under a single roof (Figure **32.24**). These "vertical cities," as stripped of decorative details as the sculptures of Brancusi, have become hallmarks of urban modernism.

Early Twentieth-Century Music

As with poetry, painting, and architecture, musical composition underwent dramatic changes in the first decades of this century. The assaults on traditional verse rhythms in poetry and on representational forms in painting and sculpture were paralleled in music by radical experiments in tonality and meter. Until the late nineteenth century, most music was tonal, that is, structured on a single key or tonal center; but by the second decade of the twentieth century, musical compositions might be **polytonal** (having several tonal centers) or **atonal** (without a tonal center). Further, instead of following a single meter, a composition might be **polyrhythmic** (having two or more different meters at

the same time), or (as with imagist poems) it might obey no fixed or regular metrical pattern.

Modern composers rejected conventional modes of expression, including traditional harmonies and instrumentation. Melody—like recognizable subject matter in painting—became of secondary importance to formal considerations of composition. Modern composers invented no new forms comparable to the fugue or the sonata; rather, they explored innovative effects based on dissonance, the free use of meter, and the unorthodox combination of musical instruments, some of which they borrowed from non-Western cultures. They employed unorthodox sources of sound, such as sirens, bullhorns, and doorbells; and they began to incorporate silence in their compositions, much as cubist sculptors introduced negative space into mass. The results were as startling to the ear as cubism was to the eye.

Schoenberg

The most radical figure in twentieth-century music was the Austrian composer Arnold Schoenberg (1874–1951). Schoenberg was born in Vienna, the city of Mozart and Beethoven. He learned to play the violin at the age of eight and began composing music in his late teens. Schoenberg's early compositions were conceived in the romantic tradition, but by 1909 he was writing music punctuated by dissonant and unfamiliar chords. Instead of organizing tones around a home key (the tonal center) in the time-honored tradition of Western musical composition, he treated all twelve notes of the chromatic scale equally. Schoenberg's atonal works use abrupt changes in rhythm, tone color, and dynamics—features evidenced in his expressionistic song cycle *Pierrot Lunaire* (*Moonstruck Pierrot*; see also chapter 33) and in his *Five Pieces for Orchestra*, Opus 16, both written in 1912. In the former work, which one critic described as "incomprehensible as a Tibetan poem," the instruments produce a succession of individual, contrasting tones that, like the nonobjective canvases of his good friend Kandinsky, resist harmony and resolution.

During the 1920s, Schoenberg formulated a unifying system for atonal composition based on **serial technique**. His type of *serialism*, called "**the twelve-tone system**," demanded that the composer use all twelve tones of the chromatic scale either melodically or in chords before any one of the other eleven notes might be repeated. The twelve-tone row might be inverted or played upside down or backwards—there are actually forty-eight possible musical combinations for each tone row. Serialism, like quantum theory or Mondrian's "equivalence of opposites," involved the strategic use of a sparse and elemental language of form. It engaged the composer in the highly controlled (even mathematical) disposition of musical elements. In theory, the serial technique invited creative invention rather than mechanical application. Nevertheless, to the average listener, who could no longer leave the concert hall humming a melody, Schoenberg's atonal compositions seemed forbidding and obscure.

Stravinsky

In 1913, one year after Schoenberg's Opus 16 was first performed—and the same year Ezra Pound issued his *Imagist Manifesto* and Malevich and Kandinsky painted their first nonobjective canvases—a Paris audience witnessed the premiere of the ballet *Le Sacre du printemps* (*The Rite of Spring*). The ballet was performed by the *Ballets Russes*, a company of expatriate Russians led by Sergei Diaghilev (1872–1929), and the music was written by the Russian composer Igor Stravinsky (1882–1971; Figure **32.25**). Shortly after the music began, catcalls, hissing, and booing disrupted the performance, as members of the audience protested the "shocking" sounds that were coming from the orchestra. By the time the police arrived, Stravinsky had disappeared through a backstage window. What offended this otherwise sophisticated audience was Stravinsky's bold combination of throbbing rhythms and dissonant harmonies, which, along with the jarring effects of a new style in choreography, ushered in the birth of modern music.

Stravinsky was one of the most influential figures in the history of twentieth-century music. Like

See Music Listening Selections at end of chapter.

Figure 32.25 Pablo Picasso, *Igor Stravinsky*, 1920. Drawing. Private collection. © Succession Picasso/DACS 1997.

Schoenberg, he studied music at a young age. His family pressed him to pursue a career in law, but Stravinsky was intent on becoming a composer. At the age of twenty-eight, he left Russia for Paris, where he joined the company of the *Ballets Russes*. Allied with some of the greatest artists of the time, including Picasso, the writer Jean Cocteau, and the choreographer Vaslav Nijinsky (1888–1950), Stravinsky was instrumental in making the *Ballets Russes* a leading force in modern dance theater. His influence on American music was equally great, especially after 1939, when he moved permanently to the United States.

Russian folk tales and songs provided inspiration for many of Stravinsky's early compositions, including *The Rite of Spring*. Subtitled *Pictures from Pagan Russia*, this piece was based on ancient Slavonic ceremonies that invoked the birth of spring by the ritual sacrifice of a young girl. The theme of death and resurrection traditionally associated with primeval celebrations of seasonal change provided the structure of the suite, which was divided into two parts: "The Fertility of the Earth" and "The Sacrifice." Such themes had been brilliantly analyzed by Sir James Frazer in his widely acclaimed book, *The Golden Bough* (1890), which had been reissued in twelve volumes between 1911 and 1915. Captivated by primitivism, Stravinsky shared the fascination with ancient and tribal folk customs (see chapter 31) that had gripped Europe and had engaged artists from Gauguin to Picasso.

The Rite of Spring had an impact on twentieth-century music comparable to that of Picasso's *Les Demoiselles d'Avignon* on painting. It shattered the syntax of traditional musical languages with the same force that cubism had shattered traditional pictorial norms. Although not atonal, the piece featured ambiguous tonality (especially in the opening portion) and polytonal melodies. *The Rite* deliberately appropriated a pastoral theme, but its music lacked the calm grace traditionally associated with that genre—indeed, Cocteau called the piece "a pastoral of the prehistoric world." The harsh chordal combinations and unexpected shifts of meter set *The Rite of Spring* apart from earlier pastorals such as Debussy's *Prelude to "The Afternoon of a Faun."* While Debussy's rhythms are gentle and ebbing, Stravinsky's are percussive and pulsing. And whereas Debussy's tonal shifts are as subtle and nuanced as the colors in Monet's *Impression: Sunrise*, Stravinsky's are as abrupt as the planes in Picasso's *Les Demoiselles* and the phrases in an imagist poem. Stravinsky's disjunctive arrangement of melodic fragments led critics to object that the composer was incapable of writing transitions in music. If the pounding rhythms and unconventional phrasing of *The Rite* are (as critics complained) "savage," so are its orchestral effects: Its unorthodox instrumentation includes eighteen woodwinds, eighteen brasses, and a *quiro* (a Latin American gourd that is scraped with a wooden stick).

The Beginnings of Modern Dance

The brilliant dancer and choreographer Vaslav Nijinsky had already earned acclaim for the choreography of the *Prélude à "L'Après-midi d'un faune,"* his debut piece. He had shocked audiences by violating the canon of classical dance with erotic movements that he rightly conceived as appropriate to Mallarmé's poem (see chapter 31). And in Russia, he had scandalized the Saint Petersburg ballet by refusing to wear the traditional pair of floppy shorts over his ballet tights. Nijinsky's choreography for *The Rite of Spring* was equally controversial: He experimented with angular dance movements that imitated the flattened appearance of cubist painting (see Figure 31.1). At the same time (and to Stravinsky's dismay), he took the pulsing rhythms of the music as inspiration for a series of frenzied leaps and wild, wheeling rounds. Like *The Rite* itself, Nijinsky's choreography seemed to express what one critic called "the hidden primitive in man." Tragically, Nijinsky's career was aborted in 1917, when the dancer became incurably insane.

In the same way that early twentieth-century poets, painters, architects, and composers found inspiration in non-Western forms of artistic expression, so too did choreographers. They drew freely on the dance traditions of Asia, Africa, and Native America, among others. The eclectic and innovative character of early modern dance is best illustrated in the work of the pioneer American choreographer Martha Graham (1894–1991). Graham once defined dance as "making visible the interior landscape." Following Isadora Duncan and Nijinsky, Graham rejected the conventional positions of classical ballet and explored the expressive power of natural movements of the body. But Graham went even further—she sought in dance a direct correspondence between body movement and human emotion. Just as Pound tried to capture the ideal "rhythmical arrangement of words" to convey an emotional "shape," so Graham attempted to find definitive gestures for feeling states. Dramatic abstraction, along with a fierce, earthy expressiveness, was a major feature of Graham's style and of early modern dance in general. While classical dancers try to conceal any display of the physical effort that goes into creating the dance, modern dancers, like modern artists, exalt the process and the techniques of dancing, thus making new the art of dance.

SUMMARY

During the first decade of the twentieth century, atomic physicists provided a model of the universe that was both more dynamic and more complex than any previously conceived. Matter, they explained, is a form of energy; time and space are relative to the position of the individual observer; and the universe itself is subject to changes that occur abruptly and without transition. Writers, painters, and composers of the first decades of the twentieth century may have been unfamiliar with the particulars of atomic physics, but they sensed its unsettling implications. Like the physicists, they challenged the established way of viewing the indifferent cosmos that they occupied. The fragmentation of form and the disjunctive juxtaposition of motifs in the poetry, art, music, and dance of this period seem to mirror the modern physicist's image of an atomic universe, whose laws are relative and whose operations lack smooth and predictable transitions.

Abstraction and formalism characterize the modernist aesthetic. In the poems of the imagists, as in the cubist paintings of Picasso and the sculpture of Brancusi, a concentrated reduction of form overtook naturalism and representation. With Kandinsky, Malevich, and Mondrian, painting freed itself entirely of recognizable objects and became an exercise in the organization of essential colors, lines, and shapes. In architecture, Frank Lloyd Wright combined the tools of glass and steel technology with the aesthetics of Asian art to invent a style of unprecedented simplicity. Gropius, founder of the Bauhaus, and Le Corbusier, pioneer of the vertical city, developed the international style, which proclaimed the credo of functional design. The austere formalism of the international style would come to dominate much of the urban architecture of the twentieth century. In music and dance, the modernist assault was equally evident. Arnold Schoenberg and Igor Stravinsky were the founders of modern music. They introduced atonality, polytonality, and polyrhythm as formal alternatives to the time-honored Western traditions of pleasing harmonies and uniform meter. Vaslav Nijinsky and Martha Graham liberated dance from academic strictures.

If early twentieth-century artists abandoned conventional and exclusively Western modes of representation, they also challenged outmoded habits of thinking and perceiving. Armed with up-to-date concepts of time and space, modernists rallied to "make it new." Pound's poems, Picasso's cubist compositions, and Stravinsky's early scores remain exemplary of the modernist search for powerful new kinds of expression. And while such works may have seemed as strange and forbidding as modern physics, they were equally effective in shattering the time-honored principles and values of the humanistic tradition.

GLOSSARY

abstraction the process by which subject matter is pared down or simplified in order to capture intrinsic or essential qualities; also, any work of art that reflects this process

avant-garde (French, "vanguard") those who create or produce styles and ideas ahead of their time; also, an unconventional movement or style

atonality in music, the absence of a tonal center or definite key

collage (French, *coller*, "to paste") a composition created by pasting materials such as newspaper, wallpaper, photographs, or cloth on a flat surface or canvas

ferroconcrete a cement building material reinforced by embedding wire or iron rods; also called "reinforced concrete"

haiku a Japanese light verse form consisting of seventeen syllables (three lines of five, seven, and five)

nonobjective art art that lacks recognizable subject matter; also called "nonrepresentational art"

polyrhythm in music, the device of using two or more different rhythms at the same time; also known as "polymeter"

polytonality in music, the simultaneous use of multiple tonal centers or keys; for compositions using only two tonal centers, the word "bitonality" applies

serial technique in music, a technique that involves the use of a particular series of notes, rhythms, and other elements that are repeated over and over throughout the piece

twelve-tone system a kind of serial music that demands the use of all twelve notes of the chromatic scale (all twelve half-tones in an octave) in a particular order or series; no one note can be used again until all eleven have appeared

MUSIC LISTENING SELECTIONS

Cassette II Selection 16 Schoenberg, *Pierrot Lunaire*, Op. 21, Part 3, No. 15, "Heimweh," 1912.
Cassette II Selection 17 Stravinsky, *The Rite of Spring*, "Sacrificial Dance," 1913, excerpt.

SUGGESTIONS FOR READING

Austin, William. *Music in the Twentieth Century from Debussy through Stravinsky.* New York: Norton, 1966.
Calder, Nigel. *Einstein's Universe.* New York: Greenwich House, 1982.
Giedion, Siegfried. *Space, Time and Architecture: The Growth of a New Tradition.* Cambridge, Mass.: Harvard University Press, 1962.
Hertz, Richard, and Norman M. Klein, eds. *Twentieth-Century Art Theory: Urbanism, Politics, and Mass Culture.* Englewood Cliffs, N.J.: Prentice-Hall, 1990.
Howe, Irving, ed. *The Idea of the Modern in Literature and the Arts.* New York: Horizon Press, 1937.
Hughes, Glenn. *Imagism and the Imagists. A Study in Modern Poetry.* New York: Humanities Press, 1960.
Hughes, Robert. *The Shock of the New: Art and the Century of Change.* New York: Knopf, 1993.
Kern, Stephen. *The Culture of Time and Space, 1880–1918.* Cambridge, Mass.: Harvard University Press, 1983.
Nute, Kevin. *Frank Lloyd Wright and Japan: The Role of Traditional Japanese Art and Architecture in the Work of Frank Lloyd Wright.* New York: Van Nostrand Reinhold, 1994.
Perkins, David. *A History of Modern Poetry: From the 1890s to the High Modernist Mode.* Cambridge, Mass.: Harvard University Press, 1976.
Perry, Gil. *Women Artists and the Parisian Avant Garde.* New York: St. Martin's Press, 1996.
Peyser, Joan. *The New Music: The Sense Behind the Sound.* New York: Delacorte Press, 1971.
Russell, John. *The Meaning of Modern Art.* New York: Harper, 1981.
Salzman, Eric. *Twentieth-Century Music: An Introduction,* 3rd ed. Englewood Cliffs, N.J.: Prentice-Hall, 1988.
Torgovnick, Marianna. *Gone Primitive: Savage Intellects, Modern Lives.* Chicago: University of Chicago Press, 1995.
Taruskin, Richard. *Stravinsky and the Russian Traditions.* 2 vols. Berkeley, Calif.: University of California Press, 1996.
Waddington, C. H. *Behind Appearance: A Study of the Relations between Painting and the Natural Sciences in this Century.* Cambridge, Mass.: MIT Press, 1969.
Weiss, Jeffrey. *The Popular Culture of Modern Art: Picasso, Duchamp, and Avant-Gardism, 1909–1917.* New Haven: Yale University Press, 1994.
Yablonskaya, M. N. *Women Artists of Russia's New Age.* New York: Rizzoli, 1990.

33
The Freudian Revolution

Freud and the Psyche

No other figure in modern Western history has had more influence on our perception of ourselves than Sigmund Freud (1865–1939). Freud, a Jewish intellectual who graduated in medicine from the University of Vienna, Austria, in 1880, was the first to map the subconscious geography of the human psyche (or mind). His early work with severely disturbed patients, followed by a period of intensive self-analysis, led him to develop a systematic procedure for treating and curing emotional illnesses. Freud was the founder of *psychoanalysis*, a therapeutic method by which repressed desires are brought to the conscious level to reveal the sources of emotional disturbance. Freud invented the principal tools of this method—dream analysis and "free association" (the spontaneous verbalization of thoughts)—and found these techniques superior to hypnosis in uncovering hidden disorders.

Freud theorized that instinctual drives, especially the libido, or sex drive, governed human behavior. According to Freud, guilt from the repression of instinctual urges dominates the subconscious life of human beings and manifests itself in emotional illness. Most psychic disorders, he argued, were the result of sexual traumas stemming from the child's subconscious attachment to the parent of the opposite sex and jealousy of the parent of the same sex, a phenomenon Freud called the Oedipus complex (in reference to the ancient Greek legend in which Oedipus, king of Thebes, unwittingly kills his father and marries his mother). Freud shocked the world with his analysis of infant sexuality and, more generally, with his proclamation that the psychic lives of human beings were formed by the time they were five years old.

Of all his discoveries, Freud considered his research on dream analysis most important. In 1900 he published *The Interpretation of Dreams*, in which he defended the significance of dreams in deciphering the unconscious life of the individual. But Freud's more speculative investigations were equally significant. In *Totem and Taboo* (1913), he examined the function of the subconscious in the evolution of the earliest forms of religion and morality. And in "The Sexual Life of Human Beings," a lecture presented to medical students at the University of Vienna in 1916, he examined the psychological roots of sadism, homosexuality, fetishism, and voyeurism—subjects that are still considered taboo in some social circles. Freud's theories not only opened the door to the clinical appraisal of previously guarded types of human behavior; they irrevocably altered popular attitudes toward human sexuality. His controversial writings also had a major impact on the treatment of the mentally ill. Until at least the eighteenth century, people generally regarded psychotic behavior as evidence of possession by demonic or evil spirits, and the mentally ill were often locked up like animals. Freud's studies proved that neuroses and psychoses were illnesses that required medical treatment. Freud also broke ground in neuropsychiatry, the branch of medicine that deals with diseases involving the mind and the nervous system. But Freud's most significant contribution to the development of modern intellectual thought was his insistence that the inner recesses of the mind were valid and meaningful parts of the personality and that dreams and fantasies were as vital to human life as reason itself.

In describing the activities of the human psyche, Freud proposed a theoretical model, the terms of which (though often oversimplified and misunderstood) have become basic to *psychology* (the study of mind and behavior) and fundamental to our everyday vocabulary. This model pictures the psyche as consisting of three parts: the *id*, the *ego*, and the *superego*. The id, according to Freud, is the seat of human instincts and the source of all physical desires, including nourishment and sexual satisfaction. Seeking fulfillment in accordance with the pleasure principle, the id is the driving force of the subconscious realm. Freud perceived the second part of the psyche, the ego, as the administrator of the id: The ego is the "manager" that attempts to adapt the needs of the id to the real world. Whether by dreams or by **sublimation** (the positive modification and redirection of primal urges), the ego mediates between potentially destructive desires and social necessities. In Freud's view, civilization was the product of the ego's effort to modify the primal urges of the id. The third agent in the psychic life of the human being, the superego, is the moral monitor commonly called the "conscience." The superego monitors human behavior according to principles inculcated by parents, teachers, and other authority figures.

Freud's tripartite psyche constituted the most radical explanation of human behavior since Darwin's law of natural selection. Freud's theories not only threatened to unleash what the nineteenth-century German philosopher Nietzsche had called the "wild dogs howling in the cellar" of the soul (see chapter 31); they asserted that the individual's conscious life was only the tip of a large iceberg, the submerged body of which might be laid bare through clinical analysis. Copernicus had dislodged human beings from their central location in the cosmos, and Darwin had deposed *Homo sapiens* from a special place over and above other living creatures; now Freud dealt the final blow: He attacked the traditional notion that human reason and rational thought governed human behaviour. Indeed, while Freud himself believed as firmly as any Enlightenment rationalist in the reforming power of science, his theories challenged the centuries-old belief in the supremacy of human reason.

In challenging reason as the governor of human action, Freud questioned the very nature of human morality. He described benevolent action and altruistic conduct as mere masks for self-gratification, and religion as a form of mass delusion. Such views were central to the essay *Civilization and Its Discontents* (1930), in which Freud explored at length the relationship between psychic activity and human society. Enumerating the various ways in which all human beings attempt to escape the "pain and unpleasure" of life, Freud argued that civilization itself was the collective product of sublimated instincts. The greatest impediment to civilization, he claimed, was human aggression, which he defined as "an original, self-subsisting instinctual disposition in man." The following excerpts offer some idea of Freud's incisive analysis of the psychic life of human beings.

READING 6.3

From Freud's *Civilization and Its Discontents*

We will . . . turn to the less ambitious question of what 1
men themselves show by their behavior to be the purpose
and intention of their lives. What do they demand of life
and wish to achieve in it? The answer to this can hardly
be in doubt. They strive after happiness; they want to
become happy and to remain so. This endeavor has two

sides, a positive and a negative aim. It aims, on the one
hand, at an absence of pain and unpleasure, and, on the
other, at the experiencing of strong feelings of pleasure.
In its narrower sense the word "happiness" only relates to 10
the last. In conformity with this dichotomy in his aims,
man's activity develops in two directions, according as it
seeks to realize—in the main, or even exclusively—the
one or the other of these aims.

As we see, what decides the purpose of life is simply
the programme of the pleasure principle. This principle
dominates the operation of the mental apparatus from the
start. There can be no doubt about its efficacy, and yet its
programme is at loggerheads with the whole world, with
the macrocosm as much as with the microcosm. There is 20
no possibility at all of its being carried through; all the
regulations of the universe run counter to it. One feels
inclined to say that the intention that man should be
"happy" is not included in the plan of "Creation." What
we call happiness in the strictest sense comes from the
(preferably sudden) satisfaction of needs which have been
dammed up to a high degree, and it is from its nature only
possible as an episodic phenomenon. When any situation
that is desired by the pleasure principle is prolonged, it
only produces a feeling of mild contentment. We are so 30
made that we can derive intense enjoyment only from a
contrast and very little from a state of things. Thus our
possibilities of happiness are already restricted by our
constitution. Unhappiness is much less difficult to
experience. We are threatened with suffering from three
directions: from our own body, which is doomed to decay
and dissolution and which cannot even do without pain
and anxiety as warning signals; from the external world,
which may rage against us with overwhelming and
merciless forces of destruction; and finally from our 40
relations to other men. The suffering which comes from
this last source is perhaps more painful to us than any
other. We tend to regard it as a kind of gratuitous addition,
although it cannot be any less fatefully inevitable than
the suffering which comes from elsewhere. . . .

An unrestricted satisfaction of every need presents
itself as the most enticing method of conducting one's
life, but it means putting enjoyment before caution, and
soon brings its own punishment. The other methods in
which avoidance of unpleasure is the main purpose, are 50
differentiated according to the source of unpleasure to
which their attention is chiefly turned. Some of these
methods are extreme and some moderate; some are one-
sided and some attack the problem simultaneously at
several points. Against the suffering which may come
upon one from human relationships the readiest
safeguard is voluntary isolation, keeping oneself aloof
from other people. The happiness which can be achieved
along this path is, as we see, the happiness of quietness.
Against the dreaded external world one can only defend 60
oneself by some kind of turning away from it, if one
intends to solve the task by oneself. There is, indeed,
another and better path: that of becoming a member of
the human community, and, with the help of a technique
guided by science, going over to the attack against
nature and subjecting her to the human will. Then one is
working with all for the good of all. But the most
interesting methods of averting suffering are those which
seek to influence our own organism. In the last analysis,

all suffering is nothing else than sensation; it only exists in so far as we feel it, and we only feel it in consequence of certain ways in which our organism is regulated. 70

The crudest, but also the most effective among these methods of influence is the chemical one—intoxication. I do not think that anyone completely understands its mechanism, but it is a fact that there are foreign substances which, when present in the blood or tissues, directly cause us pleasurable sensations; and they also so alter the conditions governing our sensibility that we become incapable of receiving unpleasurable impulses. 80 The two effects not only occur simultaneously, but seem to be intimately bound up with each other. But there must be substances in the chemistry of our own bodies which have similar effects, for we know at least one pathological state, mania, in which a condition similar to intoxication arises without the administration of any intoxicating drug. Besides this, our normal mental life exhibits oscillations between a comparatively easy liberation of pleasure and a comparatively difficult one, parallel with which there goes a diminished or an increased receptivity to unpleasure. It 90 is greatly to be regretted that this toxic side of mental processes has so far escaped scientific examination. The service rendered by intoxicating media in the struggle for happiness and in keeping misery at a distance is so highly prized as a benefit that individuals and people alike have given them an established place in the economics of their libido.[1] We owe to such media not merely the immediate yield of pleasure, but also a greatly desired degree of independence from the external world. For one knows that, with the help of this "drowner of cares," one can at 100 any time withdraw from the pressure of reality and find refuge in a world of one's own with better conditions of sensibility. As is well known, it is precisely this property of intoxicants which also determines their danger and their injuriousness. They are responsible, in certain circumstances, for the useless waste of a large quota of energy which might have been employed for the improvement of the human lot. . . .

Another technique for fending off suffering is the employment of the displacements of libido which our 110 mental apparatus permits of and through which its function gains so much in flexibility. The task here is that of shifting the instinctual aims in such a way that they cannot come up against frustration from the external world. In this, sublimation of the instincts lends its assistance. One gains the most if one can sufficiently heighten the yield of pleasure from the sources of psychical and intellectual work. When that is so, fate can do little against one. A satisfaction of this kind, such as an artist's joy in creating, in giving his phantasies body, 120 or a scientist's in solving problems or discovering truths, has a special quality which we shall certainly one day be able to characterize in metapsychological terms. At present we can only say figuratively that such satisfactions seem "finer and higher." But their intensity is mild as compared with that derived from the sating of crude and primary instinctual impulses; it does not convulse our physical being. And the weak point of this method is that it is not applicable generally: it is accessible to only a few

people. It presupposes the possession of special 130 dispositions and gifts which are far from being common to any practical degree. And even to the few who do possess them, this method cannot give complete protection from suffering. It creates no impenetrable armor against the arrows of fortune, and it habitually fails when the source of suffering is a person's own body. . . .

Another procedure operates more energetically and more thoroughly. It regards reality as the sole enemy and as the source of all suffering, with which it is impossible to live, so that one must break off all relations with it if one 140 is to be in any way happy. The hermit turns his back on the world and will have no truck with it. But one can do more than that; one can try to re-create the world, to build up in its stead another world in which its most unbearable features are eliminated and replaced by others that are in conformity with one's own wishes. But whoever, in desperate defiance, sets out upon this path to happiness will as a rule attain nothing. Reality is too strong for him. He becomes a madman, who for the most part finds no one to help him in carrying through his delusion. It is 150 asserted, however, that each one of us behaves in some one respect like a paranoiac, corrects some aspect of the world which is unbearable to him by the construction of a wish and introduces this delusion into reality. A special importance attaches to the case in which this attempt to procure a certainty of happiness and a protection against suffering through a delusional remoulding of reality is made by a considerable number of people in common. The religions of mankind must be classed among the mass-delusions of this kind. No one, needless to say, 160 who shares a delusion ever recognizes it as such. . . .

Religion restricts this play of choice and adaptation, since it imposes equally on everyone its own path to the acquisition of happiness and protection from suffering. Its technique consists in depressing the value of life and distorting the picture of the real world in a delusional manner—which presupposes an intimidation of the intelligence. At this price, by forcibly fixing them in a state of psychical infantilism and by drawing them into a mass-delusion, religion succeeds in sparing many people 170 an individual neurosis. But hardly anything more. . . . During the last few generations mankind has made an extraordinary advance in the natural sciences and in their technical application and has established his control over nature in a way never before imagined. The single steps of this advance are common knowledge and it is unnecessary to enumerate them. Men are proud of those achievements, and have a right to be. But they seem to have observed that this newly-won power over space and time, this subjugation of the forces of nature, which is the fulfillment 180 of a longing that goes back thousands of years, has not increased the amount of pleasurable satisfaction which they may expect from life and has not made them feel happier. From the recognition of this fact we ought to be content to conclude that power over nature is not the *only* precondition of human happiness, just as it is not the *only* goal of cultural endeavor; we ought not to infer from it that technical progress is without value for the economics of our happiness. One would like to ask: is there, then, no positive gain in pleasure, no unequivocal increase in my 190 feeling of happiness, if I can, as often as I please, hear the voice of a child of mine who is living hundreds of miles

---

[1]The instinctual desires of the id, most specifically, the sexual urge.

away or if I can learn in the shortest possible time after a friend has reached his destination that he has come through the long and difficult voyage unharmed? Does it mean nothing that medicine has succeeded in enormously reducing infant mortality and the danger of infection for women in childbirth and, indeed, in considerably lengthening the average life of a civilized man? And there is a long list that might be added to benefits of this kind 200 which we owe to the much-despised era of scientific and technical advances. But here the voice of pessimistic criticism makes itself heard and warns us that most of these satisfactions follow the model of the "cheap enjoyment" extolled in the anecdote—the enjoyment obtained by putting a bare leg from under the bedclothes on a cold winter night and drawing it in again. If there had been no railway to conquer distances, my child would never have left his native town and I should need no telephone to hear his voice; if travelling across the ocean 210 by ship had not been introduced, my friend would not have embarked on his sea-voyage and I should not need a cable to relieve my anxiety about him. What is the use of reducing infantile mortality when it is precisely that reduction which imposes the greatest restraint on us in the begetting of children, so that, taken all round, we nevertheless rear no more children than in the days before the reign of hygiene, while at the same time we have created difficult conditions for our sexual life in marriage, and have probably worked against the beneficial effects of 220 natural selection? And, finally, what good to us is a long life if it is difficult and barren of joys, and if it is so full of misery that we can only welcome death as a deliverer? . . .

. . . men are not gentle creatures who want to be loved, and who at the most can defend themselves if they are attacked; they are, on the contrary, creatures among whose instinctual endowments is to be reckoned a powerful share of aggressiveness. As a result, their neighbor is for them not only a potential helper or sexual object, but also someone who tempts them to satisfy 230 their aggressiveness on him, to exploit his capacity for work without compensation, to use him sexually without his consent, to seize his possessions, to humiliate him, to cause him pain, to torture and to kill him. . . .

The existence of this inclination to aggression, which we can detect in ourselves and justly assume to be present in others, is the factor which disturbs our relations with our neighbor and which forces civilization into such a high expenditure [of energy]. In consequence of this primary mutual hostility of human beings, civilized 240 society is perpetually threatened with disintegration. The interest of work in common would not hold it together; instinctual passions are stronger than reasonable interests. Civilization has to use its utmost efforts in order to set limits to man's aggressive instincts and to hold the manifestations of them in check by psychical reaction-formations. Hence, therefore, the use of methods intended to incite people into identifications and aim-inhibited relationships of love, hence the restriction upon sexual life, and hence too the [idealist] commandment to 250 love one's neighbor as oneself—a commandment which is really justified by the fact that nothing else runs so strongly counter to the original nature of man. In spite of every effort, these endeavors of civilization have not so far achieved very much. It hopes to prevent the crudest excesses of brutal violence by itself assuming the right to use violence against criminals, but the law is not able to lay hold of the more cautious and refined manifestations of human aggressiveness. The time comes when each one of us has to give up as illusions the expectations which, 260 in his youth, he pinned upon his fellowmen, and when he may learn how much difficulty and pain has been added to his life by their ill-will. . . .

◆

Freud's Followers

Freud's writings explored so many aspects of human experience that, inevitably, his theories would be tested and laid open to assault. In the second half of the twentieth century, for instance, some physicians have questioned the scientific validity of psychoanalysis and its usefulness as a form of treatment. At the same time, feminists, whose movement for women's liberation (see chapter 36) clearly owes much to Freud's critique of sexual morality, have attacked Freud's patriarchal image of the female as passive, weak, and dependent. Nevertheless, Freud's immediate followers recognized that they stood in the shadow of an intellectual giant. Although some psychoanalysts disagreed with Freud's dogmatic theory that all neuroses stemmed from the traumas of the id, most took his discoveries as the starting point for their own inquiries into human behavior. For instance, Freud's Viennese associate Alfred Adler (1870–1937), who pioneered the field of individual psychology, sought to explain the ego's efforts to adapt to its environment. Coining the term "inferiority complex," Adler concentrated on analyzing problems related to the ego's failure to achieve its operational goals in everyday life.

Another of Freud's colleagues, the Swiss physician Carl Gustav Jung (1875–1961), found Freud's view of the psyche too narrow and overly deterministic. Jung argued that the personal, unconscious life of the individual rested on a deeper and more universal layer of the human psyche, which he called the **collective unconscious**. According to Jung, the collective unconscious belongs to humankind at large, that is, to the human family. It manifests itself throughout history in the form of dreams, myths, and fairy tales. The **archetypes** of that realm—primal patterns that reflect the deep psychic needs of humankind as a species—reveal themselves as familiar motifs and characters, such as "the child-god," "the hero," and "the wise old man." Jung's investigations into the cultural history of humankind disclosed endless similarities among the symbols and myths of different religions and bodies of folklore. These he took to support his theory that the archetypes were the innate, inherited contents of the human mind.

Some of Jung's most convincing observations concerning the life of the collective unconscious appear in his essay "Psychological Aspects of the Mother Archetype" (1938). In this essay, Jung discusses the manifestations of the female archetype in personal life, as mother, grandmother, stepmother, nurse, or governess; in religion, as the redemptive Mother of God, the Virgin, Holy Wisdom, and the various nature deities of ancient myth and religion; and in the universal symbolism of things and places associated with fertility and fruitfulness, such as the cornucopia, the garden, the fountain, the cave, the rose, the lotus, the magic circle, and the uterus. The negative aspect of the female archetype, observed Jung, usually manifests itself as the witch in traditional fairy tales and legends. Jung emphasized the role of the collective unconscious in reflecting the "psychic unity" of all cultures. He treated the personal psyche as part of the larger human family, and, unlike Freud, he insisted on the positive value of religion in satisfying humankind's deepest psychic desires.

The New Psychology and Literature

The impact of the new psychology was felt throughout Europe. Freud's theories, and particularly his pessimistic view of human nature, intensified the mood of uncertainty produced by the startling revelations of atomic physics and the outbreak of World War I. The Freudian revolution affected all aspects of artistic expression, not the least of which was literature. A great many figures in early twentieth-century fiction were profoundly influenced by Freud; three of the most famous of these are Marcel Proust, Franz Kafka, and James Joyce. In the works of these novelists the most significant events are those that take place in the psychic life of dreams and memory. The narrative line of the story may be interrupted by unexpected leaps of thought, intrusive recollections, self-reflections, and sudden dead ends. Fantasy may alternate freely with rational thought. The lives of the heroes—or, more exactly, antiheroes—in these stories are often inconsequential, while their concerns, though commonplace or trivial, may be obsessive, bizarre, and charged with passion.

Proust's Quest for Lost Time

Born in Paris, Marcel Proust (1871–1922) spent his youth troubled by severe attacks of asthma and recurring insecurities over his sexual orientation. Devastated by the death of his mother in 1905, Proust withdrew completely from Parisian society. He retreated into the semidarkness of a cork-lined room, where, shielded from noise, light, and frivolous society, he pursued a life of introspection and literary endeavor. Between 1913 and 1927 Proust produced a seven-volume novel entitled *A la Recherche du temps perdu* (literally, "The Quest for Lost Time," but usually translated as *The Remembrance of Things Past*). This lengthy masterpiece provides a reflection of the society of turn-of-the-century France, but its perception of reality is wholly internal. Its central theme is the role of memory in retrieving past experience and in shaping the private life of the individual. Proust's mission was to rediscover a sense of the past by reviving sensory experiences buried deep within his psyche, that is, to bring the unconscious life to the conscious level. "For me," explained Proust, "the novel is . . . psychology in space and time."

In the first volume of *A la Recherche du temps perdu*, entitled *Swann's Way*, Proust employs the Freudian technique of "free association" to recapture from the recesses of memory the intense moment of pleasure occasioned by the taste of a piece of cake soaked in tea. The following excerpt illustrates Proust's ability to free experience from the rigid order of mechanical time and invade the richly textured storehouse of the psyche. It also illustrates the modern notion of the mental process as a "stream of thought," a concept that had appeared as early as 1884 in the writings of the American psychologist William James (1842–1910) and in the works of Henri Bergson (1859–1941), who argued that reality is best understood as a perpetual flux in which past and present are inseparable (see chapter 31).

READING 6.4

From Proust's *Swann's Way*

The past is hidden somewhere outside the realm, beyond   1
the reach of intellect, in some material object (in the
sensation which that material object will give us) which
we do not suspect. And as for that object, it depends on
chance whether we come upon it or not before we
ourselves must die.

Many years had elapsed during which nothing of
Combray, save what was comprised in the theatre and
the drama of my going to bed there, had any existence
for me, when one day in winter, as I came home, my   10
mother, seeing that I was cold, offered me some tea, a
thing I did not ordinarily take. I declined at first, and
then, for no particular reason, changed my mind. She
sent out for one of those short, plump little cakes called
"petites madeleines," which look as though they had
been moulded in the fluted scallop of a pilgrim's shell.
And soon, mechanically, weary after a dull day with the
prospect of a depressing morrow, I raised to my lips a
spoonful of the tea in which I had soaked a morsel of the
cake. No sooner had the warm liquid, and the crumbs   20
with it, touched my palate than a shudder ran through
my whole body, and I stopped, intent upon the
extraordinary changes that were taking place. An
exquisite pleasure had invaded my senses, but

individual, detached, with no suggestion of its origin. And at once the vicissitudes of life had become indifferent to me, its disasters innocuous, its brevity illusory—this new sensation having had on me the effect which love has of filling me with a precious essence; or rather this essence was not in me, it was myself. I had ceased now to feel mediocre, accidental, mortal. Whence could it have come to me, this all-powerful joy? I was conscious that it was connected with the taste of tea and cake, but that it infinitely transcended those savours, could not, indeed, be of the same nature as theirs. Whence did it come? What did it signify? How could I seize upon and define it?

I drink a second mouthful, in which I find nothing more than in the first, a third, which gives me rather less than the second. It is time to stop; the potion is losing its magic. It is plain that the object of my quest, the truth, lies not in the cup but in myself. The tea has called up in me, but does not itself understand, and can only repeat indefinitely with a gradual loss of strength, the same testimony; which I, too, cannot interpret, though I hope at least to be able to call upon the tea for it again and to find it there presently, intact and at my disposal, for my final enlightenment. I put down my cup and examine my own mind. It is for it to discover the truth. But how? What an abyss of uncertainty whenever the mind feels that some part of it has strayed beyond its own borders; when it, the seeker, is at once the dark region through which it must go seeking, where all its equipment will avail it nothing. Seek? More than that: create. It is face to face with something which does not so far exist, to which it alone can give reality and substance, which it alone can bring into the light of day.

And I begin again to ask myself what it could have been, this unremembered state which brought with it no logical proof of its existence, but only the sense that it was a happy, that it was a real state in whose presence other states of consciousness melted and vanished. I decide to attempt to make it reappear. I retrace my thoughts to the moment at which I drank the first spoonful of tea. I find again the same state, illumined by no fresh light. I compel my mind to make one further effort, to follow and recapture once again the fleeting sensation. And that nothing may interrupt it in its course I shut out every obstacle, every extraneous idea, I stop my ears and inhibit all attention to the sounds which come from the next room. And then, feeling that my mind is growing fatigued without having any success to report, I compel it for a change to enjoy that distraction which I have just denied it, to think of other things, to rest and refresh itself before the supreme attempt. And then for the second time I clear an empty space in front of it. I place in position before my mind's eye the still recent taste of that first mouthful, and I feel something start within me, something that leaves its resting-place and attempts to rise, something that has been embedded like an anchor at a great depth; I do not know yet what it is, but I can feel it mounting slowly; I can measure the resistance, I can hear the echo of great spaces traversed.

Undoubtedly what is thus palpitating in the depths of my being must be the image, the visual memory which, being linked to that taste, has tried to follow it into my conscious mind. But its struggles are too far off, too much confused; scarcely can I perceive the colorless reflection in which are blended the uncaptchurable whirling medley of radiant hues, and I cannot distinguish its form, cannot invite it, as the one possible interpreter, to translate to me the evidence of its contemporary, its inseparable paramour, the taste of cake soaked in tea; cannot ask it to inform me what special circumstance is in question, of what period in my past life.

Will it ultimately reach the clear surface of my consciousness, this memory, this old, dead moment which the magnetism of an identical moment has travelled so far to importune, to disturb, to raise up out of the very depths of my being? I cannot tell. Now that I feel nothing, it has stopped, has perhaps gone down again into its darkness, from which who can say whether it will ever rise? Ten times over I must essay the task, must lean down over the abyss. And each time the natural laziness which deters us from every difficult enterprise, every work of importance, has urged me to leave the thing alone, to drink my tea and to think merely of the worries of to-day and of my hopes for to-morrow, which let themselves be pondered over without effort or distress of mind.

And suddenly the memory returns. The taste was that of the little crumb of madeleine which on Sunday mornings at Combray (because on those mornings I did not go out before church-time), when I went to say good day to her in her bedroom, my aunt Léonie used to give me, dipping it first in her own cup of real or of lime-flower tea. The sight of the little madeleine had recalled nothing to my mind before I tasted it; perhaps because I had so often seen such things in the interval, without tasting them, on the trays in pastry-cooks' windows, that their image had dissociated itself from those Combray days to take its place among others more recent; perhaps because of those memories, so long abandoned and put out of mind, nothing now survived, everything was scattered; the forms of things, including that of the little scallop-shell of pastry, so richly sensual under its severe, religious folds, were either obliterated or had been so long dormant as to have lost the power of expansion which would have allowed them to resume their place in my consciousness. But when from a long-distant past nothing subsists, after the people are dead, after the things are broken and scattered, still, alone, more fragile, but with more vitality, more unsubstantial, more persistent, more faithful, the smell and taste of things remain poised a long time, like souls, ready to remind us, waiting and hoping for their moment, amid the ruins of all the rest; and bear unfaltering, in the tiny and almost impalpable drop of their essence, the vast structure of recollection.

And once I had recognized the taste of the crumb of madeleine soaked in her decoction of lime-flowers which my aunt used to give me (although I did not yet know and must long postpone the discovery of why this memory made me so happy) immediately the old grey house upon the street, where her room was, rose up like the scenery of a theatre to attach itself to the little pavilion, opening on to the garden, which had been built out behind it for my parents (the isolated panel which until that moment had been all that I could see); and with the house the town, from morning to night and in all weathers, the Square where I was sent before luncheon, the streets along which I used to run errands, the country roads we took when it was fine. And just as the Japanese amuse themselves by filling a porcelain bowl with water and steeping in it little crumbs of paper which until then are without character or form, but, the moment they become wet, stretch themselves and bend, take on color and distinctive shape, become flowers or   160 houses or people, permanent and recognisable, so in that moment all the flowers in our garden and in M. Swann's park, and the water-lilies on the Vivonne and the good folk of the village and their little dwellings and the parish church and the whole of Combray and of its surroundings, taking their proper shapes and growing solid, sprang into being, towns and gardens alike, from my cup of tea. . . .

◆

The Nightmare Reality of Kafka

For Proust, memory was a life-enriching phenomenon, but for the Czechoslovakian novelist Franz Kafka (1883–1924), the subconscious life gave conscious experience bizarre and threatening gravity. Written in the German language, Kafka's novels and short stories take on the reality of dreams in which characters are nameless, details are precise but grotesque, and events lack logical consistency. Kafka's novels create a nightmarish world in which the central characters become victims of unknown or imprecisely understood forces. They may be caught in absurd but commonplace circumstances involving guilt and frustration, or they may be threatened by menacing events that appear to have neither meaning nor purpose. In Kafka's novel *The Trial* (1925), for instance, the protagonist is arrested, convicted, and executed, without ever knowing the nature of his crime. In "The Metamorphosis" (1915), one of the most disquieting short stories of the twentieth century, the central character, Gregor Samsa, wakes one morning to discover that he has turned into a large beetle. The themes of insecurity and vulnerability that recur in Kafka's novels reflect the mood that prevailed during the early decades of the century. Kafka himself was afflicted with this insecurity: Shortly before he died in 1924, he asked a close friend to burn all of his manuscripts; the friend disregarded the request and saw to it that Kafka's works, even some that were unfinished, were published. Consequently, Kafka's style—a style that anticipates *magic realism* (a term coined in 1925) in its unexpected juxtapositions of events and images—has had a major influence on modern fiction. Although "The Metamorphosis" is too long to reproduce here in full, the excerpt that follows conveys some idea of Kafka's surreal narrative style.

READING 6.5

From Kafka's "The Metamorphosis"

As Gregor Samsa awoke one morning from uneasy dreams   1 he found himself transformed in his bed into a gigantic insect. He was lying on his hard, as it were armor-plated, back and when he lifted his head a little he could see his dome-like brown belly divided into stiff arched segments on top of which the bed quilt could hardly keep in position and was about to slide off completely. His numerous legs, which were pitifully thin compared to the rest of his bulk, waved helplessly before his eyes.

What has happened to me? he thought. It was no   10 dream. His room, a regular human bedroom, only rather too small, lay quiet between the four familiar walls. Above the table on which a collection of cloth samples was unpacked and spread out—Samsa was a commercial traveler—hung the picture, which he had recently cut out of an illustrated magazine and put into a pretty gilt frame. It showed a lady, with a fur cap on and a fur stole, sitting upright and holding out to the spectator a huge fur muff into which the whole of her forearm had vanished!

Gregor's eyes turned next to the window, and the   20 overcast sky—one could hear raindrops beating on the window gutter—made him quite melancholy. What about sleeping a little longer and forgetting all this nonsense, he thought, but it could not be done, for he was accustomed to sleep on his right side and in his present condition he could not turn himself over. However violently he forced himself towards his right side he always rolled on to his back again. He tried it at least a hundred times, shutting his eyes to keep from seeing his struggling legs, and only desisted when he began to feel in his side a faint dull   30 ache he had never experienced before.

Oh God, he thought, what an exhausting job I've picked on! Traveling about day in, day out. It's much more irritating work than doing the actual business in the office, and on top of that there's the trouble of constant traveling, of worrying about train connections, the bed and irregular meals, casual acquaintances that are always new and never become intimate friends. The devil take it all! He felt a slight itching upon his belly; slowly pushed himself on his back nearer to the top of the bed so that   40 he could lift his head more easily; identified the itching place which was surrounded by many small white spots the nature of which he could not understand and made to touch it with a leg, but drew the leg back immediately, for the contact made a cold shiver run through him. . . .

He looked at the alarm clock ticking on the chest. Heavenly Father! he thought. It was half-past six o'clock and the hands were quietly moving on, it was even past the half-hour, it was getting on toward a quarter to seven. Had the alarm clock not gone off? From the bed one   50 could see that it had been properly set for four o'clock; of course it must have gone off. Yes, but was it possible to sleep quietly through that ear-splitting noise? Well, he had not slept quietly, yet apparently all the more soundly for that. But what was he to do now? The next train went at seven o'clock; to catch that he would need to hurry like mad and his samples weren't even packed up, and he himself wasn't feeling particularly fresh and active.

And even if he did catch the train he wouldn't avoid a row with the chief, since the firm's porter would have been waiting for the five o'clock train and would have long since reported his failure to turn up. . . . 60

As all this was running through his mind at top speed without his being able to decide to leave his bed—the alarm clock had just struck a quarter to seven—there came a cautious tap at the door behind the head of his bed. "Gregor," said a voice—it was his mother's—"it's a quarter to seven. Hadn't you a train to catch?" That gentle voice! Gregor had a shock as he heard his own voice answering hers, unmistakably his own voice, it was 70 true, but with a persistent horrible twittering squeak behind it like an undertone, that left the words in their clear shape only for the first moment and then rose up reverberating round them to destroy their sense, so that one could not be sure one had heard them rightly. Gregor wanted to answer at length and explain everything, but in the circumstances he confined himself to saying: "Yes, yes, thank you, Mother, I'm getting up now." The wooden door between them must have kept the change in his voice from being noticeable outside, for his mother 80 contented herself with this statement and shuffled away. Yet this brief exchange of words had made the other members of the family aware that Gregor was still in the house, as they had not expected, and at one of the side doors his father was already knocking, gently, yet with his fist. "Gregor, Gregor," he called, "what's the matter with you?" And after a little while he called again in a deeper voice: "Gregor! Gregor!" At the other side door his sister was saying in a low, plaintive tone: "Gregor? Aren't you well? Are you needing anything?" He answered them both 90 at once: "I'm just ready," and did his best to make his voice sound as normal as possible by enunciating the words very clearly and leaving long pauses between them. So his father went back to his breakfast, but his sister whispered: "Gregor, open the door, do.". . .

[Unexpectedly, the chief clerk arrives to find out why Gregor is not at work. He demands to see him.]

Slowly Gregor pushed the chair towards the door, then let go of it, caught hold of the door for support—the soles at the end of his little legs were somewhat sticky—and rested against it for a moment after his efforts. Then he set himself to turning the key in the lock with his 100 mouth. It seemed, unhappily, that he hadn't really any teeth—what could he grip the key with?—but on the other hand his jaws were certainly very strong; with their help he did manage to set the key in motion, heedless of the fact that he was undoubtedly damaging them somewhere, since a brown fluid issued from his mouth, flowed over the key and dripped on the floor. "Just listen to that," said the chief clerk next door; "he's turning the key." That was a great encouragement to Gregor; but they should all have shouted encouragement to him, his 110 father and mother too: "Go on Gregor," they should have called out, "keep going, hold on to that key!" And in the belief that they were all following his efforts intently, he clenched his jaws recklessly on the key with all the force at his command. As the turning of the key progressed he circled round the lock, holding on now only with his mouth, pushing on the key, as required, or pulling it

down again with all the weight of his body. The louder click of the finally yielding lock literally quickened Gregor. With a deep breath of relief he said to himself: 120 "So I didn't need the locksmith," and laid his head on the handle to open the door wide.

Since he had to pull the door towards him, he was still invisible when it was really wide open. He had to edge himself slowly round the near half of the double door, and to do it very carefully if he was not to fall plump upon his back just on the threshold. He was still carrying out this difficult manoeuvre, with no time to observe anything else, when he heard the chief clerk utter a loud "Oh!"—it sounded like a gust of wind—and now he 130 could see the man, standing as he was nearest to the door, clapping one hand before his open mouth and slowly backing away as if driven by some invisible steady pressure. His mother—in spite of the chief clerk's being there her hair was still undone and sticking up in all directions—first clasped her hands and looked at his father, then took two steps towards Gregor and fell on the floor among her outspread skirts, her face quite hidden on her breast. His father knotted his fist with a fierce expression on his face as if he meant to knock 140 Gregor back into his room, then looked uncertainly round the living room, covered his eyes with his hands and wept till his great chest heaved. . . .

———————————————◆———————————————

Joyce and Stream of Consciousness Prose

One of the most influential writers of the early twentieth century, and also one of the most challenging, was the Irish expatriate James Joyce (1882–1941). Born in Dublin and educated in Jesuit schools, Joyce abandoned Ireland in 1905 to live abroad. In Paris, he studied medicine and music but made his livelihood there and elsewhere by teaching foreign languages and writing short stories. Joyce's style reflects his genius as a linguist and his keen sensitivity to the musical potential of words. His treatment of plot and character is deeply indebted to Freud, whose earliest publications Joyce had consumed with interest. Joyce was the master of the **interior monologue**, a literary device consisting of the private musings of a character in the form of a "stream of consciousness"—a succession of images and ideas connected by free association rather than by logical argument or narrative sequence. The stream of consciousness device resembles the free association technique used by Freud in psychotherapy; it also recalls the discontinuous verse style of the imagist poets (see chapter 32). In a stream of consciousness novel, the action is developed through the mind of the principal character as he or she responds to the dual play of conscious and subconscious stimuli. The following passage from Joyce's six-hundred-page novel *Ulysses* (1922) provides a brief example:

He crossed to the bright side, avoiding the loose cellarflap of number seventy-five. The sun was nearing the steeple of George's church. Be a warm day I fancy, Specially in these black clothes feel it more. Black conducts, reflects (refracts is it?), the heat. But I couldn't go in that light suit. Make a picnic of it. His Boland's breadvan delivering with trays our daily but she prefers yesterday's loaves turnovers crisp crowns hot. Makes you feel young. Somewhere in the east: early morning: set off at dawn, travel round in front of the sun, steal a day's march on him. Keep it up for ever never grow a day older technically. . . . Wander along all day. Meet a robber or two. Well, meet him. Getting on to sundown. The shadows of the mosques along the pillars: priest with a scroll rolled up. A shiver of the trees, signal, the evening wind. I pass on. Fading gold sky. A mother watches from her doorway. She calls her children home in their dark language. High wall: beyond strings twanged. Night sky moon, violet, colour of Molly's new garters. Strings. Listen. A girl playing one of these instruments what do you call them: dulcimers. I pass. . . .*

Joyce modeled his sprawling novel on the Homeric epic, the *Odyssey*. But Joyce's modern version differs profoundly from Homer's. Leopold Bloom, the main character of *Ulysses*, is as ordinary as Homer's Odysseus was heroic; his adventures seem trivial and insignificant by comparison with those of his classical counterpart. Bloom's commonplace experiences, as he wanders from home to office, pub, and brothel, and then home again—a one-day "voyage" through the streets of Dublin—constitute the plot of the novel. The real "action" of *Ulysses* takes place in the minds of its principal characters: Bloom, his acquaintances, and his wife Molly. Their collective ruminations produce an overwhelming sense of desolation and a startling awareness that the human psyche can never extricate itself from the timeless blur of experience. Joyce's stream of consciousness technique and his dense accumulation of unfamiliar and oddly compounded words make this monumental novel difficult to grasp—yet it remains more accessible than his experimental, baffling prose work, *Finnegans Wake*. Initially, however, it was censorship that made *Ulysses* inaccessible to the public: Since Joyce treated sexual matters as freely as all other aspects of human experience, critics judged his language obscene. The novel was banned in the United States until 1933.

The combined influence of Freud and Joyce was visible in much of the first-ranking literature of the twentieth century. Writers such as Gertrude Stein (1874–1946) and the Nobel laureates Thomas Mann (1875–1955) and William Faulkner (1897–1962) extended the use of the stream of consciousness technique. In theater the American playwright Eugene O'Neill (1888–1953) fused Greek myth with Freudian concepts of guilt and repression in the dramatic trilogy *Mourning Becomes Electra* (1931). He devised dramatic techniques that revealed the characters' buried emotions, such as two actors playing different aspects of a single individual, the use of masks, and the embellishment of dialogue with accompanying asides. The new psychology extended its influence to performance style as well: Freud's emphasis on the interior life inspired the development of **method acting**, a style of modern theatrical performance that tried to harness "true emotion" and "affective memory" from childhood experience in the interpretation of dramatic roles. The pioneer in method acting was the Russian director and actor Konstantin Stanislavsky (1863–1938), whose innovative techniques as head of the Moscow Art Theater spread to the United States in the early 1930s.

The New Freedom in Poetry

Modern poets avidly seized upon stream of consciousness techniques to emancipate poetry from syntactical and grammatical bonds—a mission that had been initiated by the symbolists and refined by the imagists. The French writer Guillaume Apollinaire (1880–1918), a close friend of Picasso and an admirer of cubism, wrote poems that not only liberated words from their traditional placement in the sentence but also freed sentences from their traditional arrangement on the page. Inspired by the designs of ordinary handbills, billboards, and signs, Apollinaire created **concrete poems**, that is, poems produced in the shape of external objects, such as watches, neckties, and pigeons. He arranged the words in the poem "Il Pleut" ("It Rains"), for instance, as if they had fallen onto the page like raindrops from the heavens. Such word-pictures, which Apollinaire called "lyrical ideograms," inspired the poet to exult, "I too am a painter!"

The American poet e. e. cummings (1894–1962) arrived in France in 1917 as a volunteer ambulance driver for the Red Cross. Like Apollinaire, cummings wrote poems that violated the traditional rules of verse composition. To sharpen the focus of a poem, he subjected typography and syntax to acrobatic distortions that challenged the eye as well as the ear. cummings poked fun at modern society by packing his verse with slang, jargon, and sexual innuendo. As the following poem of 1926 suggests, his lyrics are often infused with large doses of playful humor.

---

*James Joyce, *Ulysses*. New York: Vintage Books edition, Knopf, 1966, 57.

READING 6.6
cummings' [she being Brand]

```
she being Brand                                        1

-new;and you
know consequently a
little stiff i was
careful of her and(having                              5
thoroughly oiled the universal
joint tested my gas felt of
her radiator made sure her springs were O.

K.)i went right to it flooded-the-carburetor cranked her

up,slipped the                                        10
clutch(and then somehow got into reverse she
kicked what
the hell)next
minute i was back in neutral tried and

again slo-wly;bare,ly nudg.   ing(my                  15

lev-er Right-
oh and her gears being in
A 1 shape passed
from low through
second-in-to-high like                                20
greasedlightning) just as we turned the corner of Divinity

avenue i touched the accelerator and give

her the juice,good

                                        (it

was the first ride and believe i we was                25
happy to see how nice she acted right up to
the last minute coming back down by the Public
Gardens i slammed on

the
internalexpanding                                      30
&
externalcontracting
brakes Bothatonce and

brought allofher tremB
-ling                                                  35
to a: dead.

stand-
;Still)
```

◆

The New Psychology and the Visual Arts

It was in the visual arts that the new psychology made its most dramatic and long-lasting impact. Artists adopted Freud's theory of the unconscious mind to put into their paintings not only their hidden emotions and repressed desires but their dreams and fantasies as well. The irrational and antirational forces of the id became the subject and the inspiration for an assortment of styles that have dominated the century. These include expressionism, metaphysical art, dada, and surrealism. Expressionism and surrealism have had particularly important effects on photography and film, as well as on the fields of commercial and applied arts that have flourished in the second half of the century. Indeed, in every aspect of our daily experience, from fashion designs to magazine and television advertisements, the evidence of the Freudian revolution is still visible.

Expressionism

The pioneer expressionist painter of the twentieth century was the Scandinavian Edvard Munch (1863–1944). Munch was a great admirer of Ibsen, his Norwegian contemporary, whose plays (see chapter 30) examine the inner conflicts and repressed desires of their characters. Obsessed with the traumas of puberty and frustrated sexuality, Munch was also deeply affected by personal associations with illness and death—tuberculosis had killed both his mother and sister. Such subjects provided the imagery for his paintings and woodcuts; but it was in his style—a haunting synthesis of violently distorted forms and savage colors—that Munch captured the anguished intensity of the neurosis that caused his own mental collapse in 1908. *The Scream* (Figure 33.1), a painting that has become a universal symbol of the modern condition, takes its mood of urgency and alarm from the combined effects of sinuous clouds (which Munch described as "red as blood and tongues of fire"), writhing blue-black waters, and a dramatically receding bridge. These visual rhythms suggest the resonating sound of the cry emitted by the ghostly foreground figure (possibly inspired by an Inka mummy Munch had seen in the Paris Exhibition of 1889).

Munch's impassioned style foreshadowed *German expressionism*. Like the cubists and fauves in France and the futurists in Italy, young artists in Germany rebelled against the "old-established forces" of academic art. Influenced by Freud and by the arts of Africa and Oceania, two modernist groups emerged: in Dresden, *Die Brücke* (The Bridge) was founded in 1905; the second, established in Munich in 1911, called itself *Der Blaue Reiter* (The Blue Rider). Though marked by strong personal differences, the artists of these two groups pursued a style that has come to be known as German expressionism. This style, marked by free distortions of form and color that evoke pathos, violence, and emotional intensity, flourished until the beginning of World War I. The expressionists inherited the brooding, melancholic sensibility of Goethe, Wagner, and van Gogh. They favored macabre and intimate subjects, which they rendered by means of distorted forms, harsh

Figure 33.1 Edvard Munch, *The Scream*, 1893. Oil, pastel, and casein on cardboard, 35¾ × 29 in. National Gallery, Oslo. © The Munch-Museum/The Munch-Ellingsen-Group.

colors, and the bold and haunting use of black.

Led by Ernst Ludwig Kirchner (1880–1938), members of *Die Brücke* included Erich Heckel (1883–1970), Karl Schmidt-Rotluff (1884–1976), and Emile Nolde (1867–1956). These artists, who envisioned their movement as a "bridge" to modernism, embraced art as an outpouring of "inner necessity," emotion, and ecstasy.

Seized by the prewar tensions of urban Germany, they produced probing self-portraits, tempestuous landscapes, and ominous cityscapes. In the painting *Street, Berlin* (Figure **33.2**), Kirchner's jagged lines and dissonant colors, accented by aggressive areas of black, evoke the image of urban life as crowded, impersonal, and threatening. His convulsive distortions of figural form

Figure 33.2 Ernst Ludwig Kirchner, *Street, Berlin*, 1913. Oil on canvas, 47½ × 35⅞ in. The Museum of Modern Art, New York. Purchase. Photograph © 1997 The Museum of Modern Art, New York.

reveal the influence of African sculpture, while the nervous intensity of his line style reflects his indebtedness to the German graphic tradition pioneered by Albrecht Dürer in the sixteenth century (see chapter 18). Like Dürer, Kirchner rendered many of his subjects (including portraits and cityscapes) in woodcut—the favorite medium of the German expressionists.

Metaphysical Art and Fantasy

While the German expressionists brought a new degree of subjective intensity to depicting the visible world, other artists explored the life that lay beyond sensory experience. One of these artists was Giorgio de Chirico (1888–1978). Born in Greece, de Chirico moved to Italy in 1909, where he rejected the tenets of Italian futurism (see chapter 32) and pioneered instead a style that he called "metaphysical," that is, "beyond physical reality." In canvases executed between 1910 and 1920, de Chirico attempted to bring the world of the subconscious into the realm of art. Combining sharply conceived images, contradictory perspectives, unnatural colors, and illogically cast shadows, de Chirico produced disturbing, dreamlike effects similar to those achieved by Kafka in prose. In his painting *The Nostalgia of the Infinite* (Figure **33.3**), two figures, dwarfed by eerie shadows, stand in the empty courtyard; five flags flutter mysteriously in an airless, acid green sky. The vanishing point established by the orthogonal lines of the portico on the right contradicts the low placement of the distant horizon. Of his disquieting cityscapes, de Chirico explained, "There are more enigmas in the shadow of a man who walks in the sun than in all the religions of past, present, and future." De Chirico's style anticipated a mode of visual (and literary) representation known as magic realism, in which commonplace objects and events are exaggerated or juxtaposed in unexpected ways to create an aura of fantasy.

Equally fantastic in spirit but more indebted in style to the lessons of cubism and fauvism were the paintings of the Russian-born Marc Chagall (1887–1985). Chagall arrived in Paris in 1910 and, like his countryman and fellow expatriate Igor Stravinsky, he infused his first compositions with the folk tales and customs of his native land. In Chagall's nostalgic recollection of rural Russia called *I and the Village* (Figure **33.4**), the disjunctive sizes and positions of the figures and the fantastic colors obey the logic of the subconscious world rather than the laws of physical reality. Chagall freely superimposed images upon one another or showed them floating in space, defying the laws of gravity. Autobiographical motifs, such as the fiddle player and the levitating lovers, became Chagall's hallmarks in the richly colored canvases, murals, and stained glass windows of his long and productive career.

Figure 33.3 Giorgio de Chirico, *The Nostalgia of the Infinite*, 1913–1914?; dated on painting 1911. Oil on canvas, 53¼ × 25½ in. The Museum of Modern Art, New York. Purchase. Photograph © 1997 The Museum of Modern Art, New York. © DACS 1997.

Figure 33.4 Marc Chagall, *I and the Village*, 1911. Oil on canvas, 6 ft. 3⅝ in. × 4 ft. 11⅝ in. The Museum of Modern Art, New York. Mrs. Simon Guggenheim Fund. Photograph © 1997 The Museum of Modern Art, New York. © ADAGP, Paris and DACS, London 1997.

The Dada Movement

Although expressionism and fantasy played major roles in modern art, neither broke with tradition as aggressively as the movement known as *dada*, whose proponents would undertake to challenge the very nature of art. Founded in 1916 in Zürich, Switzerland, the dada movement consisted of a loosely knit group of European painters and poets who, perceiving World War I as evidence of a world gone mad, dedicated themselves to spreading the gospel of irrationality. The nonsensical name of the movement, "dada" (French for "hobbyhorse"), which was chosen by inserting a penknife at random into the pages of a dictionary, symbolized their irreverent stance. If the world had gone mad, should not its art be equally mad? Dada answered with art that was the product of chance, accident, or outrageous behavior. Deliberately violating "good taste," dada constituted an assault on all forms of rational order and artistic convention. The dadaists met frequently at the Café Voltaire in Zürich, where they orchestrated "noise concerts" and recited poetry informed by **improvisation** and free association. The Romanian poet Tristan Tzara produced poems from words cut out of newspapers and randomly scattered on a table, while the French sculptor and poet Jean Arp constructed collages and relief sculptures from shapes arranged "according to the laws of chance." Such attacks on Western tradition and on modern technocracy in general reflected the spirit of **nihilism** (the denial of traditional and religious and moral principles) that flowered in the ashes of the war. In his "Lecture on Dada" in 1922, Tzara declared, "The acts of life have no beginning or end. Everything happens in a completely idiotic way. Simplicity is called dada. . . . Like everything in life, dada is useless."

As with poetry and painting, dada theater paid homage to Freud by liberating "everything obscure in the mind, buried deep, unrevealed," as one French playwright explained. Narrative realism and traditional characterization gave way to improvisation and the performance of random and bizarre incidents. One form of dada theater, the *theater of cruelty*, known for its violent and scatological themes, anticipated theater of the absurd plays written during the 1950s and 1960s (see chapter 35).

The spirit of the dadaists was most vividly realized in the work of the French artist Marcel Duchamp (1887–1968). Early in his career, Duchamp had flirted with cubism and futurism, producing the influential *Nude Descending a Staircase* (see Figure 32.11); but after 1912, Duchamp abandoned professional painting and turned to making—or remaking—art objects. Duchamp mocked the seriousness of high art by drawing a mustache on a reproduction of Leonardo da Vinci's

Figure 33.5 Marcel Duchamp, *L.H.O.O.Q.*, 1919. Rectified ready-made, pencil on a reproduction of the *Mona Lisa*, 7¾ × 4⅞ in. Collection of Mrs. Mary Sisler. © ADAGP, Paris and DACS, London 1997.

venerable *Mona Lisa* (see chapter 17) and adding at the bottom a series of letters, which, when recited rapidly in French, send a lewd message (Figure 33.5). His "corrected ready-made," as he called his piece, expressed his disdain for conventional values and for Western art in general. It launched the modern artist as antiartist—the self-appointed prophet and defiler of tradition.

Duchamp did more than thumb his nose at Western aesthetics; he questioned the very nature of art and its relationship to language and thought. In 1913 he mounted a bicycle wheel atop a barstool, thus producing the first ready-made sculpture, as well as the first **mobile** (a sculpture with moving parts). In 1917 he submitted a common urinal as an entry in a gallery art show. The piece, entitled *Fountain*, was rejected; but the implications of this episode were enormous. By designating "found objects" as works of art, Duchamp mocked conventional techniques of making art and, at the same time, removed the barriers between art and life. Moreover, by detaching objects from their normal, everyday contexts, he demonstrated that images—like the residue of the human subconscious—obeyed a logic of their own, a logic whose "rules" flouted traditional aesthetic norms. The nonsensical, the accidental, and the absurd—phenomena buried in the subconscious life of dreams—now besieged the hallowed domain of the arts.

In 1918 Duchamp moved to New York City, where he labored for ten years on his *magnum opus*, a large glass and wire assemblage filled with esoteric sexual symbolism. He called it *The Bride Stripped Bare by Her Bachelors, Even*. After 1920, Duchamp went "underground," spending as much time perfecting his chess game (his favorite pastime) as making art. Nevertheless, his small, pioneering body of works and his irreverent view that art "has absolutely no existence as . . . truth" have had a powerful influence on scores of avant-garde poets, painters, and composers of the twentieth century.

Figure 33.6 Pablo Picasso, *Seated Woman*, Paris, 1927. Oil on wood, 4 ft. 3⅛ in. × 3 ft. 2¼ in. The Museum of Modern Art, New York. Gift of James Thrall Soby. Photograph © 1997 The Museum of Modern Art, New York. © Succession Picasso/DACS 1997.

Surrealism and Abstract Surrealists: Picasso, Miró, and Klee

The word *surrealism*, coined by Guillaume Apollinaire in 1917, came to describe one of the century's most intriguing literary and artistic movements—a movement devoted to expressing in conscious life the workings of the subconscious mind. The French critic André Breton (1896–1966) inaugurated surrealism in the first "Surrealist Manifesto" (1924), in which he proclaimed the artist's liberation from reason and the demands of conventional society. The surrealists paid explicit homage to Freud and his writings, especially those on free association and dream analysis. Indeed, Breton himself visited Freud in Vienna in 1921. In describing the surrealist's commitment to glorifying the irrational aspect of the human psyche, Breton proclaimed,

We are still living under the reign of logic. . . .
But in this day and age logical methods are
applicable only to solving problems of secondary

Figure 33.7 Joan Miró, *Person Throwing a Stone at a Bird*, 1926. Oil on canvas, 29 × 36¼ in. The Museum of Modern Art, New York. Purchase. Photograph © 1997 The Museum of Modern Art, New York. © ADAGP, Paris and DACS, London 1997.

interest. The absolute rationalism that is still in vogue allows us to consider only facts relating directly to our experience. . . . [Experience] is protected by the sentinels of common sense. Under the pretense of civilization and progress, we have managed to banish from the mind everything that may rightly or wrongly be termed superstition, or fancy; forbidden is any kind of search for truth which is not in conformance with accepted practices. It was, apparently, by pure chance, that a part of our mental world which we pretended not to be concerned with any longer— and, in my opinion, by far the most important part—has been brought back to light. For this we must give thanks to the discoveries of Sigmund Freud. . . . The imagination is perhaps on the point of reasserting itself, of reclaiming its rights.*

Breton defined surrealism as "psychic automatism, in its pure state," that is, creative effort guided by thought functions free of rational control and "exempt from any aesthetic or moral concern." He emphasized the omnipotence of the dream state in guiding the surrealist enterprise.

Just as writers developed literary techniques such as stream of consciousness to achieve a new freedom from rational control, so visual artists devised a variety of liberating methods and processes. Some juxtaposed realistically painted objects in ways that produce a

visionary reality approximating the reality of dreams. Others explored psychic automatism, allowing the hand to move spontaneously and at random, as if casually doodling or improvising. Still others tried to recover a sense of childlike spontaneity by filling their paintings with free-spirited, biomorphic shapes. The latter two groups produced various kinds of abstract surrealism, while the former pioneered visionary surrealism. Fundamentally, however, the paradox of surrealist art rested on the artist's *conscious* effort to capture *subconscious* experience.

Breton recognized Picasso as one of the pioneers of surrealist art. As early as 1907, in *Les Demoiselles d'Avignon* (see Figure 32.2), Picasso had begun to radicalize the image of the human figure; by the mid-1920s, brutal dissection and savage distortion dominated his art. In 1927, Picasso painted the *Seated Woman* (Figure 33.6), the image of a "split personality" that seemed to symbolize Freud's three-part psyche. The head of the female consists of a frontal view, as well as at least two profile views, each of which reveals a different aspect of her personality. In scores of paintings and sculptures, as well as in the stream of consciousness prose he wrote during the 1930s, Picasso introduced double meanings and visual puns, thus securing his reputation as the master of metamorphosis in twentieth-century art. Indeed, the "split personality" motif continued to preoccupy Picasso throughout his long artistic career.

In the paintings of the Spanish artist Joan Miró (1893–1983), the surrealist's search for subconscious experience kindled the artist's personal mythology. Employing a style that suggests a child's representation, Miró made biomorphic creatures and spiny, abstract

*André Breton, "Manifesto of Surrealism" (1924). From *Manifestoes of Surrealism* by André Breton, translated by Richard Seaver and Helen R. Lane. Ann Arbor, Mich.: University of Michigan Press, 1969, 9.

Figure 33.8 Paul Klee, *Fish Magic*, 1925. Oil on canvas, mounted on board, 30⅜ × 38½ in. Philadelphia Museum of Art. The Louise and Walter Arensberg Collection ('50–134–112).

organisms the denizens of a fantastic universe. The "person" in Miró's *Person Throwing a Stone at a Bird* (Figure **33.7**) resembles a large, white, one-footed ameba; the bird is a stick figure with a flaming cock's-comb; and the stone is an egglike object whose trajectory is traced by means of a dotted line. Superficially the depiction of a playful act, the painting conjures up a dreamlike ritual that unfolds ominously against a darkened sea and sky.

The Swiss-born painter Paul Klee (1879–1940) stood on the fringes of surrealism. One of the most sophisticated artists of the century, Klee was a brilliant draftsman who created physically small artworks that resemble hieroglyphic puzzles. His abstractions, like the entries in his personal diaries, are characterized by gentle humor and exquisite finesse; they belong to the substratum of the mind—the subconscious repository of mysterious symbols. "Art does not represent the visible," Klee insisted, "rather, it renders visible [the invisible]." Klee's *Fish Magic* (Figure **33.8**), painted during his tenure as a teacher at the Bauhaus, consists of a group of carefully arranged organic motifs that resemble sacred signs. Flowers, fish, and human figures, all executed with pictographic simplicity, share the ambient space of planets whose rhythms are measured by a mysteriously suspended clock. The painting gives credence to Klee's argument that art is "a parable of Creation," the product of imagination guided by instinctual stimuli, and the bearer of illusions that (by their very elusiveness) stir the soul.

Visionary Surrealists: Magritte and Dali

While Picasso, Miró, and Klee favored abstract, organic images, other surrealists combined meticulously painted objects in ways that were often shocking or unexpected. The most notable of the European visionary surrealists were René Magritte and Salvador Dali. Both were superb draftsmen whose *trompe l'oeil* skills elicited a disquieting dream reality. Profoundly influenced by de Chirico, the Belgian artist Magritte (1898–1967) juxtaposed realistically detailed objects in startling and irrational ways. In one of Magritte's paintings, a coffin takes the place of a reclining figure; in another, a birdcage is substituted for the head of the sitter; and in still another, human toes appear on a pair of leather shoes. In a small piece entitled *The Treachery (or Perfidy) of Images* (1928), Magritte portrays with crisp and faultless accuracy a briar pipe, beneath which appears the legend "This is not a pipe." The painting addresses the age-old distinction between the real world—the world of the *actual* pipe—and the art object, whose reality is the virtual *illusion* of a pipe. The question of real space versus illusory space is also raised in Magritte's *The False Mirror*, which consists of a single large eye whose iris is the very cloud-filled sky that it perceives (Figure **33.9**). Magritte's magic realism tests assumptions about the real world, while it asserts with deadpan humor its own bizarre laws. Modern advertising, which owes much to Magritte, has transformed some of his images into contemporary icons—the "false

Figure 33.9 René Magritte, *The False Mirror* (*Le Faux Miroir*), 1928. Oil on canvas, 21¼ × 31⅞ in. The Museum of Modern Art, New York. Purchase. Photograph © 1997 The Museum of Modern Art, New York. © ADAGP, Paris and DACS, London 1997.

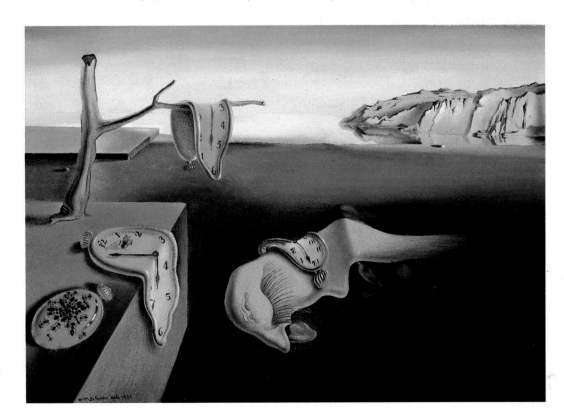

Figure 33.10 Salvador Dali, *The Persistence of Memory* (*Persistance de la Mémoire*), 1931. Oil on canvas, 9½ × 13 in. The Museum of Modern Art, New York. Given anonymously. Photograph © 1997 The Museum of Modern Art, New York. © DEMART PRO ARTE BV/DACS 1997.

mirror" serves, ironically enough, as a trademark of CBS television.

The Spanish painter and impresario Salvador Dali (1904–1989) was as much a showman as an artist. Cultivating the bizarre as a lifestyle, Dali exhibited a perverse desire to shock his audiences. Drawing motifs from his own erotic dreams and fantasies, he executed both natural and unnatural images with meticulous precision, combining them in unusual settings or giving them grotesque attributes. Dali's infamous *The Persistence of Memory* (Figure **33.10**) consists of a broad and barren landscape occupied by a leafless tree, three limp watches, and a watchcase crawling with ants. One of the timepieces plays host to a fly, while another rests upon a mass of brain matter resembling a profiled self-portrait—a motif that the artist frequently featured in his works. To seek an explicit message in this painting—even one addressing modern notions of time—would be to miss the point, for, as Dali himself observed, his "hand-painted dream photographs" were designed to "stamp themselves indelibly upon the mind."

The Women of Surrealism: Kahlo, O'Keeffe, and Oppenheim

Some of the most notable surrealist artists of the twentieth century have been women. Arguably the most celebrated female painter of the early twentieth century is Mexico's Frida Kahlo (1907–1954). Kahlo's paintings, of which more than one third are self-portraits, reflect the determined effort (shared by many modern feminists) to present the female image as something other than an erotic object of male desire. "I am the subject I know best," explained Kahlo, whose art bears testimony to what she called the "two great accidents" of her life: a bus crash that at the age of eighteen left her disabled, and her marriage to the notorious Mexican mural painter Diego Rivera (see chapter 34). Kahlo created a body of work that recorded the experience of chronic pain, both physical (her accident required some thirty surgeries and ultimately involved the amputation of her right leg) and psychic (repeated miscarriages, for example, deprived her of bearing a child). Kahlo's paintings also betray her close identification with Mexican folk culture and her deep appreciation of the beauty and expressive power of folk art. Her synthesis of fantasy and realism has much in common with magic realism, a style favored by many Latin American writers (see chapter 37). In *The Broken Column* (Figure **33.11**), Kahlo pictures herself as sufferer and savior, an emblematic figure that recalls the devotional icons of Mexico's religious shrines.

A pioneer modernist on the American scene, Georgia O'Keeffe (1887–1986) is often classified with America's regional painters. However, her treatment of

Figure 33.11 Frida Kahlo, *The Broken Column*, 1940. Oil on canvas, 15¾ × 12¼ in. Museo Frida Kahlo, Mexico City. Collection Lola Olmedo.

Figure 33.12 Georgia O'Keeffe, *Cow's Skull: Red, White, and Blue*, 1931. Oil on canvas, 39⅞ × 35⅞ in. Metropolitan Museum of Art, New York. Alfred Stieglitz Collection, 1952 (52.203). © ARS, New York and DACS, London 1997.

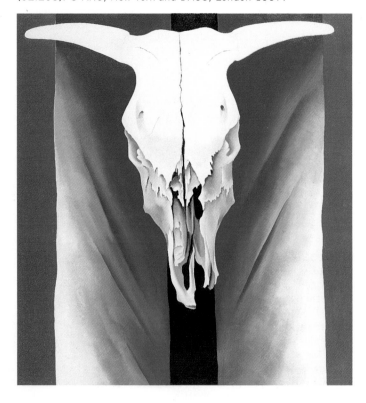

Figure 33.13 Meret Oppenheim, *Object* (*Le Déjeuner en fourrure*), 1936. Fur-covered cup, saucer, and spoon; cup 4⅜ in. diameter; saucer 9⅜ in. diameter; spoon 8 in. long; overall height 2⅞ in. The Museum of Modern Art, New York. Purchase. Photograph © 1997 The Museum of Modern Art, New York. © DACS 1997.

abstract, biomorphic shapes derived from greatly enlarged flowers and bleached animal bones gives her early paintings a haunting, menacing presence (Figure 33.12). In a fluid line style that distills the essence of the subject, the so-called "high priestess" of early modernism brought a visionary grandeur to the most ordinary ingredients of the American landscape.

Enlarging or combining commonplace objects in ways that were unexpected and shocking—the hallmark of the visionary surrealists—was a particularly effective strategy for surrealist sculptors; and in this domain as well, women made notable contributions. The furlined cup and saucer (Figure 33.13) conceived by the Swiss-German sculptor Meret Oppenheim (1913–1985) is shocking in its irreverent combination of familiar but disparate elements. Conceived in the irreverent spirit of Duchamp's modified ready-mades, Oppenheim's *Object* provokes a sequence of discomfiting and threatening narrative associations.

Surrealist Photography and Film

Photography and film were ideal media with which to explore the layers of the human subconscious. Surrealist photographers experimented with double exposure and unorthodox darkroom techniques to create unusual new effects similar to those of visionary surrealist painters and sculptors. Liberating photography from traditional pictorialism, photographers also made imaginative use of cubist collage. The German artist Hannah Höch (1889–1978) juxtaposed bits and pieces of assorted photographic images, a technique known as **photomontage**, to create antilogical compositions that

confounded the mind and the eye (Figure 33.14). A similar technique would be employed in the motion pictures of the Russian filmmaker Sergei Eisenstein (see chapter 34). In the cinema, Salvador Dali teamed up with the Spanish filmmaker Luis Buñuel (1900–1983) to create the pioneer surrealist film, *Un Chien Andalou* (1928). Violence and eroticism are the dominant motifs of this film, whose more famous scenes include ants crawling out of a hole in a man's palm (an oblique reference to Christ's stigmata), a man bleeding from the mouth as he fondles a woman, a woman poking a stick at an amputated hand that lies on the street, an eyeball being sliced with a razor blade, and two pianos filled with the mutilated carcasses of donkeys. In surrealist cinema, such special techniques as slow motion, close-up, and quick cuts from scene to scene worked to create jolting, dreamlike effects. It is no surprise that surrealism had a formative influence on some of the later twentieth century's most imaginative filmmakers, including Jean Cocteau, Jean Renoir, Ingmar Bergman, and Federico Fellini.

Figure 33.14 Hannah Höch, *Cut with the Kitchen Knife*, 1919. Collage of pasted papers, 44⅞ × 35½ in. Nationalgalerie, Staatliche Museen Preussischer Kulturbesitz, Berlin. © DACS 1997. Photo: © Bildarchiv Preussischer Kulturbesitz, Berlin.

The New Psychology and Music

During the 1920s, composers moved beyond the exotic and unorthodox instrumental forays of Stravinsky's *Rite of Spring* to explore even more outrageous experiments in sound. A group of six artists that included the French composer Eric Satie (1866–1925) incorporated into their music such "instruments" as doorbells, type-writers, and roulette wheels. Satie's style, which is typically sparse, rhythmic, and witty, has much in common with the poetry of Apollinaire and e. e. cummings. His compositions, to which he gave such titles as *Flabby Preludes, Desiccated Embryos,* and *Three Pieces in the Form of a Pear,* were, however, less eccentric than was his lifestyle—he ate nothing but white foods and wore only gray suits.

The Freudian impact on music was most evident in the medium of musical drama which, by the second decade of the century, openly explored aspects of sexuality, eroticism, female hysteria, and the life of dreams. In the opera *Salome* (1905), a modern interpretation of the martyrdom of John the Baptist, the German composer Richard Strauss (1864–1949) dramatized the obsessive erotic attachment of King Herod's beautiful niece to the Christian prophet. Revolutionary in sound (in some places the meter changes in every bar) and in its frank treatment of a biblical subject, the opera shocked critics so deeply that a performance slated for Vienna in 1905 was cancelled; in America, the opera was banned for almost thirty years after its New York performance in 1907. *Bluebeard's Castle* (1918), a one-act opera by the leading Hungarian composer of the twentieth century Béla Bartók (1881–1945), did not suffer so harsh a fate, despite the fact that the composer had boldly recast a popular fairy tale into a parable of repressed tensions and jealousy between the sexes.

The mood of anxiety and apprehension that characterized expressionist and surrealist art was, however, most powerfully realized in the song cycles of Arnold Schoenberg, whose experiments in atonality were introduced in chapter 32. Schoenberg's song cycles, or **monodramas**, were dramatic pieces written for a single (usually deeply disturbed) character. In the monodrama *Erwartung* (*Expectation*), Schoenberg took as his theme a woman's frenzied search for the lover who has deserted her. In *Pierrot Lunaire*♭ (*Moonstruck Pierrot*) of 1912, a cycle of twenty-one songs for female voice and small instrumental ensemble, Schoenberg brought to life the dreamworld of a mad clown. The texts of these and other atonal and harshly dissonant song cycles resemble stream of consciousness monologues. They are performed in *Sprechstimme* (or "speech-song"), a style in which words are spoken at different pitches. Neither

♭See Music Listening Selection at end of chapter.

exclusively song nor speech, *Sprechstimme* is a kind of operatic recitation in which pitches are approximated and the voice may glide in a wailing manner from note to note. Despite the fact that his disquieting music stirred up great controversy among audiences and critics, Schoenberg attracted a large following. Even after he moved to the United States in 1933, young composers—including many associated with Hollywood film—flocked to study with him.

Schoenberg's foremost student, Alban Berg (1885–1935), produced two of the most powerful operas of the twentieth century. Though less strictly atonal than Schoenberg's song cycles, Berg's operas *Wozzeck* (1921) and *Lulu* (1935) make use of serial techniques and the *Sprechstimme* style. Thematically, they feature the highly charged motifs of sexual frustration, murder, and suicide. The unfinished *Lulu* is the story of a sexually dominated woman who both destroys and is destroyed by her lovers. *Lulu* has been called "sordid," "psychotic," and "shocking." It explores such Freudian subjects as female hysteria and repressed sexuality, while at the same time it exploits the age-old image of woman-as-serpent. Both the music and the story of *Lulu* evoke a nightmarelike atmosphere, which, in modern multi-media productions, has been enhanced by the use of onstage film and slide projections.

SUMMARY

Sigmund Freud's theories concerning the nature of the human psyche, the significance of dreams, and the dominating role of human sexuality had a revolutionary effect on the beliefs, attitudes, and morals of modern society. They were equally influential upon the arts. In literature, Proust, Kafka, and Joyce are representative of the modern novelist's preoccupation with the subconscious life and with the role of memory in shaping reality. Their fiction reflects a fascination with the methods and principles of Freudian psychoanalysis. Stream of consciousness narrative and the interior monologue are among the literary techniques used by modern authors to develop plot and character. The poetry of e. e. cummings reveals the influence of free association in liberating words from the bounds of syntax and conventional transcription.

In the visual arts, Freud's impact generated a wide variety of styles that gave free play to fantasy and dreams. The expressionism of Munch and Kirchner, the metaphysical art of de Chirico, and the fantasies of Chagall examined the mysteries of repressed fears and desires. The dada movement spread the gospel of irrationality in randomly organized words and images. Duchamp, the most outrageous of the dada cultists, championed a nihilistic, antiart spirit that had far-reaching effects in the second half of the century. In

1924, André Breton launched surrealism, an international movement to liberate the life of the subconscious from the bonds of reason. Strongly influenced by Freud, the surrealists viewed the human subconscious as a battleground of conflicting forces dominated by the instincts. Picasso, Miró, and Klee explored the terrain of the interior life in abstract paintings filled with playful and ominous images. Dali, Magritte, Kahlo, and O'Keeffe manipulated illusions of the real world in ways that evoked the visionary incoherence of the dream life. In motion pictures, Dali, Buñuel, and others devised cinematic techniques that exposed the dark and unpredictable passions of the mind.

In music, Satie embraced mundane sounds with the same enthusiasm that e. e. cummings showed for slang in poetry and Duchamp exercised in his glorification of "found objects." But it was in the expressionistic monodramas of Schoenberg and the sexually charged operas of Strauss, Bartók, and Berg that Freud's impact was most powerfully realized. As the events of two world wars would confirm Freud's pessimistic analysis of human nature, so the arts of the twentieth century acknowledged his view that human reason was not the "keeper of the castle" and that the castle gates themselves were eternally vulnerable to the dark forces of the subconscious.

GLOSSARY

archetype the primal patterns of the collective unconscious, which Carl Jung described as "mental forms whose presence cannot be explained by anything in the individual's own life and which seem to be aboriginal, innate, and inherited shapes of the human mind"

collective unconscious according to Jung, the universal realm of the unconscious life, which contains the archetypes

concrete poetry poetry produced in the shape of ordinary, external objects

improvisation the invention of the work of art as it is being performed

interior monologue a literary device by which the stream of consciousness of a character is presented; it records the internal, emotional experience of the character on one or more levels of consciousness

method acting a modern style of theatrical performance that tries to

harness childhood emotions and memories in the service of interpreting a dramatic role

mobile a sculpture constructed so that its parts move by natural or mechanical means

monodrama in music, a dramatic piece written for only one character

nihilism a viewpoint that denies objective moral truths and traditional religious and moral principles

photomontage the combination of freely juxtaposed and usually heterogeneous photographic images (see also Glossary, chapter 34, "montage")

Sprechstimme (German, "speech-song") a style of operatic recitation in which words are spoken at different pitches

sublimation the positive modification and redirection of primal urges that Freud identified as the work of the ego

SUGGESTIONS FOR READING

Bersani, Leo. *The Freudian Body: Psychoanalysis and Art.* Irvington, N.Y.: Columbia University Press, 1986.

Chénieux-Gendron, Jacqueline. *Surrealism,* translated by Vivian Folkenflik. New York: Columbia University Press, 1990.

Clark, Ronald W. *Freud: The Man and the Cause—A Biography.* New York: Random House, 1980.

Fromm, Erich. *Sigmund Freud's Mission: An Analysis of His Personality and Influence.* New York: Grove, 1959.

Gay, Peter. *Freud for Historians.* New York: Oxford University Press, 1985.

Gordon, Donald E. *Expressionism: Art and Idea.* New Haven: Yale University Press, 1987.

Gould, Michael. *Surrealism and the Cinema.* New York: A. S. Barnes, 1976.

Hayman, Ronald. *Kafka: A Biography.* New York: Oxford University Press, 1981.

Jung, Carl Gustav. *Man and His Symbols.* New York: Doubleday, 1964.

Nadeau, Maurice. *The History of Surrealism,* translated by Richard Howard. Cambridge, Mass.: Harvard University Press, 1990.

Nelson, Benjamin. *Freud and the Twentieth Century.* New York: Meridian, 1957.

Richter, Hans. *Dada: Art and Anti-Art.* London: Thames and Hudson, 1961.

Zamora, Martha, and M. S. Smith. *Frida Kahlo: The Brush of Anguish.* San Francisco: Chronicle Books, 1990.

MUSIC LISTENING SELECTION

Cassette II Selection 16 Schoenberg, *Pierrot Lunaire,* Op. 21, Part 3, No. 15, "Heimweh," 1912.

34
Total War, Totalitarianism, and the Arts

Two fundamentally related calamities have dominated the twentieth century: total war and totalitarian dictatorship. The consequences of both have been so great that the modern world has still not recovered from them. Total war and totalitarianism, facilitated by sophisticated military technology and electronic forms of mass communication, are unique to the twentieth century. They have caused this century to be the bloodiest in world history. Unlike natural disasters—the Black Death or the Lisbon earthquake, for example—the total wars and totalitarian regimes of the modern era were disasters perpetrated on human beings by human beings. Such human-made evils not only challenged the belief that technology would improve the quality of human life; they seemed to validate Freud's theory that all mortals are driven by base instincts and the dark forces of self-destruction.

The Great War of 1914, as World War I was called, and World War II that followed in 1939 were the first *total* wars in European history. They are called total not only because they involved more nations than had ever before been engaged in armed combat, but also because they destroyed—along with military personnel—large numbers of civilians. Moreover, the wars were total in the sense that they were fought with a "no holds barred" attitude—all and any methods of destruction were utilized in the name of conquest. The weapons of advanced technology made modern wars more impersonal and more devastating than any previously fought. World War I combatants used machine guns, heavy artillery, hand grenades, poison gas, flame throwers, armored tanks, submarines, dirigibles, and airplanes. From their open cockpits, pilots fired on enemy aircraft, while on land soldiers fought from lines of trenches dug deep into the ground. The rapid-firing, fully automatic machine gun alone caused almost eighty percent of the casualties. The cost of four years of war was approximately $350 billion, and the death tolls were staggering. In all, seventy million armed men fought in World War I, and over eight million of them died. In World War II, airplanes and aerial bombs (including, ultimately, the atomic bomb) played major roles; war costs tripled those of World War I, and casualties among the armed forces alone rose to over eighteen million people.

The underlying causes of these wars were aggressive rivalries between European powers. During the nineteenth century, nationalism and industrialism had facilitated militant competition for colonies throughout the world (see chapter 29); the armed forces became the embodiment of a nation's sovereign spirit and the primary tool for imperialism. National leaders fiercely defended the notion that military might was the best safeguard of peace: *"Si vis pacem, para bellum"*—"if you want peace, prepare for war," they argued. Nations believed their safety lay in defensive alliances. They joined with their ideological or geographic neighbors to create a system of alliances that, by the early twentieth century, divided Europe into two potentially hostile camps, each equipped to mobilize their armies if threatened.

The circumstances that led to World War I involved the increasingly visible efforts of Austria-Hungary and Germany to dominate vast portions of Eastern Europe. Germany, having risen to power during the nineteenth century, rivaled all other European nations in industrial might. By the early twentieth century, German efforts to colonize markets for trade took the form of militant imperialism in Eastern Europe. And in July of 1914, Austria-Hungary, seeking to expand Austrian territory to the south, used the political assassination of Archduke Francis Ferdinand (heir to the throne of Austria-Hungary) as a pretext to declare war on Serbia. Almost immediately, two opposing alliances came into confrontation: the Central Powers of Austria-Hungary, Germany, and the Ottoman Empire versus the Allied forces of Serbia, Belgium, France, Great Britain, and Russia. It became clear that the policy of peace through military strength had not prevented war but actually encouraged it.

At the beginning of the war, the Central Powers won early victories in Belgium and Poland, but the Allies stopped the German advance at the First Battle of the Marne in September of 1914 (Map **34.1**). The opposing armies settled down to warfare along the

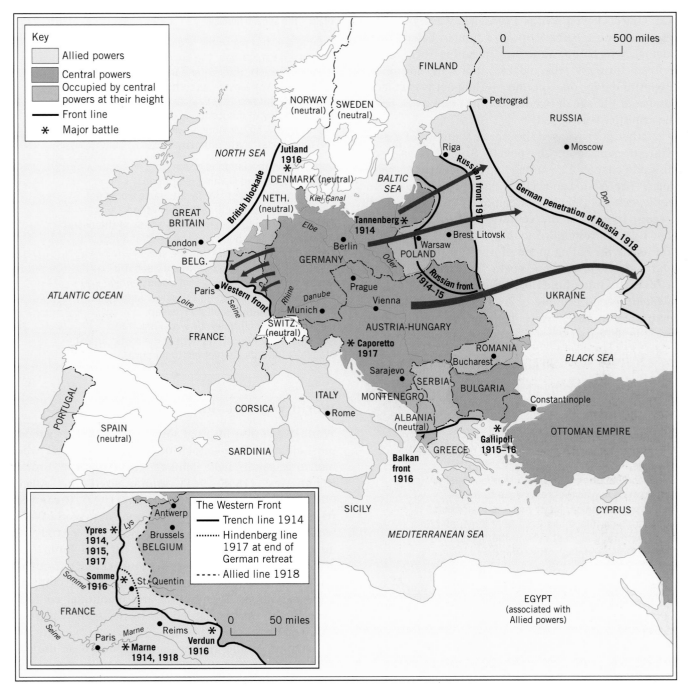

Map 34.1 World War I, 1914–1918.

Western front—a solid line of two opposing trenches that stretched 500 miles from the English Channel to the Swiss border. At the same time, on the Eastern front, Russian armies lost over a million men in combat against the combined German and Austrian forces. In the early years of the war, the United States remained neutral, but when German submarines began sinking unarmed passenger ships in 1917, the American president Woodrow Wilson opted to aid the Allies in order to "make the world safe for democracy." Fortified by American supplies and troops, the Allies moved toward victory. In November 1918, the fighting ended with an armistice.

The Literary Response to World War I

World War I Poetry

Writers responded to the war with sentiments ranging from buoyant idealism and militant patriotism to frustration and despair. The most enduring literature of the era, however, expressed the bitter anguish of the war experience itself. The poetry of the young British officer Wilfred Owen (1893–1918) reflects the sense of cynicism and futility that was voiced toward the end of the war. Owen viewed war as a senseless waste of human resources and a barbaric form of human behavior. His poems, which question the meaning of wartime heroism, unmask "the old Lie" that it is "fitting and proper to die for one's country." The poet was killed in combat at the age of twenty-five, just one week before the armistice was signed.

Other poets viewed the war as symbolic of a dying Western civilization. The poet T. S. Eliot, who is discussed in chapter 35, summed up this view in his classic poem "The Waste Land" (1922), a requiem for a dry and sterile culture. Eliot's contemporary and one of the greatest lyricists of the century, William Butler Yeats (1865–1939), responded to the violence of World War I and to the prevailing mood of unrest in his native Ireland with the apocalyptic poem "The Second Coming" (1921). The title of the poem alludes both to the long-awaited Second Coming of Jesus and to the nameless force that, in Yeats' view, threatened to enthrall the world in darkness.

READING 6.7
Poems of World War I

Owen's "Dulce Et Decorum Est"[1]

Bent double, like old beggars under sacks,	1
Knock-kneed, coughing like hags, we cursed through sludge,	
Till on the haunting flares we turned our backs,	
And towards our distant rest began to trudge.	
Men marched asleep. Many had lost their boots,	5
But limped on, blood-shod. All went lame, all blind;	
Drunk with fatigue; deaf even to the hoots	
Of gas-shells dropping softly behind.	
Gas! GAS! Quick, boys!—An ecstasy of fumbling	
Fitting the clumsy helmets just in time,	10
But someone still was yelling out and stumbling	
And flound'ring like a man in fire or lime.—	
Dim through the misty panes and thick green light,	
As under a green sea, I saw him drowning.	
In all my dreams before my helpless sight	15
He plunges at me, guttering, choking, drowning.	
If in some smothering dreams, you too could pace	
Behind the wagon that we flung him in,	
And watch the white eyes writhing in his face,	
His hanging face, like a devil's sick of sin,	20
If you could hear, at every jolt, the blood	
Come gargling from the froth-corrupted lungs	
Bitter as the cud	
Of vile, incurable sores on innocent tongues,—	
My friend, you would not tell with such high zest	25
To children ardent for some desperate glory,	
The old Lie: *Dulce et decorum est*	
Pro patria mori.	

Yeats' "The Second Coming"

Turning and turning in the widening gyre[2]	1
The falcon cannot hear the falconer;	
Things fall apart; the center cannot hold;	
Mere anarchy is loosed upon the world,	
The blood-dimmed tide is loosed, and everywhere	5
The ceremony of innocence is drowned;	
The best lack all conviction, while the worst	
Are full of passionate intensity.	
Surely some revelation is at hand;	
Surely the Second Coming is at hand.	10
The Second Coming! Hardly are those words out	
When a vast image out of Spiritus Mundi[3]	
Troubles my sight: somewhere in sands of the desert	
A shape with lion body and the head of a man,	
A gaze blank and pitiless as the sun,	15
Is moving its slow thighs, while all about it	
Reel shadows of the indignant desert birds.	
The darkness drops again; but now I know	
That twenty centuries of stony sleep	
Were vexed to nightmare by a rocking cradle,	20
And what rough beast, its hour come round at last,	
Slouches towards Bethlehem to be born?	

◆

World War I Fiction

World War I also inspired some of this century's most outstanding fiction—much of it written by men who had engaged in field combat. The American Ernest Hemingway (1898–1961) immortalized the Allied offensive in Italy in *A Farewell to Arms* (1929). The novel, whose title reflects the desperate hope that World War I would be "the war to end all wars," is a study in disillusionment and a testament to the futility of armed combat. Hemingway's prose, characterized by understatement and journalistic succinctness, and his profound respect for physical and emotional courage were forged on the battlefields of the war, which he observed firsthand.

Armed conflict had a similar influence on the life and work of the novelist Erich Maria Remarque (1898–1970). Remarque, a German soldier who was wounded in combat several times, brought firsthand experience of World War I to his book *All Quiet on the Western Front* (1929)—perhaps the finest war novel of the twentieth century. It portrays with horrifying clarity the brutal realities of trench warfare and poison gas, two of the most chilling features of the war. Remarque renders the story in first-person, present-tense narrative, a style that compels the reader to share the apprehension of the protagonist. Over one million copies of Remarque's novel were sold in Germany during the year of its publication, and similar success greeted it in

---

[1]"It is fitting and proper to die for one's country." A line from "Ode III" by the Roman poet Horace (see chapter 7).

[2]A circular course traced by the upward sweep of a falcon. The image reflects Yeats' cyclical view of history.
[3]World Spirit, similar to the Jungian Great Memory of shared archetypal images.

translation and in its three movie versions. In 1939, however, the Nazi regime in Germany condemned Remarque's outspoken antimilitarism by publicly burning his books and depriving him of German citizenship. Shortly thereafter, Remarque moved to the United States where he became an American citizen.

READING 6.8

From Remarque's *All Quiet on the Western Front*

An indigent-looking wood receives us. We pass by the soup-kitchens. Under cover of the wood we climb out. The lorries turn back. They are to collect us again in the morning, before dawn. 1

Mist and the smoke of guns lie breast-high over the fields. The moon is shining. Along the road troops file. Their helmets gleam softly in the moonlight. The heads and the rifles stand out above the white mist, nodding heads, rocking carriers of guns.

Farther on the mist ends. Here the heads become figures; coats, trousers, and boots appear out of the mist as from a milky pool. They become a column. The column marches on, straight ahead, the figures resolve themselves into a block, individuals are no longer recognizable, the dark wedge presses onward, fantastically topped by the heads and weapons floating off on the milky pool. A column—not men at all. 10

Guns and munition wagons are moving along a crossroad. The backs of the horses shine in the moonlight, their movements are beautiful, they toss their heads, and their eyes gleam. The guns and the wagons float before the dim background of the moonlit landscape, the riders in their steel helmets resemble knights of a forgotten time; it is strangely beautiful and arresting. 20

We push on to the pioneer dump. Some of us load our shoulders with pointed and twisted iron stakes; others thrust smooth iron rods through rolls of wire and go off with them. The burdens are awkward and heavy.

The ground becomes more broken. From ahead come warnings: "Look out, deep shell-holes on the left"— "Mind, trenches"— — — 30

Our eyes peer out, our feet and our sticks feel in front of us before they take the weight of the body. Suddenly the line halts; I bump my face against the roll of wire carried by the man in front and curse.

There are some shell-smashed lorries in the road. Another order: "Cigarettes and pipes out." We are getting near the line.

In the meantime it has become pitch dark. We skirt a small wood and then have the front-line immediately before us. 40

An uncertain, red glow spreads along the skyline from one end to the other. It is in perpetual movement, punctuated with the bursts of flame from the muzzles of the batteries. Balls of light rise up high above it, silver and red spheres which explode and rain down in showers of red, white, and green stars. French rockets go up, which unfold a silk parachute to the air and drift slowly down. They light up everything as bright as day, their light shines on us and we see our shadows sharply outlined on 50

the ground. They hover for the space of a minute before they burn out. Immediately fresh ones shoot up to the sky, and again, green, red, and blue stars.

"Bombardment," says Kat.

The thunder of the guns swells to a single heavy roar and then breaks up again into separate explosions. The dry bursts of the machine-guns rattle. Above us the air teems with invisible swift movements, with howls, piping, and hisses. They are the smaller shells;—and amongst them, booming through the night like an organ, go the great coal-boxes and the heavies. They have a hoarse, distant bellow like a rutting stag and make their way high above the howl and whistle of the smaller shells. It reminds me of flocks of wild geese when I hear them. Last autumn the wild geese flew day after day across the path of the shells. 60

The searchlights begin to sweep the dark sky. They slide along it like gigantic tapering rulers. One of them pauses, and quivers a little. Immediately a second is beside him, a black insect is caught between them and tries to escape— the airman. He hesitates, is blinded and falls. . . . 70

We go back. It is time we returned to the lorries. The sky is become a bit brighter. Three o'clock in the morning. The breeze is fresh and cool, the pale hour makes our faces look grey.

We trudge onward in single file through the trenches and shell-holes and come again to the zone of mist. Katczinsky is restive, that's a bad sign.

"What's up, Kat?" says Kropp.

"I wish I were back home." Home—he means the huts.

"It won't last much longer, Kat." 80

He is nervous. "I don't know, I don't know— — —"

We come to the communication-trench and then to the open fields. The little wood reappears; we know every foot of ground here. There's the cemetery with the mounds and the black crosses.

That moment it breaks out behind us, swells, roars, and thunders. We duck down—a cloud of flame shoots up a hundred yards ahead of us.

The next minute under a second explosion part of the wood rises slowly in the air, three or four trees sail up and then crash to pieces. The shells begin to hiss like safety-valves—heavy fire— — — 90

"Take cover!" yells somebody—"Cover!"

The fields are flat, the wood is too distant and dangerous—the only cover is the graveyard and the mounds. We stumble across in the dark and as though spirited away every man lies glued behind a mound.

Not a moment too soon. The dark goes mad. It heaves and raves. Darkness blacker than the night rushes on us with giant strides, over us and away. The flames of the explosions light up the graveyard. 100

There is no escape anywhere. By the light of the shells I try to get a view of the fields. They are a surging sea, daggers of flame from the explosions leap up like fountains. It is impossible for anyone to break through it.

The wood vanishes, it is pounded, crushed, torn to pieces. We must stay here in the graveyard.

The earth bursts before us. It rains clods. I feel a smack. My sleeve is torn away by a splinter. I shut my fist. No pain. Still that does not reassure me: wounds don't hurt till afterwards. I feel the arm all over. It is grazed but sound. Now a crack on the skull, I begin to lose consciousness. Like lightning the thought comes to me: Don't faint, sink 110 down in the black broth and immediately come up the top again. A splinter slashes into my helmet, but has travelled so far that it does not go through. I wipe the mud out of my eyes. A hole is torn up in front of me. Shells hardly ever land in the same hole twice, I'll get into it. With one bound I fling myself down and lie on the earth as flat as a fish; there it whistles again, quickly I crouch together, claw 120 for cover, feel something on the left, shove in beside it, it gives way, I groan, the earth leaps, the blast thunders in my ears, I creep under the yielding thing, cover myself with it, draw it over me, it is wood, cloth, cover, cover, miserable cover against the whizzing splinters.

I open my eyes—my fingers grasp a sleeve, an arm. A wounded man? I yell to him—no answer—a dead man. My hand gropes farther, splinters of wood—now I remember again that we are lying in the graveyard.

But the shelling is stronger than everything. It wipes 130 out the sensibilities, I merely crawl still deeper into the coffin, it should protect me, and especially as Death himself lies in it too.

Before me gapes the shell-hole. I grasp it with my eyes as with fists. With one leap I must be in it. There, I get a smack in the face, a hand clamps on to my shoulder—has the dead man waked up?—The hand shakes me, I turn my head, in the second of light I stare into the face of Katczinsky, he has his mouth wide open and is yelling. I hear nothing, he rattles me, comes nearer, in a 140 momentary lull his voice reaches me: "Gas—Gaas—Gaaas—Pass it on."

I grab for my gas-mask. Some distance from me there lies someone. I think of nothing but this: That fellow there must know: Gaaas—Gaaas— — —

I call, I lean toward him, I swipe at him with the satchel, he doesn't see—once again, again—he merely ducks—it's a recruit—I look at Kat desperately, he has his mask ready—I pull out mine too, my helmet falls to one side, it slips over my face, I reach the man, his 150 satchel is on the side nearest me, I seize the mask, pull it over his head, he understands, I let go and with a jump drop back into the shell-hole.

The dull thud of the gas-shells mingles with the crashes of the high explosives. A bell sounds between the explosions, gongs, and metal clappers warning everyone—Gas—Gas—Gaas.

Someone plumps down behind me, another. I wipe the goggles of my mask clear of the moist breath. It is Kat, Kropp, and someone else. All four of us lie there in heavy, 160 watchful suspense and breathe as lightly as possible.

These first minutes with the mask decide between life and death: is it tightly woven? I remember the awful sights in the hospital: the gas patients who in day-long suffocation cough their burnt lungs up in clots.

Cautiously, the mouth applied to the valve, I breathe. The gas still creeps over the ground and sinks into all hollows. Like a big, soft jelly-fish it floats into our shell-hole and lolls there obscenely. I nudge Kat, it is better to crawl out and lie on top than to stay here where the gas 170 collects most. But we don't get as far as that; a second bombardment begins. It is no longer as though the shells roared; it is the earth itself raging.

With a crash something black bears down on us. It lands close beside us; a coffin thrown up.

I see Kat move and crawl across. The coffin has hit the fourth man in our hole on his outstretched arm. He tries to tear off his gas-mask with the other hand. Kropp seizes him just in time, twists the hand sharply behind his back and holds it fast. 180

Kat and I proceed to free the wounded arm. The coffin lid is loose and bursts open, we are easily able to pull it off, we toss the corpse out, it slides to the bottom of the shell-hole, then we try to loosen the under-part.

Fortunately the man swoons and Kropp is able to help us. We no longer have to be careful, but work away till the coffin gives with a sigh before the spade that we have dug in under it.

It has grown lighter. Kat takes a piece of the lid, places it under the shattered arm, and we wrap all our bandages 190 round it. For the moment we can do no more.

Inside the gas-mask my head booms and roars—it is nigh bursting. My lungs are tight, they breathe always the same hot, used-up air, the veins on my temples are swollen, I feel I am suffocating.

A grey light filters through to us. I climb out over the edge of the shell-hole. In the dirty twilight lies a leg torn clean off; the boot is quite whole, I take that all in at a glance. Now someone stands up a few yards distant. I polish the windows, in my excitement they are 200 immediately dimmed again, I peer through them, the man there no longer wears his mask.

I wait some seconds—he has not collapsed—he looks around and makes a few paces—rattling in my throat I tear my mask off too and fall down, the air streams into me like cold water, my eyes are bursting, the wave sweeps over me and extinguishes me. . . .

———————◆———————

German Art in the War Era: Ernst and Grosz

In Germany, World War I brought protests from many visual artists. One of the most outspoken was Max Ernst (1891–1976), whose career flowered in the dada and surrealist movements. Shortly after the war, Ernst began to create unsettling visual fantasies assembled from bits of photographs and prints that he cut from magazines, books, and newspapers. In the collage-painting *Two Ambiguous Figures* (Figure **34.1**), he combined the paraphernalia of modern warfare with the equipment of the scientist's laboratory. Ernst's machine-like monsters are suspiciously reminiscent of the gas-masked soldiers that he encountered during his four-year stint in the German infantry. Sadly enough, however, Ernst's demons have become prophetic icons of modern warfare. Poison gas, used by the Iraqis in the 1980s war with Iran, received renewed international attention during the widely televised Gulf War of 1991, when images of both soldiers and civilians donning gas masks were a common, if appalling, sight.

The art of George Grosz (1893–1959) was unique in its imaginative blend of social criticism and biting satire. Discharged from the army in 1916 after a brief experience at the front, Grosz mocked the German military and its corrupt and mindless bureaucracy in sketchy, brittle compositions filled with pungent caricatures. For example, the wartime pen and ink drawing, *Fit for Active Service* (Figure **34.2**), shows a fat German army doctor pronouncing a skeletal cadaver "O.K.," hence, fit to serve in combat. Grosz evokes a sense of the macabre similar to that captured by Remarque in the novel *All Quiet on the Western Front*. Like Remarque (and hundreds of other European artists and writers), Grosz fled Nazi Germany for the United States in the 1930s, where he eventually became an American citizen.

The Russian Revolution

One of the last of the European powers to become industrialized, Russia entered World War I in 1914 under the leadership of Tzar Nicholas II. Within a single year, the Russian army lost over one million men and a million more soldiers deserted. Russian involvement in the war, compounded by problems of government corruption and a weak and essentially agrarian economy, reduced the nation to desperate straits. Food and fuel

Figure 34.1 Max Ernst, *Two Ambiguous Figures*, 1919. Collage with gouache and pencil, 9½ × 6½ in. © ADAGP, Paris and DACS, London 1997.

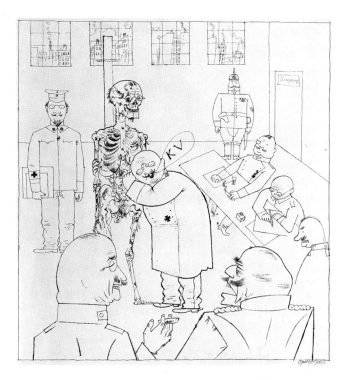

Figure 34.2 George Grosz, *Fit for Active Service*, 1916–1917. Pen and brush and ink on paper, 20 × 14⅜ in. The Museum of Modern Art, New York. A. Conger Goodyear Fund. Photograph © 1997 The Museum of Modern Art, New York. © DACS 1997.

shortages threatened the entire civilian population. By 1917, a full-scale revolution was under way: Strikes and riots broke out in the cities, while in the countryside peasants seized the land of their aristocratic landlords. The Revolution of 1917 forced the abdication of the Tzar and ushered in a new regime, which, in turn, was seized by members of the Russian Socialist party under the leadership of the Marxist revolutionary Vladimir I. Lenin (1870–1924). Between 1917 and 1921, by means of shrewd political manipulation and a reign of terror conducted by the Red Army and the secret police, Lenin installed the left-wing faction of the Marxian Socialists—the Bolsheviks—as the party that would govern a nation of more than 150 million people. By tailoring Marxian ideas to the needs of revolutionary Russia, Lenin became the architect of Soviet communism.

In his treatise *Imperialism, the Highest Stage of Capitalism* (1916), Lenin followed Marx in describing imperialism as an expression of the capitalist effort to monopolize raw materials and markets throughout the world. Lenin agreed with Marx that a "dictatorship of the proletariat" was the first step in liberating the workers from bourgeois suppression. While condemning the state as "the organ of class domination," he projected the transition to a classless society in a series of phases, which he outlined in the influential pamphlet "The State and Revolution" (1917). According to Lenin, in

Figure 34.3 A. I. Strakhov, *Emancipated Women Build Socialism! 8th March, Day of the Liberation of Women, 1926*. Colored lithograph, 42½ × 26 ¾ in.

the first phase of communist society (generally called socialism), private property would be converted into property held in common and the means of production and distribution would belong to the whole of society. Every member of society would perform a type of labor and would be entitled to a "quantity of products" (drawn from public warehouses) that corresponded to his or her "quantity of work." (A favorite Lenin slogan ran, "He who does not work does not eat.") Accordingly, as Lenin explained, "a form of state is still necessary, which, while maintaining public ownership of the means of production, would preserve the equality of labor and equality in the distribution of products." In the first phase of communism, then, the Socialist state prevailed.

In the second phase of communism, however, the state would disappear altogether. As Lenin explained,

The state will be able to wither away completely when society has realized the rule: "From each according to his ability; to each according to his needs," *i.e.*, when people have become accustomed to observe the fundamental rules of social life, and their labor is so productive that they voluntarily work *according to their ability*. . . . There will then be no need for any exact calculation by society of the quantity of products to be distributed to each of its members; each will take freely according to his needs.*

Lenin was aware that such a social order might be deemed "a pure Utopia"; yet, idealistically, he

---

The State and Revolution. New York: International Publishers, 1932, 1943, 71–80.

anticipated the victory of communist ideals throughout the world. The reality was otherwise. In early twentieth-century Russia, the Bolsheviks would create a dictatorship *over* rather than *of* the proletariat. In 1918, when the Constituent Assembly refused to approve Bolshevik power, Lenin dissolved the Assembly. (In free elections Lenin's party received less than a quarter of one percent of the vote.) He then eliminated all other parties and consolidated the communist party in the hands of five men—an elite committee called the Politburo, which Lenin himself chaired. In 1922, Russia was renamed the Union of Soviet Socialist Republics (U.S.S.R.), and in 1924 the constitution established a sovereign Congress of Soviets. But this body was actually governed by the leadership of the communist party, which maintained absolute authority well after Lenin's death.

The communist party established the first totalitarian regime of the twentieth century. This totalitarian regime subordinated the life of the individual to that of the state. Through strict government control of political, economic, and cultural life, and by means of coercive measures such as censorship and terrorism, the state imposed its will upon the conduct of the society. Soviet communists persecuted all individuals and religious groups whose activities they deemed threatening to the state. Using educational propaganda and the state-run media, they worked tirelessly to indoctrinate Soviet citizens to the virtues of communism. Under the rule of Joseph Stalin (1879–1953), who took control of the communist bureaucracy in 1926, the Soviets launched vast programs of industrialization and agricultural collectivization (the transformation of private farms into government-run units) that demanded heroic sacrifice from the Russian people. Peasants worked long hours on state-controlled farms, earning a bare subsistence wage. Stalin crushed all opposition: His secret police "purged" the state of dissidents, who were either imprisoned, exiled to *gulags* (labor camps), or executed. Between 1928 and 1938, the combination of severe famine and Stalin's inhuman policies took the lives of fifteen to twenty million Russians.

Communism enforced totalitarian control over all aspects of cultural expression. In 1934, the First All-Union Congress of Soviet Writers officially approved the style of *socialist realism* in the arts. At the same time, it condemned all expressions of "modernism" (from cubist painting to hot jazz) as "bourgeois decadence." The congress called upon Soviet artists to create "a true, historically concrete portrayal of reality in its revolutionary development." Artists—including Malevich and the pioneer Russian constructivists—were instructed to communicate simply and directly, to shun all forms of decadent (that is, modern) Western art, and to describe only the positive aspects of socialist society. In realistically conceived posters, the new Soviet man and woman were portrayed joyfully operating tractors or running factory machinery (Figure **34.3**). Thus the arts served to reinforce in the public mind the ideological benefits of communism. Socialist realism and the philosophy of art as mass propaganda lent support to almost every totalitarian regime of the twentieth century.

The Great Depression and the American Scene in the Arts

World War I left Europe devastated, and massive economic problems burdened both the Central Powers and the Allied nations. In the three years following the war, world industrial production declined by more than a third, prices dropped sharply, and over thirty million people lost their jobs. The United States emerged from the war as the great creditor nation, but its economy was inextricably tied to world conditions. Following the inevitable crash of inflated stock prices in 1929, a growing paralysis swept through the American economy which developed into the Great Depression, a world crisis that lasted until the 1940s.

The Great Depression inspired literary descriptions of economic oppression and misery that were often as much social documents as fictional narratives. The most memorable of these is the American novel *The Grapes of Wrath*, written in 1939 by John Steinbeck (1902–1968). The story recounts the odyssey of a family of Oklahoma migrant farmers who make their way to California in search of a living. In straightforward and photographically detailed prose, Steinbeck describes courageous encounters with starvation, injustice, and sheer evil. Like the soldiers in Remarque's regiment, the members of the Joad family (and especially the matriarch, Ma Joad) display heroism in sheer survival. *The Grapes of Wrath* is an example of *social realism*, a style that presents socially significant subject matter in an objective and lifelike manner. Not to be confused with socialist realism, which operated to glorify the socialist state, social realism was often the vehicle of social criticism and political protest. A writer, declared Steinbeck, is "the watchdog of society"; he must "set down his time as nearly as he can understand it."

During the depression, social realism also dominated the visual arts in America. In opposition to modernists who sacrificed subject matter to formal abstraction (Picasso, Kandinsky, and Mondrian, for instance), American social realists painted recognizable imagery that communicated the concerns of the masses. The Missouri-born Thomas Hart Benton (1889–1975) devoted his career to the depiction of American scenes that often called into question political and economic policies leading to the Great Depression. Benton was ambitious to commemorate "true" American values by immortalizing the daily lives of common men and women, whom he pictured as rugged and energetic. In three sets of public murals completed between 1930 and 1933, Benton created an extraordinary pictorial history of the United States. He portrayed steelworking, mining, farming, and other working-class activities, as well as bootlegging, gospel singing, crapshooting, and a wide variety of essentially common pastimes. Benton's *City Activities*, one section from a set of murals depicting American life during the era of Prohibition, is a montage of "clips" from such popular urban entertainments as the circus, the movie theater, and the dancehall (Figure **34.4**). A ticker-tape machine—the symbol of Wall Street commercialism and American greed—appears in the upper part of the mural; it is balanced in the lower foreground by another instrument of commercialism—

bootlegging equipment. Benton, who appears with paintbrush in hand in the lower-right corner of the painting, admired the purity of Midwestern rural life. His assessment of America's urban centers as "nothing but coffins for living and thinking" is powerfully conveyed in *City Activities*.

In Benton's hands the mural was not mere architectural decoration. It was a major form of public art, one that revealed ordinary American life as vividly as Renaissance murals mirrored the elitist world of sixteenth-century Italy. Benton drew inspiration from two great Mexican muralists: José Clemente Orozco (1883–1949) and Diego Rivera (1886–1957). The paintings of Orozco and Rivera, characterized by simple yet powerful forms and bold colors, capture the vitality and the futility of the Mexican Revolution—one of the many militant efforts at reforming economic and social conditions in Central and South America that took place during the first half of the twentieth century (Figure **34.5**).

During the Great Depression photography was

Figure 34.4 Thomas Hart Benton, *City Activities with Dance Hall*, from the mural series "America Today," 1930. Distemper and egg tempera on gessoed linen with oil glaze, 7 ft. 8 in. × 11 ft. 2½ in. Collection, The Equitable Life Assurance Society of the U.S., New York. Photo: Dorothy Zeidman 1988. © The Equitable Life Assurance Society of the U.S./Thomas Hart Benton Estate/VAGA, New York/DACS, London 1997.

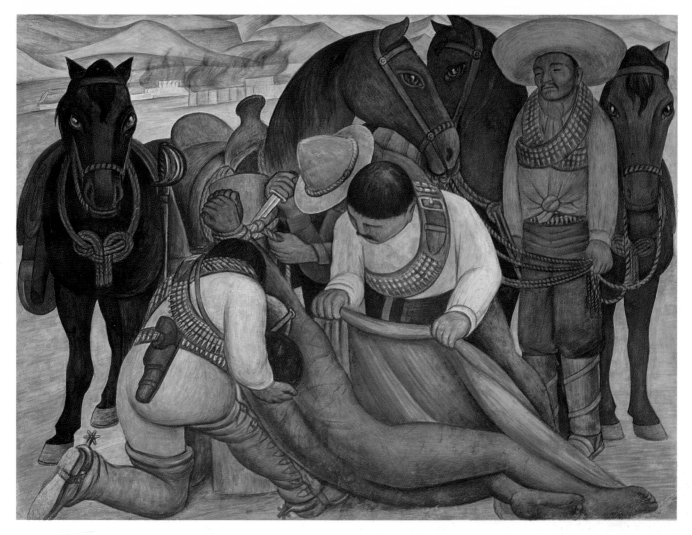

Figure 34.5 (above) Diego Rivera, *Liberation of the Peon*, 1931. Fresco, 6 ft. 2 in. × 7 ft. 11 in. Philadelphia Museum of Art. Given by Mr. and Mrs. Herbert Cameron Morris ('43–46–1).

Figure 34.6 (right) Dorothea Lange, *Migrant Mother, Nipomo, California*, 1938. Gelatin-silver print. Library of Congress, Washington, D.C.

pressed into political service. United States federal agencies sponsored a program to provide a permanent record of economic and social conditions in rural America. Migration and rural poverty—bread-lines, beggars, and the shantytowns of America's impoverished classes—became part of the straightforward style of *documentary photography*. The New York photographer Dorothea Lange (1895–1965) traveled across the country to record the conditions of destitute farmers who had fled the Midwestern Dust Bowl for the fields of California. *Migrant Mother* (Figure **34.6**), which Lange photographed at a farm camp in Nipomo, California, is the portrait of a gaunt thirty-two-year-old woman who had become the sole supporter of her six children. Forced to sell her last possessions for food, the anxious but unconquerable heroine in this photograph might have stepped out of the pages of Steinbeck's *Grapes of Wrath*. Lange's moving image reaches beyond a specific time and place to universalize the twin evils of poverty and oppression.

Nazi Totalitarianism and World War II

In Germany, widespread discontent and turmoil resulted from the combined effects of the Great Depression and the results of the humiliating peace terms dictated by the victorious Allies. Crippling debts forced German banks to close in 1931, and at the height of the depression only one-third of all Germany's workers were fully employed. In the wake of these conditions, the young ideologue Adolf Hitler (1889–1945) rose to power. By 1933, Hitler was chancellor of Germany and the leader (in German, *Führer*) of the National Socialist German Workers' party (the *Nazi* party), which would lead Germany again into world war.

A fanatic racist, Hitler shaped the Nazi platform. He blamed Germany's ills on the nation's internal "enemies," whom he identified as Jews, Marxists, bourgeois liberals, and "social deviates." Hitler promised to "purify" the German state of its "threatening" minorities and rebuild the country into a mighty empire. He manipulated public opinion by using all available means of propaganda—especially the radio, which brought his voice into every German home. In his autobiographical work *Mein Kampf* (*My Struggle*), published in 1925, Hitler set forth a fanatical theory of "Aryan racial superiority" that would inspire some of the most malevolent episodes in the history of humankind, including genocide: the systematic extermination of millions of Jews, Roman Catholics, gypsies, homosexuals, and other minorities. Justifying his racist ideology, he wrote:

> What we must fight for is to safeguard the existence and reproduction of our race and our people, the sustenance of our children and the purity of our blood, the freedom and independence of the fatherland so that our people may mature for the fulfillment of the mission allotted to it by the creator of the universe.*

Mein Kampf exalted the totalitarian state as "the guardian of a millennial future in the face of which the wishes and the selfishness of the individual must appear as nothing and submit." "The state is a means to an end," insisted Hitler. "Its end lies in the preservation and advancement of physically and psychically homogeneous creatures."

Less than twenty years after the close of World War I the second, even more devastating, world war began. The conditions that contributed to the outbreak of World War II included the failure of the peace settlement that had ended World War I and the undiminished growth of nationalism and militarism. But the specific event that initiated a renewal of hostilities was Hitler's military advance into Poland in 1939.

Once again, two opposing alliances were formed: Germany, Italy, Bulgaria, and Hungary comprised the Axis powers (the term describing the imaginary line between Rome and Berlin), while France and Britain and, in 1941, the United States and Russia, constituted the major Allied forces. Germany joined forces with totalitarian regimes in Italy (under Benito Mussolini) and in Spain (under General Francisco Franco), and the hostilities quickly spread into North Africa, the Balkans, and elsewhere (Map **34.2**). The fighting that took place during the three-year civil war in Spain (1936–1939) and in the German attack on the Netherlands in 1940 anticipated the merciless aspects of total war. In Spain, Nazi dive-bombers destroyed whole cities, while in the Netherlands, German tanks, parachute troops, and artillery overran the country in less than a week. The tempo of death was quickened as German air power attacked both military and civilian targets. France fell to Germany in 1940, and Great Britain became the target of systematic German bombing raids. At the same time, violating a Nazi-Soviet pact of 1939, Hitler invaded Russia, only to suffer massive defeat in the Battle of Stalingrad in 1941.

The United States, though supportive of the Allies, again tried to hold fast to its policy of "benevolent neutrality." It was brought into the war nevertheless by Japan, which had risen rapidly to power in the late nineteenth century. Japan had defeated the Russians in the Russo-Japanese War of 1904. The small nation had successfully invaded Manchuria in 1931 and established a foothold in China and Southeast Asia. In December of 1941, in opposition to United States efforts at restricting Japanese trade, the Japanese naval air service dropped bombs on the American air base at Pearl Harbor in Hawaii. The United States, declaring war on Japan, joined the twenty-five other nations that opposed the Axis powers and sent combat forces to fight in both Europe and the Pacific. The war against Japan was essentially a naval war, but it involved land and air attacks as well. Its climax was America's atomic bombing of two Japanese cities, Hiroshima and Nagasaki, in August of 1945. The bombing, which annihilated over 120 thousand people (mostly civilians) and forced the Japanese to surrender within a matter of days, ushered in the atomic age. Just months before the bombing of Hiroshima, as German forces gave way to

1927	the first television transmission is viewed in America	
1930	the British invent a workable jet engine	
1938	the Germans split the atom to achieve nuclear fission	
1939	British scientists produce pure penicillin	
1945	the first experimental atomic bomb is exploded at Alamogordo, New Mexico	

Mein Kampf, translated by Ralph Manheim. Boston: Houghton Mifflin, 1943, 324.

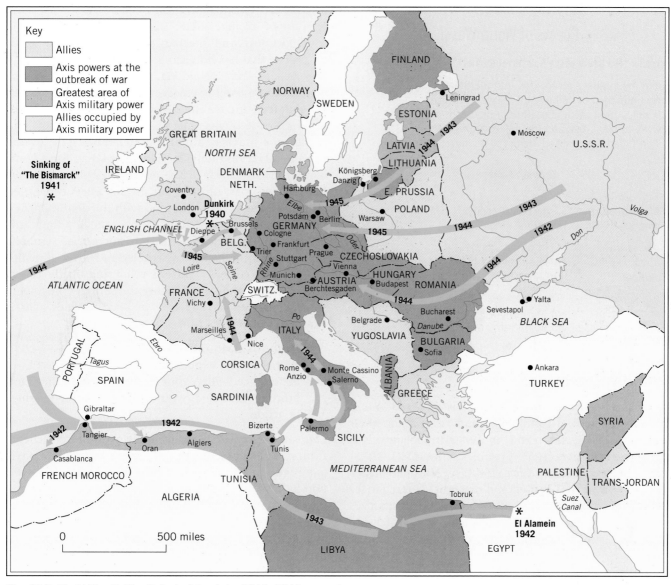

Map 34.2 World War II: The Defeat of the Axis, 1942–1945.

Allied assaults on all fronts, Hitler committed suicide. World War II came to a close with the surrender of both Germany and Japan in the summer of 1945.

World War II Poetry

World War II poetry around the globe carried to new extremes the sentiments of despair and futility. The American poet and critic Randall Jarrell (1914–1965), who served in the army air force from 1942 to 1946, described military combat as dehumanizing and degrading. In the short poem "The Death of the Ball Turret Gunner," a World War II airman, speaking from beyond the grave, recounts his fatal experience as an air force gunner. Encased in the Plexiglas bubble dome of an airplane ball turret—like an infant in his mother's womb—he "wakes" to "black flak" and dies; the startling image of birth in death fuses the states of

dreaming and waking. Jarrell observed that modern combat, fueled by sophisticated technical instruments, neither fostered pride nor affirmed human nobility. Rather, such combat turned the soldier into a technician and an instrument of war. It robbed him of personal identity and reduced him to the level of an object—a thing to be washed out by a high-pressure steam hose. The note to the title of the poem was provided by the poet himself. In Japan, lamentation preceded rage. The *haiku*, the light verse form that had traditionally enshrined such images as cherry blossoms and spring rain, now became the instrument by which Japanese poets evoked the presence of death. Kato Shuson (b. 1905) introduced the three *haikus* reproduced below with the following words: "In the middle of the night there was a heavy air raid. Carrying my sick brother on my back I wandered in the flames with my wife in search of our children."

READING 6.9

Poems of World War II

Jarrell's "The Death of the Ball Turret Gunner"[1]

From my mother's sleep I fell into the State,
And I hunched in its belly till my wet fur froze.[2]
Six miles from earth, loosed from its dream of life,
I woke to black flak and the nightmare fighters.
When I died they washed me out of the turret with a hose.

Shuson's *haikus*

Hi no oku ni	In the depths of the flames
Botan kuzururu	I saw how a peony
Sama wo mitsu	Crumbles to pieces.
Kogarashi ya	Cold winter storm—
Shōdo no kinko	A safe-door in a burnt-out site
Fukinarasu	Creaking in the wind.
Fuyu kamome	The winter sea gulls—
Sei no ie nashi	In life without a house,
Shi no haka nashi	In death without a grave.

———————◆———————

World War II Fiction

As in the poetry of Jarrell, the novels of World War II were characterized by nihilism and resignation, their heroes robbed of reason and innocence. In such novels as *From Here to Eternity* (1951) by James Jones (1921–1977) and *The Naked and the Dead* (1948) by Norman Mailer (b. 1923), war makes men and machines interchangeable—the very brutality of total war dehumanizes its heroes. Mailer's raw, naturalistic novels, which are peppered with the four-letter words that have come to characterize so much modern fiction, portray a culture dominated by violence and sexuality. Stylistically, Mailer likes to deviate from the traditional beginning-middle-and-end narrative format, using instead such cinematic techniques as flashback.

This episodic technique also prevails in the novels of Joseph Heller (b. 1923), Kurt Vonnegut (b. 1922), and other **black humor** writers. "Black" (or "gallows") humor is a form of literary satire that mocks modern life by calling attention to situations that seem too ghastly or too absurd to be true. Such fiction often describes the grotesque and the macabre in the passionless and nonchalant manner of a contemporary newspaper account. Like an elaborate hate joke, the black humor novel provokes helpless laughter at what is hideous and awful. Modern war, according to black humorists, is the greatest of all hate jokes: Dominated by bureaucratic capriciousness and mechanized destruction, it is an enterprise that has no victors, only victims.

Heller's *Catch-22* (1955), one of the most popular black humor novels to emerge from World War II, marks the shift from the realistic description of modern warfare (characteristic of the novels of Remarque, Jones, and Mailer) to its savage satirization. Heller based the events of *Catch-22* on his own experiences as an air force bombardier in World War II. The novel takes place on an air base off the coast of Italy, but its plot is less concerned with the events of the war than with the dehumanizing operations of the vast military bureaucracy that runs the war. Heller describes this bureaucracy as symbolic of "the humbug, hypocrisy, cruelty and sheer stupidity of our mass society." Heller's rendering of the classic armed forces condolence form-letter satirizes the impersonal character of modern war and provides a brief example of the black humorist's biting style:

> Dear Mrs.,/Mr.,/Miss,/or Mr. and Mrs.— — —:
> Words cannot express the deep personal grief I experienced when your husband,/son,/father,/or brother was killed,/wounded,/or reported missing in action.

Catch-22 is a caustic blend of nihilism and forced cheerfulness. The characters in the novel—including a navigator who has no sense of direction and an aviator who bombs his own air base for commercial advantage—operate at the mercy of a depersonalizing system. As they try their best to preserve their identity and their sanity, they become the enemies of the very authorities that sent them to war.

The Literary Response to Totalitarianism

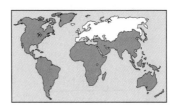

While total war became a compelling theme in twentieth-century fiction, so too did totalitarianism, especially as it was described by those who had experienced it firsthand. Until Stalin's death in 1953, a reign of terror prevailed in the Soviet Union. As many found out, the slightest deviation from orthodox Marxist-Stalinist decorum resulted in imprisonment, slave labor, or execution. Aleksandr Solzhenitsyn (b. 1918) served in the Russian army during World War II, and although he had twice received recognition for bravery in combat, Solzhenitsyn was arrested in 1945 for veiled anti-Stalinist comments he had made in a letter to a friend. He was sentenced to

---

[1] "A ball turret was a Plexiglas sphere set into the belly of a B–17 or B–24 and inhabited by two .50 caliber machine-guns and one man, a short, small man. When this gunner traced with his machine-guns a fighter attacking his bomber from below, he revolved with the turret; hunched upside-down in his little sphere, he looked like the fetus in the womb. The fighters which attacked him were armed with cannon firing explosive shells. The hose was a steam hose."

[2] The airman's fur-lined flight jacket.

eight years of imprisonment, spending half the term in a *gulag* in Siberia and the other half teaching mathematics in a Moscow prison. His Siberian experience provided the eyewitness material for his first novel, *One Day in the Life of Ivan Denisovich* (1962), which was followed in 1973 by *The Gulag Archipelago*, a documentary description of Soviet prison life. These dispassionate accounts of the grim conditions of totalitarianism are searing indictments of savage inhumanity, and testaments to the heroism of the victims of Soviet political oppression.

Like Stalin, Hitler wielded unlimited and often ruthless authority. He destroyed democratic institutions in Germany, condemned avant-garde art, modern architecture, atonal music, and jazz as "degenerate," and proceeded to eliminate—by means of the *Gestapo* (the Nazi secret police)—all opposition to his program of mass conformity. In 1933, over thirty-five thousand Germans died either by suicide or from "unexplained causes." Over the next ten years, concentration camps arose in Austria and Germany to house Hitler's "impure" minorities. It is estimated that six million Jews and five million non-Jews were put to death in Nazi gas chambers—a hideous episode in European history known as the Holocaust.

In Germany, the voices of actual witnesses to the atrocities of the Holocaust were for the most part silenced by death, but drawings by camp inmates and documentary photographs taken just after the war (Figure 34.7) provide shocking visual evidence of modern barbarism. One of the most eloquent survivors of the Holocaust is the writer Elie Wiesel (b.1928), recipient of the Nobel Peace Prize in 1986. At the age of fifteen, Wiesel, a Romanian Jew, was shipped with his entire family to the concentration camp at Auschwitz, Poland. From there the family was split up, and Wiesel and his father were sent to a labor camp in Buchenwald, Germany, where the youth saw his father and hundreds of others killed by the Nazis. Liberated in 1945, Wiesel transmuted the traumatic experiences of his childhood into prose. "Auschwitz," wrote Wiesel, "represents the negation and failure of human progress: it negates the human design and casts doubts on its validity." *Night* (1958), Wiesel's autobiographical record of the Nazi terrors, is a graphic account of Hitler's barbarism. The brief excerpt that follows reveals the anguish Wiesel and other Jews experienced in confronting what appeared to be "God's silence" in the face of brutal injustice.

READING 6.10

From Wiesel's *Night*

One day, the electric power station at Buna was blown up. The Gestapo, summoned to the spot, suspected sabotage. They found a trail. It eventually led to the Dutch Oberkapo.[1] And there, after a search, they found an important stock of arms.

The Oberkapo was arrested immediately. He was tortured for a period of weeks, but in vain. He would not give a single name. He was transferred to Auschwitz. We never heard of him again.   10

But his little servant had been left behind in the camp in prison. Also put to torture, he too would not speak. Then the SS[2] sentenced him to death, with two other prisoners who had been discovered with arms.

One day when we came back from work, we saw three gallows rearing up in the assembly place, three black crows. Roll call. SS all round us, machine guns trained: the traditional ceremony. Three victims in chains—and one of them, the little servant, the sad-eyed angel.

The SS seemed more preoccupied, more disturbed   20 than usual. To hang a young boy in front of thousands of spectators was no light matter. The head of the camp read the verdict. All eyes were on the child. He was lividly pale, almost calm, biting his lips. The gallows threw its shadow over him.

This time the Lagerkapo[3] refused to act as executioner. Three SS replaced him.

The three victims mounted together onto the chairs.

The three necks were placed at the same moment within the nooses.   30

"Long live liberty!" cried the two adults.

But the child was silent.

"Where is God? Where is He?" someone behind me asked.

At a sign from the head of the camp, the three chairs tipped over.

Figure 34.7 Lee Miller, *Buchenwald, Germany*, 30 April 1945. Photograph. Photo: © Lee Miller Archive, Penrose Film Productions, Chiddingly, East Sussex.

---

[1] The foreman of the prisoners, selected from among them by the Nazis.
[2] A special police force that operated the camps.
[3] The prisoner who acted as foreman of the warehouse.

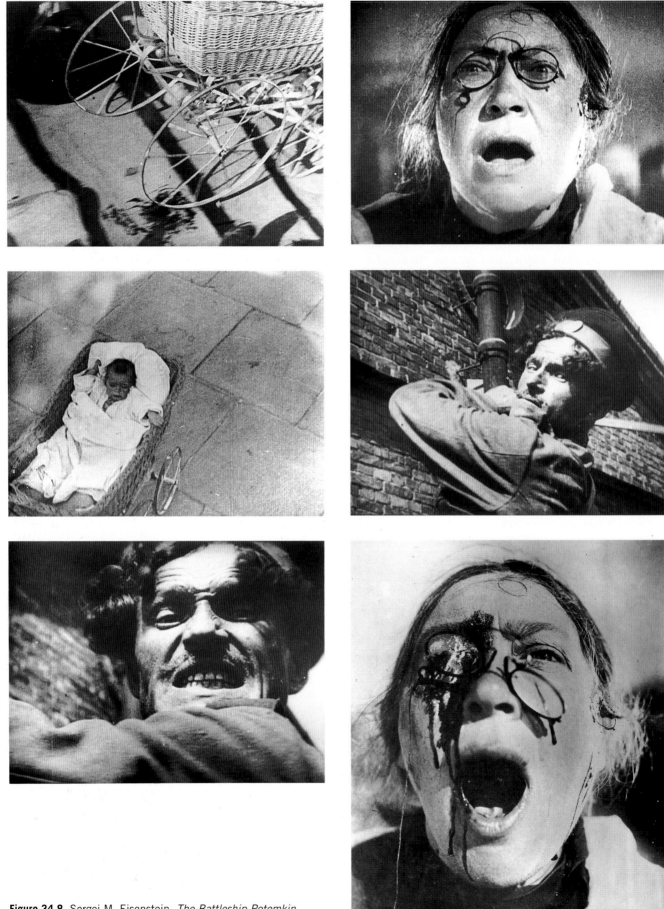

Figure 34.8 Sergei M. Eisenstein, *The Battleship Potemkin*, 1925. Film stills from Act IV, "The Odessa Steps Massacre." Courtesy, The Museum of Modern Art/Film Stills Library.

Total silence throughout the camp. On the horizon, the sun was setting.

"Bare your heads!" yelled the head of the camp. His voice was raucous. We were weeping.

"Cover your heads!"

Then the march past began. The two adults were no longer alive. Their tongues hung swollen, blue-tinged. But the third rope was still moving; being so light, the child was still alive. . . .

For more than half an hour he stayed there, struggling between life and death, dying in slow agony under our eyes. And we had to look him full in the face. He was still alive when I passed in front of him. His tongue was still red, his eyes were not yet glazed.

Behind me, I heard the same man asking:

"Where is God now?"

And I heard a voice within me answer him:

"Where is He? Here He is—He is hanging here on this gallows. . . ."

That night the soup tasted of corpses. . . .

———————◆———————

Film and Photojournalism in the War Era

Film provided a permanent historical record of the turbulent military and political events of the early twentieth century. It also became an effective medium of political propaganda. In Russia, Lenin envisioned film as an invaluable means of spreading the ideals of communism. Following the Russian Revolution, he nationalized the fledgling motion-picture industry. At the hand of the Russian filmmaker Sergei Eisenstein (1898–

1948), film operated both as a vehicle for political persuasion and as a fine art. Eisenstein shaped the social and artistic potential of cinema by combining realistic narrative with symbolic imagery. In *The Battleship Potemkin* (1925), his silent film masterpiece, Eisenstein staged the 1905 mutiny of the Tzar's soldiers to resemble an on-the-spot documentary. He used to brilliant effect the technique of **montage**, the assembling of cinematic shots in rapid succession. In the final sequence of the film, the events of a riot in the city of Odessa are captured with graphic force. Eisenstein interposed images of the advancing Tzarist police with a series of alternating close-ups and long shots of civilian victims (Figure **34.8**), including those of a mother who is killed trying to save her infant in a baby carriage that careens down a broad flight of stairs. The so-called "Odessa Steps sequence," whose rapidly increasing tempo works to evoke apprehension and terror, is an ingenious piece of editing that has been imitated with great frequency by modern filmmakers. Two years later, in 1927, Eisenstein made the Russian Revolution itself the subject of the film *Ten Days That Shook the World*.

While Eisenstein used film to glorify the collective heroism of the Soviet people, German filmmakers working for Hitler turned motion pictures into outright vehicles of state propaganda. The filmmaker and former actress Leni Riefenstahl (b. 1902) received unlimited state subsidies to produce the most famous propaganda film of all time, *The Triumph of the Will* (1934). Riefenstahl engaged a crew of 135 people to film the huge rallies and ceremonies staged by Hitler and the Nazi party, including their first meeting in Nuremberg. *The Triumph*

Figure 34.9 Leni Riefenstahl, *The Triumph of the Will*, 1934. Film still showing Himmler, Hitler, and Lutze framed by columns of people as they approach the memorial monument in Nuremberg, Germany. Courtesy, The Museum of Modern Art/Film Stills Library.

of the Will is a synthesis of documentary fact and sheer artifice. Its bold camera angles and stark compositions seem in themselves totalitarian—witness the absolute symmetry and exacting conformity of the masses of troops that frame the tiny figures of Hitler and his compatriots at the Nuremberg rally (Figure **34.9**).

In America, film served to inform, to boost morale, and to propagandize for the Allied cause; but it also served as entertainment and escape. At the height of the Depression as well as during the war era millions of Americans flocked to movie-theaters each week. While such prize-winning movies as *All Quiet on the Western Front* (1930) and *From Here to Eternity* (1953) were painfully realistic, numerous other films romanticized and glamorized the war. An exception to the standard war-movie fare was *The Great Dictator* (1940), which was directed by the multitalented British-born actor and filmmaker Charles Chaplin (1889–1977). In this hilarious satire of Fascist dictatorship, Adolf Hitler (known in the film as Adenoid Hynkel and played by Chaplin) rises to power as head of the "Double Cross Party," only to be arrested by his own troops, who mistake him for a Jewish barber.

The realities of World War II were recorded by an international array of photojournalists. One of the most gifted was Lee Miller (1907–1977), an American debutante who became the first female wartime photojournalist and an early witness to the horrors of the German concentration camps (see Figure 34.7). The American photographer Robert Capa (1897–1954) produced notable pictures of World War II paratroopers, and the French photographer Henri Cartier-Bresson (b. 1908) immortalized the plight of war-torn Europe in hundreds of aesthetically compelling social realist photographs.

Painting in the War Era

Picasso's *Guernica*

On the afternoon of April 26, 1937, in the midst of the Spanish Civil War (1936–1939) that pitted republican forces against the Fascist dictatorship of General Francisco Franco, the German air force (in league with the Spanish Fascists) dropped incendiary bombs upon Guernica, a small Basque town in Northeast Spain. The news of this first aerial bombardment of a civilian target—a rural market town—and details of the mounting death toll devastated Picasso. Earlier in the year, the artist had been invited to contribute a painting for the Spanish Pavilion of the Paris World's Fair. The bombing of Guernica provided him with inspiration for the 26- by 12-foot mural that would become this century's most memorable antiwar image (Figure **34.10**; see also Part Opener, p. xvi).

More powerful than any literary description, *Guernica* captures the grim brutality and suffering of the wartime era. Picasso used monochromatic tones—the ashen grays of incineration—which also call to mind the documentary media of mass communication: newspapers, photographs, and film. However, *Guernica* is far from documentary. Indeed, its abstract treatment of flattened, distorted forms contrasts sharply with the social realist truth-to-nature style that dominated much of the art produced in Europe and America between the wars. Picasso's style combines the cubist affection for strong, angular motifs with an expressionistic treatment of form. The bull and horse of the Spanish bullfight, Picasso's lifelong metaphor for savage discord, share the shallow stage with a broken statue of a warrior and four women, one of whom holds a dead infant. This figure,

Figure 34.10 Pablo Picasso, *Guernica*, 1937. Oil on canvas, 11 ft. 5½ in. × 25 ft. 5¾ in. Prado, Madrid. Museo Nacional Centro de Arte Reina Sofía, Madrid. © Succession Picasso/DACS 1997.

her upturned head issuing a voiceless scream, is the physical embodiment of human grief. At the center of the painting, the horse, whose body bears the gaping wound of a spear, rears its head as if to echo the woman's anguished cry. The shattered statue of a warrior at the bottom of the painting symbolizes war's corrupting effect on the artifacts of high culture, just as it mocks the militant idealism represented by traditional war monuments. Sharp contrasts of light and dark establish the geometric structure that gives drama to the composition in a manner that recalls Goya's *The Third of May, 1808* (see chapter 29). Like Goya's powerful painting, but phrased in the vocabulary of modern abstraction, *Guernica* is a universal symbol of protest. It illustrates Picasso's insistent argument for art as a "weapon against the enemy."

Music in the War Era

It seems that every totalitarian government in history has feared the power of music and condemned those musical styles that threatened mass conformity. In Nazi Germany, jazz was forbidden on the basis of its free and improvised style and its association with black musicians; in communist China, Beethoven's music was banned as the sound of the independent spirit. In Soviet Russia, Lenin's regime laid down the specific rule that composers write only music that "communicated" to the people; since atonality was associated with elitism and inscrutability, it was to be avoided, along with other expressions of Western "decadence." "Music," observed Lenin, "is a means of unifying great masses of people."

Music, however, also allows for ambiguity of meaning, as the career of the eminent Russian composer, Dmitri Shostakovich (1906–1975), illustrates. Enrolled at thirteen in the Leningrad Conservatory, Shostakovich was the product of rigorous classical training. His compositions, including fifteen symphonies, fifteen string quartets, and numerous scores for ballet, opera, plays, and motion pictures, incorporate songlike melodies and insistent rhythmic repetition. They are essentially tonal, but they make dramatic use of dissonance and frequently evoke a reflective, melancholic mood. Although Shostakovich appeared to be a loyal adherent to Russian communism, his music received constant criticism for its "bourgeois formalism." Finally, upon the performance of his Seventh ("Leningrad") Symphony in 1941, Soviet leaders hailed the work as a celebration of the Soviet triumph against the Nazi invasion of Leningrad. Only in 1979, when Shostakovich's memoirs were smuggled out of the Soviet Union, did it become apparent that the composer intended the piece as an attack on Stalin's inhumanity toward his own people.

The aesthetic philosophy of the Russian composer Sergei Prokofiev (1891–1953) also seemed to defend Soviet principles. "In my view," he wrote, "the composer . . . is in duty bound to serve man, the people. He must be a citizen first and foremost, so that his art may consciously extol human life and lead man to a radiant future." In 1948, the Soviets nevertheless denounced Prokofiev's music as "too modern." Prokofiev's compositions, most of which reveal his preference for classical form, are tonal and melodic, but they are boldly inventive in modulation and harmonic dissonance. In his scores for the ballets *Romeo and Juliet* (1935) and *Cinderella* (1944), in his cantata for the Eisenstein film *Alexander Nevsky* (1938), and in such shorter, modern-day classics as the witty *Lieutenant Kije Suite* (1934) and the orchestral fairy tale *Peter and the Wolf* (1936), Prokofiev demonstrated a talent for driving rhythms, sprightly marches, and unexpected, often whimsical shifts of tempo and melody.

Just as the music of Shostakovich and Prokofiev was rooted in Russian soil, so the music of Aaron Copland (1900–1990) drew nourishment from native American musical idioms. Copland spiced his largely tonal compositions with the unique harmonies of American folk songs and the lively rhythms of jazz and Mexican dance. Like the murals of the American scene painter Thomas Hart Benton, Copland's *Billy the Kid* (1938), *Rodeo* (1940), and *Appalachian Spring* (1944) wedded regional themes to a vigorous and readily accessible language of form.

Twentieth-century composers were frequently moved to commemorate the horrors of war in music. The most monumental example of such music is the *War Requiem* (1963) written by the British composer Benjamin Britten (1913–1976) to accompany the opening of England's renovated Coventry Cathedral, which had been partially destroyed by German bombs. Britten was a master at setting text to music. In the *War Requiem* he juxtaposed the Roman Catholic Mass for the Dead (the Latin Requiem Mass) with the war poems of Wilfred Owen in such a way that Owen's lines offer ironic commentary on traditional religious thought. Britten's imaginative union of sacred ritual and secular song calls for orchestra, chorus, boys' chorus, and three soloists. Poignant in spirit and dramatic in effect, Britten's oratorio may be seen as the musical analogue of Picasso's *Guernica*.

If it were possible to capture in music the agony of war, the Polish composer Krzystof Penderecki (b. 1933) has come closest to doing so. His *Threnody in Memory of the Victims of Hiroshima* (1960) consists of violent torrents of dissonant, percussive sound, some of which is produced by beating on the bodies of the fifty-two stringed instruments for which the piece is scored. The ten-minute song of lamentation for the dead begins with a long, screaming tone produced by playing the highest pitches possible on the violins; it is followed by passages punctuated by **tone clusters** (groups of adjacent dissonant notes). The rapid shifts in densities, timbres, rhythms, and dynamics are jarring and disquieting—effects consistent with the subject matter of the piece. Penderecki's angry blurring of tones also characterizes his *Dies Irae* (1967), subtitled *Oratorio Dedicated to the Memory of those Murdered at Auschwitz*. Like Britten's *War Requiem*, Penderecki's composition draws on Christian liturgy—here the traditional hymn of Last Judgment (the "Day of Wrath")—to convey a mood of darkness and despair. The *Dies Irae*—first performed on the grounds of a former concentration camp—is punctuated by clanking chains and piercing sirens. Painfully harsh and abrasive, it remains a symbol of the Holocaust's haunting impact.

The Communist Revolution in China

The history of totalitarianism is not confined to the West. Modern tyrants have wiped out whole populations in Cambodia, Vietnam, Iraq, Africa, and elsewhere. Of all the Asian countries, however, China has experienced the most violent kinds of change. In 1900, less than ten percent of the Chinese population owned almost eighty percent of the land. Clamoring for reform, as well as for independence from foreign domination, nationalist forces tried to redistribute land among an enormous peasant population dominated by a small number of wealthy landowners. By 1911, the National People's party had overthrown the Manchu leaders (see chapter 23) and established a republican government. But the Nationalists failed to provide an efficient land redistribution program and, after 1937, they lost much of their popular support. Following World War II, the communist forces under the leadership of Mao Zedong (1893–1976) rose to power, and in 1949 they formed the People's Republic of China.

In China as in Russia, the communist party gained exclusive control of the government, with Mao serving as both chairman of the party and head of state. Mao called upon the great masses of citizens to work toward radical reform. "The theory of Marx, Engels, Lenin and Stalin is universally applicable," wrote Mao; but, he added, "We should regard it not as a dogma, but as a guide to action." A competent poet and scholar, Mao drew up the guidelines for the new society of China, a society that practiced cooperative endeavor and self-discipline. These guidelines were published in 1963 as the *Quotations from Chairman Mao* which became the "bible" of the Chinese Revolution. On youth, Mao wrote, "The world is yours, as well as ours, but in the last analysis, it is yours. You young people, full of vigor and vitality, are in the bloom of life, like the sun at eight or nine in the morning. Our hope is placed in you." On women: "In order to build a great socialist society, it is of the utmost importance to arouse the broad masses of women to join in productive activity. Men and women must receive equal pay for equal work in production." On the masses: "The masses have boundless creative power . . . the revolutionary war is a war of the masses; it can be waged only by mobilizing the masses and relying on them."*

Mao's ambitious reforms earned the support of the landless masses, but his methods for achieving his goals struck at the foundations of traditional Chinese culture. He tried to replace the old order, and especially the Confucian veneration of the family, with new socialist values that demanded devotion to the local economic unit—and ultimately to the state. Between 1949 and 1952, in an effort to make his reforms effective, Mao authorized the execution of some two to five million people, including the wealthy landowners themselves. To carry out his series of five-year plans for economic development in industry and agriculture, Mao also instituted totalitarian practices such as indoctrination, exile, and repeated purges of the voices of opposition.

Like the century's other totalitarian leaders, Mao directed artists to infuse literature with an ideological content that celebrated the creative powers of the masses. To some extent, however, the movement for a "people's literature" furthered reforms that had been launched during the political revolution of 1911: At that time, traditional styles of writing, including the "book language" of the classics, gave way to the language of common, vernacular speech. The new naturalistic style was strongly influenced by Western literature and journalism. Chinese writers responded enthusiastically to modern European novels, surrealistic short stories, and psychological dramas—poets even imitated such Western forms as the sonnet. But during the Cultural Revolution (1966–1976) China's communist regime reinstated the policy of socialist realism as it had been defined by the First All-Union Congress of Soviet Writers in 1934. The consequences of this policy would work to foment the liberation movements of the last decades of the century (see chapter 36).

---

*Mao Tse-Tung's Quotations: The Red Guard's Handbook, introduction by Stewart Fraser. Nashville, Tenn.: Peabody International Center, 1967, 118, 256, 288, 297.

SUMMARY

The twentieth century has been molded in the crucible of total war and totalitarianism. World Wars I and II were more devastating in nature and effect than any previous wars in world history. The Russian Revolution of 1917 marked the beginnings of Soviet communism and ushered in decades of totalitarian rule. Revolutions in China and Mexico were equally traumatic in destroying agelong traditions. In Europe, the Nazi policy of militant racism under Adolf Hitler brought about the brutal deaths of millions.

Artists responded to these events with rage, disbelief, and compassion. Searing indictments of World War I are found in the poetry of Owen and Yeats, the novels of Remarque, and the visual art of Ernst and Grosz. World War II literature emphasized the dehumanizing effects of war. In the poems of Jarrell, as in the novels of black humor fiction writers, war becomes a metaphor for all modern-day varieties of cruelty and perversion; while the firsthand experiences of Solzhenitzyn in the Russian *gulags* and Wiesel in Nazi concentration camps are no less poignant and shocking.

In America, during the period between the wars, the effects of the Great Depression encouraged the rise of social realism, a style that dominates the novels of Steinbeck and the paintings of Thomas Hart Benton. Throughout the world, photographs and moving pictures documented the facts of twentieth-century warfare, even as they served ideological ends. In the Soviet Union, the pro-Bolshevik films of Sergei Eisenstein raised the art of the moving picture to new heights, while elsewhere in Europe photographs documented the tragic consequences of war. Working in Paris, Picasso was stirred by the events of the Spanish Civil War to produce the quintessential antiwar painting, *Guernica.*

Composers of the wartime era also felt the effects of current political events. Living under the critical eye of the communist regime, Shostakovich and Prokofiev produced distinctly different, but memorable, musical styles. In England, Benjamin Britten commemorated World War II in his *War Requiem,* while in Poland Penderecki wrote atonal works that immortalized the harsh realities of twentieth-century genocide. Total war and totalitarianism have touched all of the arts of the twentieth century and left upon them the indelible imprint of despair.

GLOSSARY

black humor (or "gallows humor") the use of morbid and absurd situations for comic and satirical purposes in modern fiction and drama

montage in art, music, or literature, a composite made by freely juxtaposing usually heterogeneous images; in cinema, the production of a rapid succession of images to present a stream of interconnected ideas (see also Glossary, chapter 33 "photomontage")

tone cluster a group of adjacent dissonant notes, such as the notes of a scale, sounded together

totalitarian a political regime that imposes the will of the state upon the life and conduct of the individual

SUGGESTIONS FOR READING

Andrews, Julia A. *Painters and Politics in the People's Republic of China, 1949–1979.* Berkeley, Calif.: University of California Press, 1994.

Arnold, Ben. *Music and War.* New York: Garland Publishing, 1993.

Braham, Randolph, L., ed. *Reflections of the Holocaust in Art and Literature.* Irvington, N.Y.: Columbia University Press, 1990.

Carmean, E. A., et al. *American Art at Mid-Century: The Subjects of the Artists.* Washington, D.C.: National Gallery of Art, 1978.

Cork, Richard. *A Bitter Truth: Avant-Garde Art and the Great War.* New Haven: Yale University Press, 1994.

Eksteins, Modris. *Rites of Spring: The Great War and the Birth of the Modern Age.* Boston: Houghton Mifflin, 1989.

Fussell, Paul. *The Great War and Modern Memory.* New York: Oxford University Press, 1975.

Jones, Peter G. *War and the Novelist: Appraising the American War Novel.* Columbia, Mo.: University of Missouri Press, 1976.

Langer, Lawrence L. *The Holocaust in Literary Imagination.* New Haven: Yale University Press, 1975.

Mosse, George L., ed. *Nazi Culture: Intellectual, Cultural, and Social Life in the Third Reich,* translated by Salvator Attanasio, et al. New York: Schocken Books, 1981.

Rothstein, Arthur. *Documentary Photography.* Boston: Focal Press, 1986.

Vogel, Amos. *Film as a Subversive Art.* New York: Random House, 1974.

Walsh, Jeffrey. *American War Literature 1914 to Vietnam.* New York: St. Martin's Press, 1982.

Zeman, Zbynek. *Selling the War: Art and Propaganda in World War II.* New York: Bookthrift, 1982.

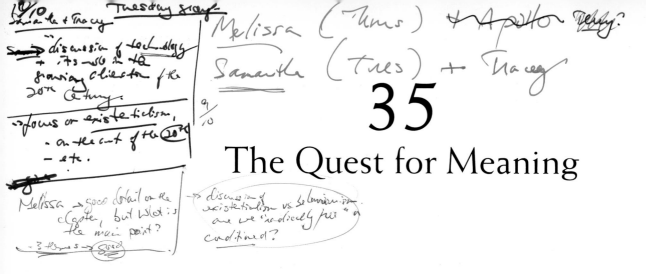
35

The Quest for Meaning

The nightmare of World War II left the world's population in a state of shock and disillusion. The Western democracies had held back the forces of totalitarian aggression, but the future seemed as threatening as ever. Communism and capitalist democracy now confronted one another in hostile distrust. And both possessed atomic weapons with the potential to extinguish the human race. The pessimism that accompanied the two world wars was compounded by a loss of faith in the bedrock beliefs of former centuries. The realities of trench warfare, the concentration camps, and Hiroshima made it difficult to maintain that human beings were rational by nature, that technology would work to advance human happiness, and that the universe was governed by a benevolent God. There is little wonder that the events of the first half of the twentieth century caused a loss of confidence in the eternal truths, including faith in a Supreme Being. The sense of estrangement from God and reason produced a condition of anxious withdrawal that has been called "alienation." Like a visitor to a foreign country, the modern individual felt estranged from all that was comforting and certain.

The condition of alienation was further aggravated by the depersonalizing influence of modern science and technology. In the mid-twentieth century, the breach between humanism and science seemed wider than ever; increasingly intellectuals questioned the social value of scientific technology to human progress. Optimists still envisioned modern technology as a liberating force for humankind. The American behavioral psychologist B. F. Skinner (1903–1990), for instance, anticipated a society in which the behavior of human beings might be scientifically engineered for the benefit of both the individual and the community. In the futuristic novel *Walden Two* (1948), Skinner created a fictional society in which the "technology of behavior" replaced traditional "prescientific" views of freedom and dignity. *Walden Two* is typical of a large body of utopian literature that exalted science as a positive force in shaping the future.

Pessimists, on the other hand, feared—and still fear—that modern technology might produce catastrophes ranging from a nuclear holocaust to the absolute loss of personal freedom. Dystopian novels, that is, novels that picture societies in which conditions are dreadful and bleak, reflect this negative outlook. *Brave New World* (1932) by the British writer Aldous Huxley (1894–1963), *1984* (1949) by England's George Orwell (the pen name of Eric Arthur Blair, 1903–1950), and *Fahrenheit 451* (1953) by the American Ray Bradbury (b. 1920) all present fictional totalitarian societies in which modern technology and the techniques of human engineering operate to destroy human freedom. *Brave New World* describes an imaginary society of the seventh century "A.F." ("after Henry Ford," the early twentieth-century American automobile manufacturer). In Huxley's futuristic society, babies are conceived in test tubes and, following the assembly line methods invented by Henry Ford for the manufacture of cars, individuals are behaviorally conditioned to perform socially beneficial tasks. From this "brave new world," the concept and practice of family life have been eradicated; human anxieties are quelled by means of *soma* (a mood-altering drug); and art, literature, and religion—all of which, according to the custodians of technology, threaten communal order and stability—have been ruthlessly purged.

Existentialism and Freedom

While *utopians* envisioned science and technology as potentially liberating and *dystopians* saw them as potentially threatening, both schools implicitly acknowledged that environment determined human behavior. "We are what we are conditioned to be," held the futurists. But partisans of the new humanist philosophy called *existentialism* argued otherwise. "We are what we choose to be," insisted the existentialists; "we create both ourselves and our freedom by our every choice." Existentialism, the most influential philosophic movement of the twentieth century, had its roots in the late nineteenth century, most notably in the writings of the Danish philosopher Søren Kierkegaard (1813–1855). But it rose to prominence through the efforts of the French left-wing intellectual, Jean-Paul Sartre.

The Philosophy of Sartre

Jean-Paul Sartre (1905–1980), the leading existentialist philosopher of the twentieth century, also made significant contributions as a playwright, novelist, journalist, and literary critic. Sartre had fought in World War II and been active in the French resistance to the German occupation of France. These experiences influenced his personal quest for meaning and identity in a universe that he perceived as devoid of moral absolutes.

Sartre's philosophy, as expounded in his classic work *Being and Nothingness* (1943), took as its basic premise the idea that existence precedes essence, that is, that one's material being exists prior to and independent of any intrinsic factors. Sartre's premise challenged the fundamentals of traditional philosophy: Plato had identified "essence" as Forms (or Ideas) that were eternal and unchanging. Aristotle had argued that the essence of the human being—that which distinguished humans from lower animals—was reason. Philosophers from Descartes through Kant followed the ancients by defending the notion that primary internal principles of being preceded being itself—a view that was metaphysically compatible with Christian theology. Sartre proposed, however, that human beings have no fixed nature. They are not imbued, by a Supreme Being, with any special divinity, nor are they (by nature) rational. They are neither imprisoned by subconscious forces (as Freud had held) nor are they determined by specific economic conditions (as Marx had maintained). Born into the world as body/matter, they proceed to make the choices by which they form their own natures. In Sartre's analysis, each individual is the sum of his or her actions. In that human beings must choose at every turn between a variety of possibilities, they are (in Sartre's words) "condemned to be free." Moreover, since every choice implies a choice for all humankind, each individual bears the overwhelming burden of total responsibility—a condition that Sartre called "anguish."

Sartre's viewpoint struck a balance between optimism and despair. While freedom and meaning depend on human action, said Sartre, all human actions, by necessity, are played out within a moral void—that is, within a universe lacking divine guidance and absolute values. To our profound despair, we seek meaning in a meaningless world. Yet, because human life is all there is, it must be cherished. According to Sartre, the human condition is one of anxiety experienced in the face of nothingness and the inevitability of death. Such anxiety is compounded because we alone are responsible for our actions. To disclaim responsibility for those actions by blaming external causes—"the Devil made me do it," "The ghetto turned me into a criminal," or "My parents were too lenient"—or to deny the possibility of alternative actions is to act in "bad faith." For Sartre, no forms of human engineering, technocratic or otherwise, can usurp the human potential for free action. To fly from freedom and responsibility is a form of self-deception and inauthenticity. "We are alone, with no excuses," according to Sartre.

In addition to his major philosophic work, Sartre wrote a number of significant novels, short stories, and plays. The most gripping of his plays, *No Exit* (1945), features three characters trapped in a "hell" they have created by their efforts to justify the acts of bad faith that have shaped their lives. The principal ideas set forth in these most famous of Sartre's writings are summarized in the lecture entitled "Existentialism," which Sartre presented in Paris in 1945. In the following excerpt from this essay, Sartre discusses existentialism as "an ethics of action and involvement" and explores the meaning of existential anguish.

READING 6.11
From Sartre's "Existentialism"

. . . Atheistic existentialism . . . states that if God does not exist, there is at least one being in whom existence precedes essence, a being who exists before he can be defined by any concept, and that this being is man, or, as Heidegger[1] says, human reality. What is meant here by saying that existence precedes essence? It means that, first of all, man exists, turns up, appears on the scene, and, only afterwards, defines himself. If man, as the existentialist conceives him, is indefinable, it is because at first he is nothing. Only afterward will he be something, and he himself will have made what he will be. Thus, there is no human nature, since there is no God to conceive it. Not only is man what he conceives himself to be, but he is also only what he wills himself to be after this thrust toward existence.

Man is nothing else but what he makes of himself. Such is the first principle of existentialism. It is also what is called subjectivity, the name we are labeled with when charges are brought against us. But what do we mean by this, if not that man has a greater dignity than a stone or table? For we mean that man first exists, that is, that man first of all is the being who hurls himself toward a future and who is conscious of imagining himself as being in the future. Man is at the start a plan which is aware of itself, rather than a patch of moss, a piece of garbage, or a cauliflower; nothing exists prior to this plan; there is nothing in heaven; man will be what he will have planned to be. Not what he will want to be. Because by

1

10

20

---

[1]A German philosopher (1889–1976) whose writings had a major influence on Sartre and other existentialists.

the word "will" we generally mean a conscious decision, which is subsequent to what we have already made of ourselves. I may want to belong to a political party, write a book, get married; but all that is only a manifestation of an earlier, more spontaneous choice that is called "will." But if existence really does precede essence, man is responsible for what he is. Thus, existentialism's first move is to make every man aware of what he is and to make the full responsibility of his existence rest on him. And when we say that a man is responsible for himself, we do not only mean that he is responsible for his own individuality, but that he is responsible for all men.

The word subjectivism has two meanings, and our opponents play on the two. Subjectivism means, on the one hand, that an individual chooses and makes himself; and, on the other, that it is impossible for man to transcend human subjectivity. The second of these is the essential meaning of existentialism. When we say that man chooses his own self, we mean that every one of us does likewise; but we also mean by that that in making this choice he also chooses all men. In fact, in creating the man that we want to be, there is not a single one of our acts which does not at the same time create an image of man as we think he ought to be. To choose to be this or that is to affirm at the same time the value of what we choose, because we can never choose evil. We always choose the good, and nothing can be good for us without being good for all.

If, on the other hand, existence precedes essence, and if we grant that we exist and fashion our image at one and the same time, the image is valid for everybody and for our whole age. Thus, our responsibility is much greater than we might have supposed, because it involves all mankind. If I am a workingman and choose to join a Christian trade-union rather than be a communist, and if by being a member I want to show that the best thing for man is resignation, that the kingdom of man is not of this world, I am not only involving my own case—I want to be resigned for everyone. As a result, my action has involved all humanity. To take a more individual matter, if I want to marry, to have children; even if this marriage depends solely on my own circumstances or passion or wish, I am involving all humanity in monogamy and not merely myself. Therefore, I am responsible for myself and for everyone else. I am creating a certain image of man of my own choosing. In choosing myself, I choose man.

This helps us understand what the actual content is of such rather grandiloquent words as anguish, forlornness, despair. As you will see, it's all quite simple.

First, what is meant by anguish? The existentialists say at once that man is anguish. What that means is this: the man who involves himself and who realizes that he is not only the person he chooses to be, but also a lawmaker who is, at the same time, choosing all mankind as well as himself, cannot escape the feeling of his total and deep responsibility. Of course, there are many people who are not anxious; but we claim that they are hiding their anxiety, that they are fleeing from it. Certainly, many people believe that when they do something, they themselves are the only ones involved, and when someone says to them, "What if everyone acted that way?" they shrug their shoulders and answer, "Everyone doesn't act that way." But really, one should always ask himself, "What would happen if everybody

looked at things that way?" There is no escaping this disturbing thought except by a kind of double-dealing. A man who lies and makes excuses for himself by saying "not everybody does that," is someone with an uneasy conscience, because the act of lying implies that a universal value is conferred upon the lie. . . .

The existentialist . . . thinks it very distressing that God does not exist, because all possibility of finding values in a heaven of ideas disappears along with Him; there can no longer be an *a priori* Good, since there is no infinite and perfect consciousness to think it. Nowhere is it written that the Good exists, that we must be honest, that we must not lie; because the fact is we are on a plane where there are only men. Dostoevsky said, "If God didn't exist, everything would be possible." That is the very starting point of existentialism. Indeed, everything is permissible if God does not exist, and as a result man is forlorn, because neither within him nor without does he find anything to cling to. He can't start making excuses for himself.

If existence really does precede essence, there is no explaining things away by reference to a fixed and given human nature. In other words, there is no determinism, man is free, man is freedom. On the other hand, if God does not exist, we find no values or commands to turn to which legitimize our conduct. So, in the bright realm of values, we have no excuse behind us, nor justification before us. We are alone, with no excuses.

That is the idea I shall try to convey when I say that man is condemned to be free. Condemned, because he did not create himself, yet, in other respects is free; because, once thrown into the world, he is responsible for everything he does. The existentialist does not believe in the power of passion. He will never agree that a sweeping passion is a ravaging torrent which fatally leads a man to certain acts and is therefore an excuse. He thinks that man is responsible for his passion.

The existentialist does not think that man is going to help himself by finding in the world some omen by which to orient himself. Because he thinks that man will interpret the omen to suit himself. Therefore, he thinks that man, with no support and no aid, is condemned every moment to invent man. Ponge,[2] in a very fine article, has said, "Man is the future of man." That's exactly it. But if it is taken to mean that this future is recorded in heaven, that God sees it, then it is false, because it would really no longer be a future. If it is taken to mean that whatever a man may be, there is a future to be forged, a virgin future before him, then this remark is sound. But then we are forlorn. . . .

Now, for the existentialist there is really no love other than one which manifests itself in a person's being in love. There is no genius other than one which is expressed in works of art; the genius of Proust is the sum of Proust's works; the genius of Racine is his series of tragedies. Outside of that, there is nothing. Why say that Racine could have written another tragedy, when he didn't write it? A man is involved in life, leaves his impress on it, and outside of that there is nothing. To be sure, this may seem a harsh thought to someone whose life hasn't been a success. But, on the other hand, it prompts people to understand that reality alone is what

---

[2]Francis Ponge (b. 1899) was a French poet and critic.

counts, that dreams, expectations, and hopes warrant no more than to define a man as a disappointed dream, as miscarried hopes, as vain expectations. In other words, to define him negatively and not positively. However, when we say, "You are nothing else than your life," that does not imply that the artist will be judged solely on the basis of his works of art; a thousand other things will contribute toward summing him up. What we mean is [160] that a man is nothing else than a series of undertakings, that he is the sum, the organization, the ensemble of the relationships which make up these undertakings. . . .

If it is impossible to find in every man some universal essence which would be human nature, yet there does exist a universal human condition. It's not by chance that today's thinkers speak more readily of man's condition than of his nature. By condition they mean, more or less definitely, the *a priori* limits which outline man's fundamental situation in the universe. Historical [170] situations vary; a man may be born a slave in a pagan society or a feudal lord or a proletarian. What does not vary is the necessity for him to exist in the world, to be at work there, to be there in the midst of other people, and to be mortal there. . . .

But there is another meaning of humanism. Fundamentally it is this: man is constantly outside of himself; in projecting himself, in losing himself outside of himself, he makes for man's existing; and, on the other hand, it is by pursuing transcendent goals that he [180] is able to exist; man, being this state of passing-beyond, and seizing upon things only as they bear upon this passing-beyond, is at the heart, at the center of this passing-beyond. There is no universe other than a human universe, the universe of human subjectivity. This connection between transcendency, as a constituent element of man—not in the sense that God is transcendent, but in the sense of passing beyond—and subjectivity, in the sense that man is not closed in on himself but is always present in a human universe, is [190] what we call existentialist humanism. Humanism, because we remind man that there is no lawmaker other than himself, and that in his forlornness he will decide by himself; because we point out that man will fulfill himself as man, not in turning toward himself, but in seeking outside of himself a goal which is just this liberation, just this particular fulfillment.

From these few reflections it is evident that nothing is more unjust than the objections that have been raised against us. Existentialism is nothing else than an [200] attempt to draw all the consequences of a coherent atheistic position. It isn't trying to plunge man into despair at all. But if one calls every attitude of unbelief despair, like the Christians, then the word is not being used in its original sense. Existentialism isn't so atheistic that it wears itself out showing that God doesn't exist. Rather, it declares that even if God did exist, that would change nothing. There you've got our point of view. Not that we believe that God exists, but we think that the problem of His existence is not the issue. In this [210] sense existentialism is optimistic, a doctrine of action, and it is plain dishonesty for Christians to make no distinction between their own despair and ours and then to call us despairing.

◆

Christian Existentialism

While Sartre excluded the question of God's existence from his speculations, Christian existentialists saw little contradiction between the belief in a Supreme Being and the ethics of human freedom and responsibility. They held that religious philosophy need not concern itself with the proof or disproof of God's existence; rather, it should focus on the moral life of the individual. Beyond what Kierkegaard had called the "leap of faith" from which all religious belief proceeded, there lay a continuing moral responsibility for one's own life. According to the philosophers Karl Jaspers (1883–1969) and Gabriel Marcel (1889–1973), God had challenged human beings to act as free and responsible creatures.

Among Christian theologians, a similar concern for the moral life of the individual moved religion out of the seminaries and into the streets. The Protestant theologian Reinhold Niebuhr (1892–1971) criticized doctrinaire theology and called for the revival of moral conduct in an immoral society. Convinced that human participation was essential to social redemption, Niebuhr urged Christians to cultivate the roles of humility and justice in modern life. Niebuhr's contemporary and fellow Lutheran Paul Tillich (1886–1965) boldly rejected the concept of a personal god. For Tillich, anxiety and alienation were conditions preliminary to the mystical apprehension of a "God above the God of theism."

Existentialism and Literature

Sartre's secular philosophy inspired a new kind of literary hero: a hero who, deprived of traditional values and religious beliefs, bears the burden of freedom and the total responsibility for his actions. The existential hero—or, more exactly, antihero—took up the quest for meaning: Alienated by nature and circumstance, this hero makes choices in a world lacking moral absolutes, a world in which no act might be called "good" unless it is chosen in conscious preference to its alternatives. Unlike the heroes of old, the modern antihero is neither divinely inspired nor sure of purpose and design. He might act decisively, but with full recognition of the absence of shared cultural values and moral absolutes. Trapped rather than liberated by freedom, the antihero might have trouble getting along with others or simply making it through the day—"Hell," says one of Sartre's characters in *No Exit*, "is other people." Encountering the frustrating conditions of meaninglessness and irrationality, the antihero might achieve nothing other than the awful recognition of the absurdity of the life experience.

Twentieth-century literature is filled with antiheroes—characters whose lives illustrate the absurdity of the human condition. Sartre's compatriot Albert Camus (1913–1960) defined the absurd as the "divorce between man and life, actor and setting." In Camus' short stories and novels, including his classic work, *The Stranger* (1942), the antihero inevitably confronts the basic existential imperatives: "Recognize your dignity as a human being"; "Choose and commit yourself to action." The central character of Camus' *The Stranger* is the quintessential alienated man: He is estranged from traditional social values and unable to establish his sense of being except through continual rebellion. Camus' view of human nature was less cynical than Sartre's and more concerned with the value of benevolent reconciliation between human beings. At the same time, the situations described by Camus in his novels—and his own death in an automobile crash—seem inescapably arbitrary and absurd.

Although existentialism was an essentially European phenomenon, the existential hero appears in the literature of twentieth-century writers throughout the world, most notably in the novels of Argentina's Jorge Luis Borges and Japan's Oē Kenzaburo. In postwar America, the existential perspective cut across regional lines, from the deep South of William Faulkner and Walker Percy to John Cheever's New England, and from the urban Midwest of Saul Bellow to California's Beat Generation writers. The antihero assumes a quintessentially American flavor in the powerful drama *The Death of a Salesman* by Arthur Miller. In the short story genre, Bernard Malamud (1914–1986) offered an especially cogent view of the existential condition in mid-century America, especially as it affected the lives of Jews and other ethnic minorities. Malamud's "A Summer's Reading" (1956) is a particularly good example of the existential condition. The story brings to life the transformation of a high school dropout whose actions in bad faith ultimately drive him to discover that meaning in life demands choice and commitment.

READING 6.12
Malamud's "A Summer's Reading"

George Stoyonovich was a neighborhood boy who had [1] quit high school on an impulse when he was sixteen, run out of patience, and though he was ashamed everytime he went looking for a job, when people asked him if he had finished and he had to say no, he never went back to school. This summer was a hard time for jobs and he had none. Having so much time on his hands, George thought of going to summer school, but the kids in his classes would be too young. He also considered registering in a night high school, only he didn't like the [10] idea of the teachers always telling him what to do. He felt they had not respected him. The result was he stayed off the streets and in his room most of the day.

He was close to twenty and had needs with the neighborhood girls, but no money to spend, and he couldn't get more than an occasional few cents because his father was poor, and his sister Sophie, who resembled George, a tall bony girl of twenty-three, earned very little and what she had she kept for herself. Their mother was dead, and Sophie had to take care of [20] the house.

Very early in the morning George's father got up to go to work in a fish market. Sophie left about eight for her long ride in the subway to a cafeteria in the Bronx. George had his coffee by himself, then hung around in the house. When the house, a five-room railroad flat above a butcher store, got on his nerves he cleaned it up—mopped the floors with a wet mop and put things away. But most of the time he sat in his room. In the afternoons he listened to the ball game. Otherwise he [30] had a couple of old copies of the *World Almanac* he had bought long ago, and he liked to read in them and also the magazines and newspapers that Sophie brought home, that had been left on the tables in the cafeteria. They were mostly picture magazines about movie stars and sports figures, also usually the *News* and *Mirror*. Sophie herself read whatever fell into her hands, although she sometimes read good books.

She once asked George what he did in his room all day and he said he read a lot too. [40]

"Of what besides what I bring home? Do you ever read any worthwhile books?"

"Some," George answered, although he really didn't. He had tried to read a book or two that Sophie had in the house but found he was in no mood for them. Lately he couldn't stand made-up stories, they got on his nerves. He wished he had some hobby to work at—as a kid he was good in carpentry, but where could he work at it? Sometimes during the day he went for walks, but mostly he did his walking after the hot sun had gone down and [50] it was cooler in the streets.

In the evening after supper George left the house and wandered in the neighborhood. During the sultry days some of the storekeepers and their wives sat in chairs on the thick, broken sidewalks in front of their shops, fanning themselves, and George walked past them and the guys hanging out on the candy store corner. A couple of them he had known his whole life, but nobody recognized each other. He had no place special to go, but generally, saving it till the last, he left the [60] neighborhood and walked for blocks till he came to a darkly lit little park with benches and trees and an iron railing, giving it a feeling of privacy. He sat on a bench here, watching the leafy trees and the flowers blooming on the inside of the railing, thinking of a better life for himself. He thought of the jobs he had had since he had quit school—delivery boy, stock clerk, runner, lately working in a factory—and he was dissatisfied with all of them. He felt he would someday like to have a good job and live in a private house with a porch, on a street with [70] trees. He wanted to have some dough in his pocket to buy things with, and a girl to go with, so as not to be so lonely, especially on Saturday nights. He wanted people to like and respect him. He thought about these things often but mostly when he was alone at night. Around midnight he got up and drifted back to his hot and stony neighborhood.

One time while on his walk George met Mr. Cattanzara coming home very late from work. He wondered if he was drunk but then could tell he wasn't. Mr. Cattanzara, a stocky, bald-headed man who worked in a change booth on an IRT station, lived on the next block after George's, above a shoe repair store. Nights, during the hot weather, he sat on his stoop in an undershirt, reading the *New York Times* in the light of the shoemaker's window. He read it from the first page to the last, then went up to sleep. And all the time he was reading the paper, his wife, a fat woman with a white face, leaned out of the window, gazing into the street, her thick white arms folded under her loose breast, on the window ledge.

Once in a while Mr. Cattanzara came home drunk, but it was a quiet drunk. He never made any trouble, only walked stiffly up the street and slowly climbed the stairs into the hall. Though drunk, he looked the same as always, except for his tight walk, the quietness, and that his eyes were wet. George liked Mr. Cattanzara because he remembered him giving him nickels to buy lemon ice with when he was a squirt. Mr. Cattanzara was a different type than those in the neighborhood. He asked different questions than the others when he met you, and he seemed to know what went on in all the newspapers. He read them, as his fat sick wife watched from the window.

"What are you doing with yourself this summer, George?" Mr. Cattanzara asked. "I see you walkin' around at nights."

George felt embarrassed. "I like to walk."

"What are you doin' in the day now?"

"Nothin much just right now. I'm waiting for a job." Since it shamed him to admit he wasn't working, George said, "I'm staying home—but I'm reading a lot to pick up my education."

Mr. Cattanzara looked interested. He mopped his hot face with a red handkerchief.

"What are you readin'?"

George hesitated, then said, "I got a list of books in the library once, and now I'm gonna read them this summer." He felt strange and a little unhappy saying this, but he wanted Mr. Cattanzara to respect him.

"How many books are there on it?"

"I never counted them. Maybe around a hundred."

Mr. Cattanzara whistled through his teeth.

"I figure if I did that," George went on earnestly, "it would help me in my education. I don't mean the kind they give you in high school. I want to know different things than they learn there, if you know what I mean."

The change maker nodded. "Still and all, one hundred books is a pretty big load for one summer."

"It might take longer."

"After you're finished with some, maybe you and I can shoot the breeze about them?" said Mr. Cattanzara.

"When I'm finished," George answered.

Mr. Cattanzara went home and George continued on his walk. After that, though he had the urge to, George did nothing different from usual. He still took his walks at night, ending up in the little park. But one evening the shoemaker on the next block stopped George to say he was a good boy, and George figured that Mr.

Cattanzara had told him all about the books he was reading. From the shoemaker it must have gone down the street, because George saw a couple of people smiling kindly at him, though nobody spoke to him personally. He felt a little better around the neighborhood and liked it more, though not so much he would want to live in it forever. He had never exactly disliked the people in it, yet he had never liked them very much either. It was the fault of the neighborhood. To his surprise, George found out that his father and Sophie knew about his reading too. His father was too shy to say anything about it—he was never much of a talker in his whole life—but Sophie was softer to George, and she showed him in other ways she was proud of him.

As the summer went on George felt in a good mood about things. He cleaned the house every day, as a favor to Sophie, and he enjoyed the ball games more. Sophie gave him a buck a week allowance, and though it still wasn't enough and he had to use it carefully, it was a helluva lot better than just having two bits now and then. What he bought with the money—cigarettes mostly, an occasional beer or movie ticket—he got a big kick out of. Life wasn't so bad if you knew how to appreciate it. Occasionally he bought a paperback book from the newsstand, but he never got around to reading it, though he was glad to have a couple of books in his room. But he read thoroughly Sophie's magazines and newspapers. And at night was the most enjoyable time, because when he passed the storekeepers sitting outside their stores, he could tell they regarded him highly. He walked erect, and though he did not say much to them, or they to him, he could feel approval on all sides. A couple of nights he felt so good that he skipped the park at the end of the evening. He just wandered in the neighborhood, where people had known him from the time he was a kid playing punchball whenever there was a game of it going; he wandered there, then came home and got undressed for bed, feeling fine.

For a few weeks he had talked only once with Mr. Cattanzara, and though the change maker had said nothing more about the books, asked no questions, his silence made George a little uneasy. For a while George didn't pass in front of Mr. Cattanzara's house anymore, until one night, forgetting himself, he approached it from a different direction than he usually did when he did. It was already past midnight. The street, except for one or two people, was deserted, and George was surprised when he saw Mr. Cattanzara still reading his newspaper by the light of the street lamp overhead. His impulse was to stop at the stoop and talk to him. He wasn't sure what he wanted to say, though he felt the words would come when he began to talk; but the more he thought about it, the more the idea scared him, and he decided he'd better not. He even considered beating it home by another street, but he was too near Mr. Cattanzara, and the change maker might see him as he ran, and get annoyed. So George unobtrusively crossed the street, trying to make it seem as if he had to look in a store window on the other side, which he did, and then went on, uncomfortable at what he was doing. He feared Mr. Cattanzara would glance up from his paper and call him a dirty rat for walking on the other side of the street, but

all he did was sit there, sweating through his 200
undershirt, his bald head shining in the dim light as
he read his *Times*, and upstairs his fat wife leaned out
of the window, seeming to read the paper along with
him. George thought she would spy him and yell out
to Mr. Cattanzara, but she never moved her eyes off
her husband.

George made up his mind to stay away from the
change maker until he had got some of his softback
books read, but when he started them and saw they were
mostly story books, he lost his interest and didn't bother 210
to finish them. He lost his interest in reading other
things too. Sophie's magazines and newspapers went
unread. She saw them piling up on a chair in his room
and asked why he was no longer looking at them, and
George told her it was because of all the other reading he
had to do. Sophie said she had guessed that was it. So
for most of the day, George had the radio on, turning to
music when he was sick of the human voice. He kept the
house fairly neat, and Sophie said nothing on the days
when he neglected it. She was still kind and gave him 220
his extra buck, though things weren't so good for him as
they had been before.

But they were good enough, considering. Also his night
walks invariably picked him up, no matter how bad the
day was. Then one night George saw Mr. Cattanzara
coming down the street toward him. George was about to
turn and run but he recognized from Mr. Cattanzara's
walk that he was drunk, and if so, probably he would not
even bother to notice him. So George kept on walking
straight ahead until he came abreast of Mr. Cattanzara 230
and though he felt wound up enough to pop into the sky,
he was not surprised when Mr. Cattanzara passed him
without a word, walking slowly, his face and body stiff.
George drew a breath in relief at his narrow escape,
when he heard his name called, and there stood Mr.
Cattanzara at his elbow, smelling like the inside of a beer
barrel. His eyes were sad as he gazed at George, and
George felt so intensely uncomfortable he was tempted
to shove the drunk aside and continue on his walk.

But he couldn't act that way to him, and, besides, Mr. 240
Cattanzara took a nickel out of his pants pocket and
handed it to him.

"Go buy yourself a lemon ice, Georgie."

"It's not that time anymore, Mr. Cattanzara," George
said, "I am a big guy now."

"No, you ain't," said Mr. Cattanzara, to which George
made no reply he could think of.

"How are all your books comin' along now?" Mr.
Cattanzara asked. Though he tried to stand steady, he
swayed a little. 250

"Fine, I guess," said George, feeling the red crawling
up his face.

"You ain't sure?" The change maker smiled slyly, a way
George had never seen him smile.

"Sure I'm sure. They're fine."

Though his head swayed in little arcs, Mr. Cattanzara's
eyes were steady. He had small blue eyes which could
hurt if you looked at them too long.

"George," he said, "name me one book on that
list that you read this summer, and I will drink to 260
your health."

"I don't want anybody drinking to me."

"Name me one so I can ask you a question on it. Who
can tell, if it's a good book maybe I might wanna read
it myself."

George knew he looked passable on the outside, but
inside he was crumbling apart.

Unable to reply, he shut his eyes, but when—years
later—he opened them, he saw that Mr. Cattanzara had,
out of pity, gone away, but in his ears he still heard the 270
words he had said when he had left: "George, don't do
what I did."

The next night he was afraid to leave his room, and
though Sophie argued with him he wouldn't open
the door.

"What are you doing in there?" she asked.

"Nothing."

"Aren't you reading?"

"No."

She was silent a minute, then asked, "Where do you 280
keep the books you read? I never see any in your room
outside of a few cheap trashy ones."

He wouldn't tell her.

"In that case you're not worth a buck of my hard-
earned money. Why should I break my back for you? Go
on out, you bum, and get a job."

He stayed in his room for almost a week, except to
sneak into the kitchen when nobody was home. Sophie
railed at him, then begged him to come out, and his old
father wept, but George wouldn't budge, though the 290
weather was terrible and his small room stifling. He
found it very hard to breathe, each breath was like
drawing a flame into his lungs.

One night, unable to stand the heat anymore, he burst
into the street at one A.M., a shadow of himself. He
hoped to sneak to the park without being seen, but there
were people all over the block, wilted and listless,
waiting for a breeze. George lowered his eyes and
walked, in disgrace, away from them, but before long he
discovered they were still friendly to him. He figured Mr. 300
Cattanzara hadn't told on him. Maybe when he woke up
out of his drunk the next morning, he had forgotten all
about meeting George. George felt his confidence slowly
come back to him.

That same night a man on a street corner asked him if
it was true that he had finished reading so many books,
and George admitted he had. The man said it was a
wonderful thing for a boy his age to read so much.

"Yeah," George said, but he felt relieved. He hoped
nobody would mention the books anymore, and when, 310
after a couple of days, he accidentally met Mr.
Cattanzara again, *he* didn't, though George had the idea
he was the one who had started the rumor that he had
finished all the books.

One evening in the fall, George ran out of his house to
the library, where he hadn't been in years. There were
books all over the place, wherever he looked, and though
he was struggling to control an inward trembling, he
easily counted off a hundred, then sat down at a table
to read. 320

———————————◆———————————

The Quest for Meaning in Modern Poetry

T. S. Eliot

The theme of alienation permeates the poetry of the twentieth century; however, no English-speaking poet captured the mood of anxiety and the modern quest for meaning more powerfully than the American-born writer T. S. (Thomas Stearns) Eliot (1888–1965). In the verse drama *The Rock*, written in 1935, Eliot summed up the crisis that threatened to engulf the modern world:

> All our knowledge brings us nearer to our
>   ignorance,
> All our ignorance brings us nearer to death,
> But nearness to death no nearer to GOD.
> Where is the wisdom we have lost in knowledge?
> Where is the knowledge we have lost in
>   information?
> The cycles of Heaven in twenty centuries
> Bring us farther from God and nearer to the
>   Dust.*

Educated at Harvard University in philosophy and the classics, Eliot was studying at Oxford when World War I broke out. He remained in England after the war, becoming a British citizen in 1927 and converting to the Anglican church in the same year. Eliot's grasp of modern philosophy, world religions, anthropology, and the classical literature of Asia and the West made him the most esteemed literary critic of his time. His erudition also informed his poetic style. Like his colleague Ezra Pound, whom he met in 1914, Eliot tried to rid modern poetry of romantic sentiment. He insisted that the poet must seek the verbal formula or "objective correlative" (as he called it) that gives precise shape to feeling. Eliot's poetry features inventive rhythms, irregular cadences, and startling images that appear pieced together like fragments of a jigsaw puzzle. Many of his poems are densely packed with personal reminiscences and intriguing literary allusions. His poem "The Waste Land" (1922), which takes as its theme the aridity of modern life, had the effect—as one of his contemporaries remarked—of an atom bomb. While it did not wipe away all earlier poetic styles, it established the idiom of modern poetry as compressed, complex, demanding, and serious.

The poem "The Love Song of J. Alfred Prufrock," though written as early as 1915, belongs in this chapter because it so perfectly captures the condition of the existential antihero. The "love song" is actually the dramatic monologue of a timid and neurotic middle-aged man who has little faith in himself or his capacity for effective action. Prufrock's cynicism and despair presage the failure of nerve and the sense of impotence that marked the postwar generation. At the same time, his sense of powerlessness and moral inertia have made Prufrock an archetype of the spiritual loss that some critics associate with the modern condition in general.

Eliot sets the tone of Prufrock's monologue with a montage of powerfully compressed and gloomy images: "one-night cheap hotels," "sawdust restaurants," "soot that falls from chimneys," "narrow streets," "lonely men in shirt-sleeves." Throughout the poem, he interweaves literary vignettes that illuminate Prufrock's bankrupt idealism. Prufrock's lack of heroic vision is underscored, for instance, by allusions to the biblical prophets and to the heroes of history and art, such as Michelangelo and Hamlet. Repeatedly, Prufrock laments his self-conscious retreat from action. Finally, in the last lines of the poem, he reflects on his loss of faith in the conventional sources of wisdom. He observes that the voices of inspiration have been submerged by all-too-human voices, including his own. The despairing final lines of the poem are Eliot's epitaph for the modern antihero.

READING 6.13

Eliot's "Love Song of J. Alfred Prufrock"

S'io credesse che mia risposta fosse
A persona che mai tornasse al mondo,
Questa fiamma staria senza piu scosse.
Ma perciocche giammai di questo fondo
Non torno vivo alcun s'i'odo il vero,
Senza tema d'infamia ti rispondo.[1]

Let us go then, you and I,	1
When the evening is spread out against the sky	
Like a patient etherised upon a table;	
Let us go, through certain half-deserted streets,	
The muttering retreats	5
Of restless nights in one-night cheap hotels	
And sawdust restaurants with oyster-shells:	
Streets that follow like a tedious argument	
Of insidious intent	
To lead you to an overwhelming question . . .	10
Oh, do not ask, "What is it?"	
Let us go and make our visit.	

In the room the women come and go
Talking of Michelangelo.

**T. S. Eliot, choruses from *The Rock* in *The Complete Poems and Plays 1909–1950*. New York: Harcourt, Brace and Company, 1952, 96.

[1]Lines from Dante's "Inferno," Canto 27, 61–66, spoken by Guido da Montefeltro, who was condemned to Hell for the sin of false counseling. In explaining his punishment to Dante, Guido is still apprehensive of the judgment of society.

The yellow fog that rubs its back upon the window-
    panes,   15
The yellow smoke that rubs its muzzle on the window-panes
Licked its tongue into the corners of the evening,
Lingered upon the pools that stand in drains,
Let fall upon its back the soot that falls from chimneys,
Slipped by the terrace, made a sudden leap,   20
And seeing that it was a soft October night,
Curled once about the house, and fell asleep.

    And indeed there will be time
For the yellow smoke that slides along the street,
Rubbing its back upon the window-panes;   25
There will be time, there will be time
To prepare a face to meet the faces that you meet;
There will be time to murder and create,
And time for all the works and days of hands[2]
That lift and drop a question on your plate;   30
Time for you and time for me,
And time yet for a hundred indecisions,
And for a hundred visions and revisions,
Before the taking of a toast and tea.

    In the room the women come and go   35
Talking of Michelangelo.

    And indeed there will be time
To wonder, "Do I dare?" and, "Do I dare?"
Time to turn back and descend the stair,
With a bald spot in the middle of my hair—   40
(They will say: "How his hair is growing thin!")
My morning coat, my collar mounting firmly to the chin,
My necktie rich and modest, but asserted by a simple pin—
(They will say: "But how his arms and legs are thin!")
Do I dare   45
Disturb the universe?
In a minute there is time
For decisions and revisions which a minute will reverse.

    For I have known them all already, known them all—
Have known the evenings, mornings, afternoons,   50
I have measured out my life with coffee spoons;
I know the voices dying with a dying fall
Beneath the music from a farther room.
    So how should I presume?

    And I have known the eyes already, known them all—   55
The eyes that fix you in a formulated phrase,
And when I am formulated, sprawling on a pin,
When I am pinned and wriggling on the wall,
Then how should I begin
To spit out all the butt-ends of my days and ways?   60
    And how should I presume?

    And I have known the arms already, known them all—
Arms that are braceleted and white and bare
(But in the lamplight, downed with light brown hair!)
Is it perfume from a dress   65
That makes me so digress?
Arms that lie along a table, or wrap about a shawl.
    And should I then presume?
    And how should I begin?

              . . . . .

Shall I say, I have gone at dusk through narrow streets   70
And watched the smoke that rises from the pipes
Of lonely men in shirt-sleeves, leaning out of windows? . . .

    I should have been a pair of ragged claws
Scuttling across the floors of silent seas.

              . . . . .

    And the afternoon, the evening, sleeps so peacefully! 75
Smoothed by long fingers,
Asleep . . . tired . . . or it malingers,
Stretched on the floor, here beside you and me.
Should I, after tea and cakes and ices,
Have the strength to force the moment to its crisis?   80
But though I have wept and fasted, wept and prayed,
Though I have seen my head (grown slightly bald)
    brought in upon a platter,
I am no prophet—and here's no great matter;[3]
I have seen the moment of my greatness flicker,
And I have seen the eternal Footman hold my coat, and
    snicker,   85
And in short, I was afraid.

    And would it have been worth it, after all,
After the cups, the marmalade, the tea,
Among the porcelain, among some talk of you and me,
Would it have been worth while,   90
To have bitten off the matter with a smile,
To have squeezed the universe into a ball[4]
To roll it toward some overwhelming question,
To say: "I am Lazarus, come from the dead,[5]
Come back to tell you all, I shall tell you all"—   95
If one, settling a pillow by her head,
    Should say: "That is not what I meant at all,
    That is not it, at all."

              . . . . .

    And would it have been worth it, after all,
Would it have been worth while,   100
After the sunsets and the dooryards and the sprinkled
    streets,
After the novels, after the teacups, after the skirts that
    trail along the floor—
And this, and so much more?—
It is impossible to say just what I mean!
But as if a magic lantern threw the nerves in patterns on
    a screen: 105
Would it have been worth while
If one, settling a pillow or throwing off a shawl,
And turning towards the window, should say:
    "That is not it at all,
    That is not what I meant, at all."   110

              . . . . .

---

[2]An ironic allusion to the poem "Works and Days" by the eighth-century
B.C.E. poet Hesiod, which celebrates the virtues of hard labor on the land.

[3]A reference to John the Baptist, who was beheaded by Herod (Matthew
14.3–11). Prufrock perceives himself as victim but as neither saint
nor martyr.
[4]A reference to the line "Let us roll all our strength and all our sweetness
up into a ball," from the poem "To a Coy Mistress," by the seventeenth-
century English poet Andrew Marvell, in which Marvell presses his lover to
"seize the day."
[5]According to the Gospel of John (11.1–44), Jesus raised Lazarus from
the grave.

No! I am not Prince Hamlet, nor was meant to be;
Am an attendant lord, one that will do
To swell a progress, start a scene or two,
Advise the prince; no doubt, an easy tool,[6]
Deferential, glad to be of use,   115
Politic, cautious, and meticulous;
Full of high sentence, but a bit obtuse;
At times, indeed, almost ridiculous—
Almost, at times, the Fool.

    I grow old . . . I grow old . . .   120
I shall wear the bottoms of my trousers rolled.[7]

    Shall I part my hair behind? Do I dare to eat a peach?
I shall wear white flannel trousers, and walk upon the
    beach.
I have heard the mermaids singing, each to each.

I do not think that they will sing to me.   125

I have seen them riding seaward on the waves
Combing the white hair of the waves blown back
When the wind blows the water white and black.

We have lingered in the chambers of the sea
By sea-girls wreathed with seaweed red and brown   130
Till human voices wake us, and we drown.

◆

Dylan Thomas

The moral inertia that afflicted Eliot's Prufrock was not shared by the poet Dylan Thomas (1914–1953), who proclaimed himself a Welshman first and a drunkard second. One of the twentieth century's most powerful wordsmiths, Thomas took an exuberant approach to the modern condition. His poem "Do Not Go Gentle Into That Good Night," published just after the death of his father in 1951, makes a plea for life-affirming action even in the face of death. Thomas creates a musical litany with the phrases "wise men," "good men," "wild men," "grave men"—resolving four of the six stanzas with the imperative: "rage against the dying of the light." The reference to those "who see with blinding sight" was probably inspired by the loss of vision that the poet's schoolteacher father suffered during his last years of life, but it also may be taken as an allusion to his father's agnosticism, that is, to his spiritual blindness—and, more generally, to the mood of alienation afflicting a generation of modern disbelievers. In 1954, Igor Stravinsky used this poem as the basis for *In Memoriam Dylan Thomas*, a piece written for tenor, string orchestra, and two trombones.

---

[6]A reference to Polonius, the king's adviser in Shakespeare's *Hamlet*, as well as to Guido da Montefeltro—both of them false counselors.
[7]In Eliot's time, rolled or cuffed trousers were considered fashionable.

READING 6.14

Thomas' "Do Not Go Gentle Into That Good Night"

Do not go gentle into that good night,   1
Old age should burn and rave at close of day;
Rage, rage against the dying of the light.

Though wise men at their end know dark is right,
Because their words had forked no lightning they   5
Do not go gentle into that good night.

Good men, the last wave by, crying how bright
Their frail deeds might have danced in a green bay,
Rage, rage against the dying of the light.

Wild men who caught and sang the sun in flight,   10
And learn, too late, they grieved it on its way,
Do not go gentle into that good night.

Grave men, near death, who see with blinding sight
Blind eyes could blaze like meteors and be gay,
Rage, rage against the dying of the light.   15

And you, my father, there on the sad height,
Curse, bless, me now with your fierce tears, I pray.
Do not go gentle into that good night.
Rage, rage against the dying of the light.

◆

Rabindranath Tagore

T. S. Eliot's Asian contemporary Rabindranath Tagore (1861–1941) shared Eliot's perception of a world in spiritual deterioration. For Tagore, the crisis of modern society lay in a set of misplaced values that prized the rush of business and the acquisition of material comforts at the expense of beauty, creativity, and spiritual harmony. Born in Bengal (while the province was still under British control), Tagore was raised in a family of artists, musicians, and social reformers. After a brief stay in England, he returned to India, where he became a prolific writer, publishing some sixty volumes of poetry, plays, stories, and novels. In India, Tagore pursued his ambition to foster a "spiritual unity of all races" by founding an international educational institute for the exchange of ideas between Western scholars and Indian students. Awarded the Nobel Prize for literature in 1913, Tagore left a body of writings that offers an Eastern, and specifically Hindu, approach to the modern quest for meaning. In his provocative allegory, "The Man Had No Useful Work," Tagore deals gently with the existential responsibility for individual choice. The narrative poem questions the value of the practical, goal-oriented pursuits that drive most modern societies. It also plays on the ironic truth that works of art may be both meaningless and essential.

READING 6.15

Tagore's "The Man Had No Useful Work"

The man had no useful work, only vagaries of various kinds. 1
Therefore it surprised him to find himself in Paradise
  after a life spent perfecting trifles.
Now the guide had taken him by mistake to the wrong
  Paradise—one meant only for good, busy souls.

In this Paradise, our man saunters along the road only to
  obstruct the rush of business.
He stands aside from the path and is warned that he
  tramples on sown seed. Pushed, he starts up: hustled,
  he moves on. 5
A very busy girl comes to fetch water from the well. Her feet
  run on the pavement like rapid fingers over harp-strings.
  Hastily she ties a negligent knot with her hair, and loose
  locks on her forehead pry into the dark of her eyes.
The man says to her, "Would you lend me your pitcher?"
"My pitcher?" she asks, "to draw water?"
"No, to paint patterns on."
"I have no time to waste," the girl retorts in contempt. 10

Now a busy soul has no chance against one who is
  supremely idle.
Every day she meets him at the well, and every day he
  repeats the same request, till at last she yields.
Our man paints the pitcher with curious colors in a
  mysterious maze of lines.
The girl takes it up, turns it round and asks, "What does
  it mean?"
"It has no meaning," he answers. 15

The girl carries the pitcher home. She holds it up in
  different lights and tries to con its mystery.
At night she leaves her bed, lights a lamp, and gazes at
  it from all points of view.
This is the first time she has met with something without
  meaning.

On the next day the man is again near the well.
The girl asks, "What do you want?" 20
"To do more work for you!"
"What work?" she enquires.
"Allow me to weave colored strands into a ribbon to bind
  your hair."
"Is there any need?" she asks.
"None whatever," he allows. 25
The ribbon is made, and thenceforward she spends a
  great deal of time over her hair.

The even stretch of well-employed time in that Paradise
  begins to show irregular rents.
The elders are troubled; they meet in council.
The guide confesses his blunder, saying that he has
  brought the wrong man to the wrong place.
The wrong man is called. His turban, flaming with color,
  shows plainly how great that blunder has been. 30
The chief of the elders says, "You must go back to the earth."
The man heaves a sigh of relief: "I am ready."
The girl with the ribbon round her hair chimes in: "I also!"
For the first time the chief of the elders is faced with a
  situation which has no sense in it.

———————◆———————

Islamic Poetry: Anwar and Iqbal

In the Muslim world, where Western technology and Western imperialism have weighed heavily in the transition from ancient to modern ways, Islamic culture and religious devotion have not only endured, but flourished. In spite of political and social challenges to traditional belief and practice, Islam has become the world's fastest growing faith, a response perhaps to the vigorous pan-Islamic movement that began in the late nineteenth century. Recent Islamic literature (written in Arabic, Persian, English, and other languages) has tended to be geographically and socially representative of Muslims throughout the world. Modern Islamic poetry, much of which remains untranslated, has departed considerably from its ancient forms; but the rich harvest of twentieth-century Islamic poets suggests the beginnings of a new golden age.

Muhammad Iqbal (1873–1938), who died before the outbreak of World War II, is regarded as the most eminent writer of Muslim India. Like Tagore, Iqbal studied law and philosophy in Europe, then returned to his native India to make a lasting mark in literature. His prose and poetry are written in Urdu (the language of present-day Pakistan), Persian, and English. In tracts that reflect his close study of both Muslim and European thought, Iqbal championed the civilizing role of Islam in modern life. He urged the formation of an independent Muslim state in Hindu India, but emphasized the importance of achieving brotherhood among India's Muslim, Christian, and Hindu populations. While he defended the centrality of Islamic law in the Muslim community, he envisioned an ideal community that transcended ethnic, racial, and national loyalties. The poet-philosopher urged his readers to replace the mystical ideals of passive contemplation and withdrawal with a modern doctrine of choice and action that might make Islam the leading moral force in South Asia. Deeply critical of injustice, godlessness, and false ideals—all of which he equated with a failing Western morality—he infused the pan-Islamic ideals of early modernism with new fervor. Although the language of Iqbal's verse lacks the immediacy of vernacular speech, it conveys the lyric passion of one of Asia's most gifted poets.

Indonesia, whose majority population is Muslim, produced its greatest poet, Chairil Anwar (1922–1949), in the first half of the twentieth century. Anwar was greatly influenced by Western literature and the modern taste for colloquial verse. "At the Mosque," one of seventy poems written during the course of his twenty-six years, reflects his personal struggle to maintain an intimate relationship with God in the face of doubt and despair.

READING 6.16

Islamic Poems

Iqbal's "Revolution"

Death to man's soul is Europe, death is Asia
To man's will: neither feels the vital current.
In man's hearts stirs a revolution's torrent;
Maybe our old world too is nearing death.

(1938)

Iqbal's "Europe and Syria"

This land of Syria gave the West a Prophet
Of purity and pity and innocence;
And Syria from the West as recompense
Gets dice and drink and troops of prostitutes.

(1936)

Anwar's "At the Mosque"

I shouted at Him   1
Until He came.

We met face to face.

Afterwards He burned in my breast.
All my strength struggles to extinguish Him.   5
My body, which won't be driven, is soaked with sweat.

This room
Is the arena where we fight,

Destroying each other,
One hurling insults, the other gone mad.   10

(1943)

◆

Theater of the Absurd

Among the most anguished portrayals of modern society were those generated by the *theater of the absurd*, an international movement that has been called "the true theater of our time." Working in the postwar era, absurdist playwrights portrayed reality as devoid of meaning and moral order, and infested with macabre and bizarre circumstances. Their plays, which usually lack the traditional plot and character development that marks the works of Sophocles, Shakespeare, and Ibsen, drew stylistic inspiration from dada performance art and surrealist film (see chapter 33). Unlike classical theater, in which dramatic structure is established by action that takes place over a clearly defined period of time, absurdist plays (much like a modern art and music) seem devoid of direction and resolution. Characters undergo little or no change, words often contradict actions, and events might assume no logical order. Dramatic action, leavened with black humor, can consist exclusively of irrational and grotesque situations that remain unresolved at the end of the performance—as is often the case with real life.

The principal figures of absurdist theater reflect the international character of the movement: They include Samuel Beckett (Irish), Eugène Ionesco (Romanian), Harold Pinter (British), Fernando Arrabal (Spanish), Jean Genet (French), and Edward Albee (American). Of these, Samuel Beckett (1906–1989), recipient of the Nobel Prize in 1969, has the greatest distinction. Early in his career, Beckett came under the influence of James Joyce, parts of whose novel *Finnegans Wake* he recorded from dictation, as the aging Joyce was losing his eyesight. Beckett admired Joyce's experimental use of language. He also shared the views of the Austrian linguistic philosopher Ludwig Wittgenstein (see chapter 37), who held that human beings were imprisoned by language and consequently cut off from the possibility of understanding. The concept of language as the prisonhouse of the mind—a point of view that had far-reaching consequences in postmodern philosophy—was fundamental to Beckett's dramatic style. It is particularly apparent in his most notable work, *Waiting for Godot*, written in 1948 and first staged in 1952. The main "action" of the play consists of a running dialogue—terse, repetitious, and often comical—between two tramps as they await the mysterious "Godot" (who, despite their anxious expectations, never arrives). Critics find in Godot a symbol of salvation, revelation, or, most commonly, God—an interpretation that Beckett himself rejects. Nevertheless, the absent "deliverer" (perhaps by his very absence) gives a modicum of meaning to the lives of the central characters. Their longings and delusions, their paralysis and ignorance, are anticipated in the opening line, "Nothing to be done." The progress of the play, animated by an extraordinary blend of biblical references, broad slapstick, comic wordplay, Zenlike propositions, and crude jokes, gives life to Sartre's observation that "man first of all is the being who hurls himself toward a future" (see Reading 6.11). A parable of the existential condition, *Waiting for Godot* dwells on the divorce between expectation and event. At the same time (and as the brief excerpt from the end of Act Two illustrates), the play underscores the futility of communication between the very creatures who choose to cling (and wait) together.

READING 6.17

From Beckett's *Waiting for Godot*

ESTRAGON: Where shall we go?   1
VLADIMIR: Not far.
ESTRAGON: Oh yes, let's go far away from here.
VLADIMIR: We can't.
ESTRAGON: Why not?
VLADIMIR: We have to come back to-morrow.
ESTRAGON: What for?
VLADIMIR: To wait for Godot.

ESTRAGON: Ah! (*Silence.*) He didn't come?
VLADIMIR: No.   10
ESTRAGON: And now it's too late.
VLADIMIR: Yes, now it's night.
ESTRAGON: And if we dropped him. (*Pause.*) If we dropped him?
VLADIMIR: He'd punish us. (*Silence. He looks at the tree.*) Everything's dead but the tree.
ESTRAGON (*Looking at the tree*): What is it?
VLADIMIR: It's the tree.
ESTRAGON: Yes, but what kind?
VLADIMIR: I don't know. A willow.   20
(*Estragon draws Vladimir towards the tree. They stand motionless before it. Silence.*)
ESTRAGON: Why don't we hang ourselves?
VLADIMIR: With what?
ESTRAGON: You haven't got a bit of rope?
VLADIMIR: No.
ESTRAGON: Then we can't.
(*Silence.*)
VLADIMIR: Let's go.
ESTRAGON: Wait, there's my belt.
VLADIMIR: It's too short.
ESTRAGON: You could hang on to my legs.
VLADIMIR: And who'd hang on to mine?   30
ESTRAGON: True.
VLADIMIR: Show all the same. (*Estragon loosens the cord that holds up his trousers which, much too big for him, fall about his ankles. They look at the cord.*) It might do at a pinch. But is it strong enough?
ESTRAGON: We'll soon see. Here.
(*They each take an end of the cord and pull. It breaks. They almost fall.*)
VLADIMIR: Not worth a curse.
(*Silence.*)
ESTRAGON: You say we have to come back to-morrow?
VLADIMIR: Yes.
ESTRAGON: Then we can bring a good bit of rope.   40
VLADIMIR: Yes.
(*Silence.*)
ESTRAGON: Didi.
VLADIMIR: Yes.
ESTRAGON: I can't go on like this.
VLADIMIR: That's what you think.
ESTRAGON: If we parted? That might be better for us.
VLADIMIR: We'll hang ourselves tomorrow. (*Pause.*) Unless Godot comes.
ESTRAGON: And if he comes?
VLADIMIR: We'll be saved.   50
(*Vladimir takes off his hat (Lucky's), peers inside it, feels about inside it, shakes it, knocks on the crown, puts it on again.*)
ESTRAGON: Well? Shall we go?
VLADIMIR: Pull on your trousers.
ESTRAGON: What?
VLADIMIR: Pull on your trousers.
ESTRAGON: You want me to pull off my trousers?
VLADIMIR: Pull ON your trousers.
ESTRAGON (*Realizing his trousers are down*): True. (*He pulls up his trousers.*)
VLADIMIR: Well? Shall we go?
ESTRAGON: Yes, let's go.   60
(*They do not move.*)
(*Curtain.*)

◆

The Visual Arts at Mid-Century
Film

At mid-century, filmmakers broadened the art of cinema to explore the moral and psychological crises of modern society. A pioneer experimental filmmaker of this century, the Japanese Kurasawa Akira (1910–1993), used film as a vehicle for examining the ambiguities of modern life. A highly skilled director with a talent for fine editing, Kurasawa brought to his films technical virtuosity (evident in his unusual camera angles and flashbacks) and a stringent economy of expression. In the classic films *Rashomon* (1950), *Ikiru* (1952), and *Seven Samurai* (1954), Kurasawa suggests that the world's evils can only be redeemed by positive social action.

The Swedish filmmaker Ingmar Bergman (b. 1918) wrote and directed landmark films that probed into the troubled lives of modern men and women. The loss of God, the acknowledgment of spiritual and emotional isolation, and the quest for self-knowledge are the principal themes of Bergman's films, the most notable of which are *The Seventh Seal* (1956), *Wild Strawberries* (1957), *The Silence* (1963), and *Persona* (1966). Bergman's black-and-white cinema triumph *The Seventh Seal* is an allegorical tale of despair in the face of death. Set in medieval Europe, the story (inspired by the Revelation of Saint John) involves a medieval knight who returns home from the Crusades, only to confront widespread plague and human suffering. Ultimately, the disillusioned knight challenges Death to a chess game, the stakes of which are life itself. In *The Seventh Seal*, Bergman abandoned traditional narrative techniques—he compared filmmaking to writing music—so as to capture the spirit of an apocalyptic vision.

Painting

During the first half of the century, almost all important new styles in painting had originated in Paris or other European cities. After 1945, however, the United States, and New York City in particular, took the lead in the production of a radical new art style called *abstract expressionism*. Abstract expressionism had its roots in the modern artist's assault on traditional, representational art. It took inspiration from the reductionist abstractions of Picasso and Matisse, the colorist experiments of Wasily Kandinsky, the random performances of dada, and the "automatic" art of the surrealists. At the same time, it reflected new evidence concerning the role of choice and chance in the operation of the physical universe: By mid-century, research in particle physics confirmed the

Figure 35.1 Willem de Kooning, *Woman I*, 1950–1952. Oil on canvas, 6 ft. 3⅞ in. × 4 ft. 10 in. The Museum of Modern Art, New York. Purchase. Photograph © 1997 The Museum of Modern Art, New York. © Willem de Kooning/ARS, New York and DACS, London 1997.

theory that quantum reality consists of random patterns that evolve in a process of continuous change. Whether or not such theories directly influenced the visual arts, they paralleled the experiments in random art that occurred at this time in more than one part of the world. In postwar Japan, members of the radical group known as the Gutai Bijutsu Kyokai (Concrete Art Association) harnessed physical action to chance in dynamic performance-centered works. Gutai "action events," which featured the energetic and sometimes outrageous manipulation of paint (flung or hurled at the canvas), allied the random techniques of surrealism to native Japanese traditions in spontaneous, gestural Zen painting (see Figure 35.3).

In America, where abstract expressionism ushered in the so-called "heroic age of American painting," the pioneers of the movement were a group of talented immigrants who had escaped Nazi oppression and the perils of war-torn Europe. These artists included Arshile Gorky (1905–1948), Hans Hofmann (1880–1966), and Willem de Kooning (1904–1997), all of whom migrated to New York between 1920 and 1930. Working on large canvases and using oversized brushes, Gorky, Hofmann,

and de Kooning applied paint in a loose, free, and instinctive manner that emphasized the physical gesture—the *act* of painting. Abstract expressionist paintings were usually nonrepresentational, but where recognizable subject matter appeared, as in de Kooning's series of fierce, totemic women—one of his favorite subjects—it was rendered with frenzied, subjective urgency (Figure **35.1**). De Kooning's wide-eyed females, taken by some to suggest the artist's negative view of women, were actually inspired by Sumerian votive sculptures and Earth Mother fetishes (see chapters 1, 2). By contrast, the huge black-and-white canvases of Franz Kline (1910–1962) consist entirely of imposing, abstract shapes. Though wholly nonrepresentational, they call to mind the powerful angularity of bridges, steel mills, and other monuments of postwar urban expansion (Figure **35.2**). Kline, who used housepainters' brushes on canvases that often measured over 10 feet square, tried to achieve a sense of rugged immediacy (which he called "snap") similar to that found in the calligraphy of Zen masters, famous for their unique balance of improvisation and control (Figure **35.3**).

The best known of the abstract expressionists was Wyoming-born Jackson Pollock (1912–1956). His early paintings reveal a coarse figural style and brutal brushwork similar to de Kooning's, but, by 1945, Pollock had devised a technique that made action itself the subject of the painting. Instead of mounting the canvas on an easel, he spread it on the floor of his studio and proceeded to drip, splash, pour, and spread oil, enamel, and commercial aluminum paints across its surface (Figure **35.4**). Layered filaments of paint—the artist's seductive "handwriting"—mingled with sand, nails, matches, bottle shards, and occasional cigarette butts. This daring, allover technique enabled Pollock (as he explained) "to walk around [the canvas], work from the four sides and literally be *in* the painting," a method he compared to Native American sand painting in its union of intuition, improvisation, and rigorous control. "It seems to me," observed Pollock, "that the modern painter cannot express his age, the airplane, the atom bomb, the radio, in the old forms of the Renaissance or of any other past culture. Each age finds its own technique." Pollock's *action paintings* may strike us as baffling studies in

1944	a Canadian bacteriologist proves DNA is fundamental in determining heredity	
1946	the first functional electronic digital computer is tested in America	
1947	quantum electrodynamics (QED) studies "irregular" behavior of subatomic particles	
1948	Bell Laboratories develop the transistor	
1951	nuclear reactors are utilized successfully to produce electricity	
1951	color television first appears in the U.S.A.	

Figure 35.2 (above) Franz Kline, *New York, N.Y.*, ca. 1953. Oil on canvas, 6 ft. 7 in. × 4 ft. 3 in. Albright-Knox Art Gallery, Buffalo, New York. Gift of Seymour H. Knox, 1995.

Figure 35.3 Torei Enji, *Calligraphic Talisman*, late eighteenth century. Sumi on paper, 50¾ × 10⅞ in. Courtesy of the New Orleans Museum of Art. Gitter Collection.

sensation, density, and rhythm (Figure **35.5**), but they are apt metaphors for an age that describes physical reality in terms of process, uncertainty, and molecular energy. Like the currents in some cosmic whirlpool, Pollock's galactic threads seem to expand beyond the limits of the canvas, as if to mirror postwar theories of quantum forces in an expanding universe (oddly enough, Pollock's compositions anticipate the photographs of outer space taken in 1995 by the Hubble Space Telescope). Pollock viewed each of his works of art as having "a life of its own," but he insisted that *he* controlled its direction: "There is no accident, just as there is no beginning and no end."

While Pollock pioneered action painting, other mid-century artists explored *color field painting*, a type of abstract expressionism that involved the application of large, often transparent layers of paint to the surface of the canvas. The paintings of Mark Rothko (1903–1970) consist of translucent, soft-edged rectangles of color that float mysteriously on the surfaces of yet other fields of color (Figure **35.7**). Rothko's huge, sensuous compositions derive their power from the subtle interaction of a few elusive colors, but they are not mere exercises in color. As Rothko himself explained, "The people who weep before my pictures are having the same religious experience I had when I painted them, and if you . . . are moved only by their color relationships, then you miss the point."

Figure 35.4 Jackson Pollock at work in his Long Island Studio, 1950. Photo: © Hans Namuth, New York, 1983.

Figure 35.5 Jackson Pollock, *Convergence*, 1952. Oil on canvas, 8 ft. × 13 ft. Albright-Knox Art Gallery, Buffalo, New York. Gift of Seymour H. Knox, 1956. © ARS, New York and DACS, London 1997.

Figure 35.6 Helen Frankenthaler, *Interior Landscape*, 1964. Acrylic on canvas, 8 ft. 8⅞ in. × 7 ft. 8⅝ in. San Francisco Museum of Modern Art. Gift of the Women's Board (68.52).

While Rothko's abstract shapes are usually self-contained, those of Helen Frankenthaler (b. 1928) tend to swell and expand like exotic blooms (Figure **35.6**). Frankenthaler cultivated the practice of pouring thin washes of paint directly from coffee tins onto raw or **unprimed** (without gesso undercoat) canvas. Her lyrical compositions, often heroic in scale, capture the transparent freshness of watercolors.

In a culture increasingly dominated by mass mechanization, abstract expressionists asserted their preference for an art of spontaneous action. They sought a balance between choice and chance that obeyed the existential credo of self-actualization. They elevated the *process* of making art to a status that was almost as important as the *product*. As the movement developed, the size of the canvas expanded as if to accommodate the heroic ambitions of the artists themselves. Abstract expressionists seemed to turn their backs on bourgeois taste by creating artworks that were simply too large to hang in the average living room. Ironically, however, this style, which opposed the depersonalizing effects of capitalist technology, came to be prized by the guardians of that technology. Abstract expressionist paintings, which now hang in large numbers of corporate offices and banks, have become hallmarks of modern sophistication.

The abstract expressionists represented a decisive break with the realist tradition in American painting and with social realism in particular. Nevertheless, throughout the century, representational art continued to flourish, especially among the regionalists, that is,

Figure 35.7 Mark Rothko, *Untitled*, 1960. Oil on canvas, 5 ft. 9 in. × 4 ft. 2⅛ in. San Francisco Museum of Modern Art. Acquired through a gift of Peggy Guggenheim. © ARS, New York and DACS, London 1997.

artists associated with specific geographic locations. The paintings of the New York artist Edward Hopper (1882–1967), for instance, present a figurative view of an urban America that is bleak and empty of meaningful relationships. Hopper's fondness for American cinema and theater is reflected in compositions that often resemble film stills. In *Nighthawks* (Figure **35.8**), Hopper depicts a harshly lit all-night diner, whose occupants share a small space but little intimacy. His characters, estranged and isolated in the mundane interiors of "one-night cheap hotels" and "sawdust restaurants," call to mind Eliot's Prufrock.

Sculpture

The mood of existential anxiety also dominated international sculpture. What the art critic Herbert Read called a "geometry of fear" was evident in both the figurative and the nonfigurative sculpture of the Swiss artist Alberto Giacometti (1901–1966). In 1930 Giacometti came under the influence of surrealism, but in the postwar era he devised a new language with which to describe the human figure and the human condition. In both small and large clay works, thereafter cast in bronze, he transformed his subjects into haunting, spindly creatures that seem to symbolize the existential solitude of the individual amidst the modern metropolis (Figure **35.9**). Giacometti's disengaged and ravaged

Figure 35.8 Edward Hopper, *Nighthawks*, 1942. Oil on canvas, 33³⁄₁₆ × 60⅛ in. Art Institute of Chicago. Chicago Friends of American Art Collection, 1942.51.

Figure 35.9 Alberto Giacometti, *City Square* (*La Place*), 1948. Bronze, 8½ × 25⅜ × 17¼ in. The Museum of Modern Art, New York. Purchase. Photograph © 1997 The Museum of Modern Art, New York. © ADAGP, Paris and DACS, London 1997.

Figure 35.10 George Segal, *Bus Riders*, 1962. Plaster, cottongauze, steel, wood, and vinyl, 5 ft. 10 in. × 3 ft. 6⅜ in. × 7 ft. 6¾ in. Hirshhorn Museum and Sculpture Garden, Smithsonian Institution, Washington, D.C. Gift of Joseph H. Hirshhorn, 1966. Photo: Lee Stalsworth. © George Segal/DACS, London/ VAGA, New York 1997.

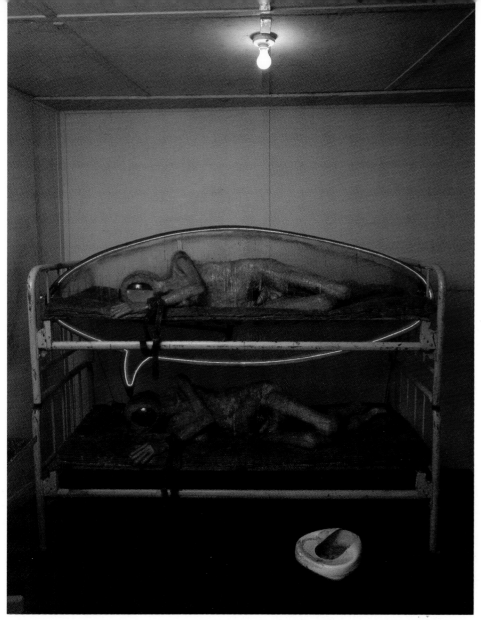

Figure 35.11 Edward Kienholz, *The State Hospital*, 1964–1966. Mixed media, 8 ft. × 12 ft. × 10 ft. Moderna Museet, Stockholm. Photo: Statens Konstmuseer.

figures were greatly admired by Sartre, who wrote the introduction to the catalogue for the artist's one-man exhibition in New York City in 1948. The artist's ties to existentialist writers secured his commission to design the set for the original production of Beckett's *Waiting for Godot*.

In America, the haunting works of George Segal (b. 1924) were among the first to capture the modern mood of alienation. Segal devised a unique method of constructing life-sized figures from plaster casts of live models. He then installed them, unpainted, in such ordinary settings as bedrooms, buses, and diners (Figure **35.10**). Even more startling than Segal's ghostly scenarios are the arresting tableaux of Edward Kienholz (1927–1994), which anticipate the politically explicit installations and conceptual projects of the last quarter of the twentieth century (see chapter 37). *The State Hospital* (Figure **35.11**) is a "concept tableau" that shows a man's naked figure strapped to the institutional cot of a mental hospital. A glass bowl filled with two black fish replaces his head, from which emerges a neon tube in the shape of a thought bubble that surrounds his own

gruesome image—as if the patient were contemplating his dire condition. Kienholz appended to the tableau a detailed description based, in part, on firsthand experience—in 1948, he had worked briefly as an orderly in a mental hospital. Like theater sets, the installations of Segal and Kienholz engage the viewer in dramatic time, thus intensifying the continuity between art and life.

The nonfigurative sculpture of the postwar era shared the vitality and subjectivity of abstract expressionist painting. American sculptors, exploiting such industrial materials as welded iron and steel, constructed abstract objects that were monumental in size and dynamic in spirit. Among the pioneers in the domain of *constructed sculpture* was the American artist David Smith (1906–1965). Smith learned to weld in an automobile plant and became familiar with a variety of other industrial processes while working in a wartime locomotive factory. Smith made imaginative use of industrial techniques. His early pieces were large, welded iron forms sprayed with multiple layers of automobile enamel. During the 1950s, he began to construct stainless steel sculptures whose surfaces he rubbed and

Figure 35.12 (left) David Smith, *Cubi XIX*, 1964.
Stainless steel, 113⅛ × 21¾ × 20¾ in. Krauss #667.
Collection, The Tate Gallery, London. Photo: David Smith.
© Estate of David Smith/DACS, London/VAGA, New York 1997.

Figure 35.13 (below) Alexander Calder, *Big Red*, 1959.
Sheet metal and steel wire, 6 ft. 2 in. × 9 ft. 6 in.
Collection of Whitney Museum of American Art, New York.
Purchase, with funds from the Friends of the Whitney Museum
of American Art, and exchange. 61.46. Photograph copyright
© 1997 Whitney Museum of American Art.
Photograph by Geoffrey Clements, New York.

scraped with motorized tools so that they reflected the colors of their surroundings (Figure **35.12**). Smith's heroic forms share the calligraphic energy of Franz Kline's abstractions: They capture a sense of aggressive movement, even as they animate the space around them. While the art of Segal and Kienholz evokes a mood of existential despair, Smith's style symbolizes the optimistic spirit of postwar America.

The American sculptor Alexander Calder (1898–1976) was a contemporary of the surrealists, whom he met in Paris in 1926. Influenced by the work of Miró, Calder created whimsical wire constructions, which he then motorized or hung from ceilings so that they floated freely in the air. Calder's wind-driven mobiles, which range from a few feet in size to enormous proportions, take advantage of the "chance" effects of air currents to create constantly changing relationships between volumes and voids, that is, between solid masses of brightly colored aluminum shapes and the surrounding space (Figure **35.13**).

Architecture at Mid-Century

By the middle of the twentieth century public architecture assumed a distinctly international character. The principles of international style architecture, based on the use of structural steel, ferroconcrete, and glass, had gained popularity through the influence of Bauhaus-trained architects and Le Corbusier (see chapter 32). Standardization and machinelike efficiency became the hallmarks of high-rise urban apartment buildings, constructed in their thousands to provide low-rent housing in the decades after 1930 (Figure **35.14**). In the building of schools, factories, and offices, the simplicity and austerity of the international style echoed the mood of depersonalization that prevailed in the arts. International style skyscrapers became symbols of corporate wealth and modern technocracy. They reflected the ideals of the twentieth century as powerfully as the Gothic cathedral summed up the spirit of the High Middle Ages. Among the most daring of the international style proponents was the Dutch architect (and the last director of the Bauhaus) Ludwig Mies van der Rohe (1886–1969). Mies' credo "less is more" inspired austere structures such as the Seagram Building in New York City, designed in partnership with Philip Johnson (b. 1906) in 1958 (Figure **35.15**). This sleek, unadorned slab of metallic bronze and amber glass was "the last word" in sophisticated machine engineering and a monument to the "form follows function" mandate of

Figure 35.14 (above) Irwin Chanin and Gilmore Clarke, Stuyvesant Town and Peter Cooper Village, New York, 1947. Photo: © The Bettmann Archive, New York.

Figure 35.15 (below) Ludwig Mies van der Rohe, Seagram Building, New York City, 1954–1958. Metallic bronze and amber glass. Photo: Ezra Stoller/© Esto. Courtesy Joseph E. Seagram & Sons, Inc.

the international style. The proportions of the building are as impeccable as those of any classical structure: The raised level at the bottom is balanced at the top by a four-story band of darker glass. For decades, the Seagram Building influenced glass-and-steel-box architecture; unfortunately, in many of its imitators, it was the cool, impersonal quality of the building and not its poetic simplicity that prevailed.

At mid-century, some of the world's leading architects (including Le Corbusier, Frank Lloyd Wright, and the Finnish architect Eero Saarinen) reacted against the strict geometry and functional purism of international style architecture. Instead, they provided subjective, personal, and even romantic alternatives to the cool rationalism of the international style. Using the medium of cast concrete, they created organically shaped structures that were as gestural as the sculptures of Smith and the paintings of Frankenthaler. The Trans World Airlines Terminal at New York's Kennedy Airport (Figure 35.16), for example, designed by Saarinen (1910–1961), is a metaphor for flight: Its cross-vaulted roof—a steel structure surfaced with concrete—flares upward like a gigantic bird. The interior of the terminal unfolds gradually and mysteriously to embrace fluid, uninterrupted space. Equally inventive in both design and function is Frank Lloyd Wright's Guggenheim Museum in Manhattan (Figure 35.17). Its interior, which resembles the inside of a huge snail shell, consists

Figure 35.16 Eero Saarinen, Trans World Airlines Terminal, Kennedy Airport, New York, 1962.
Photo: Balthazar Korab, Troy, Michigan.

Figure 35.17 Frank Lloyd
Wright, The Solomon
R. Guggenheim Museum,
New York, 1957–1959.
Photo: David Heald/
Courtesy of the Solomon
R. Guggenheim Museum.

Figure 35.18 Frank Lloyd Wright, The Solomon R. Guggenheim Museum interior, 1957–1959. Photo: Robert E. Mates/ Courtesy of the Solomon R. Guggenheim Museum.

of a continuous spiral ramp fixed around an open, central well (Figure **35.18**). A clear glass dome at the top allows natural light to bathe interior space, whose breathtaking enclosure competes seductively with almost any artwork exhibited therein. And while the ten-story limestone extension added in 1992 reduces the dramatic contrast between the rotunda and its urban setting, it does not detract from the uniqueness of the total enterprise. The Guggenheim remains the definitive example of the modern architectural imagination.

Music and Dance at Mid-Century

Many of the artworks discussed in this chapter reflect the modern artist's quest for a balance between freedom and control and between meaninglessness and purposeful action. In the domain of music, the American writer/composer John Cage (1912–1992) epitomized that quest. Cage styled himself a student of architecture and gardening, and a devotee of Zen Buddhism but, beyond this, he was a concert pianist and one of the most influential avant-garde composers of the twentieth century. A leading spokesperson for inventive creativity in modern music, Cage embraced chance and experimentation as fundamental to artistic expression. "Everything we do is music," argued Cage, whose dadaesque definition exalted music as a combination of sounds (specific pitches), noise (non-pitched sounds), and silence, with rhythm as the common denominator.

Cage's approach to music—like Pollock's to painting

—made process and accident central to the work of art. In 1938 Cage invented the prepared piano, a traditional Steinway piano "prepared" by attaching to its strings pieces of rubber, bamboo slats, bolts, and other objects. When played, the prepared piano becomes something like a percussion instrument, the sounds of which resemble those of a Balinese orchestra; it is, as Cage observed, "a percussive orchestra under the control of a single player." Influenced by Schoenberg as well as by Indian and Chinese music, Cage's early compositions—including his *Sonata V*[♮] (1948)—are delicate in timbre and texture and elegant in percussive rhythms. However, his later works were radically experimental, especially in their effort to accommodate silence and non-pitched sound. In 1953, Cage composed *4' 33"*, a piece in which a performer sits motionless before the piano for four minutes and thirty-three seconds. The "music" of *4' 33"* consists of the fleeting sounds that occur during the designated time period—the breathing of the pianist, the shuffling of the audience's feet, or, perhaps, the distant hum of traffic outside of the concert hall.

Like *4' 33"*, much of Cage's music is **aleatory**, that is, based on chance or random procedures. To determine the placement of notes in a musical composition, Cage might apply the numbers dictated in a throw of the dice or incorporate the surface stains and imperfections on an otherwise blank piece of sheet music. Cage found inspiration for random techniques in the *I Ching*, the

[♮]See Music Listening Selection at end of chapter.

Figure 35.19 Merce Cunningham, set and costumes by Robert Rauschenberg, *Summerspace*, 1958. © Robert Rauschenberg/VAGA, New York 1998.

ancient oracular Chinese *Book of Changes*, and in the psychic automatism of dada and surrealist art. Unpredictability and improvisation are basic to Cage's *Music of Changes* (1951), written for piano, and to his *Imaginary Landscape No. 4* (1951), a composition that calls for twelve radios playing simultaneously with twenty-four performers (two at each radio) randomly turning the volume and selector controls. Such antimusical music celebrates the absurd and random nature of experience. At the same time, it tests the traditional relationship between composers and performers, and between artistic conception and execution. Ultimately, Cage's music embraces the existential notion that every creative act, and even the decision *not* to act, requires choice. The very decision in favor of chance engages the act of choosing and, further, of deciding whether to roll dice, toss coins, or employ some other random method.

Cage's ideas, as publicized in his numerous essays and lectures, have been more influential than his music. The impact of these ideas has been especially great in the areas of dance and the visual arts. In the mid-1940s, Cage met the American choreographer Merce Cunningham (b. 1922) and the young painter Robert Rauschenberg (b. 1925). At Black Mountain College in North Carolina, the three artists collaborated in staging performances that employed improvisational techniques. As the director of Cunningham's dance company until 1966, Cage combined dance, mime, poetry, music, slide projections, and moving pictures to produce some of the first and most innovative mixed media performances of the century.

Cunningham's contribution to modern choreography was equally revolutionary. Rejecting the representational and storytelling dance style of his teacher, Martha Graham (see chapter 32), along with her use of the body to express psychological states, he concentrated exclusively on movement and form. Cunningham's choreography disavowed the traditional association between music and dance. In a Cunningham piece, music may coexist with dance, but its rhythms do not necessarily determine those of the dancers. Cunningham treats all body movements, even such ordinary ones as running, jumping, and falling, as equally important to dance. He may combine physical forces in ways that are unexpected or determined by chance, favoring expansive body gestures that shift and unfold in large, lateral areas of space. Though his choreography is technically rigorous, his compositions may appear fragmentary, discontinuous, and devoid of purpose or shape. Just as Cunningham disclaims traditional dance positions, so he ignores traditional staging (whereby dancers are assigned to specific spaces). He creates a spatial continuum, which—like a Pollock painting or a Cage composition—lacks a fixed center. In *Summerspace* (1958), for instance, for which Rauschenberg designed the sets and costumes, dancers travel confidently through an uncertain spatial field (Figure **35.19**). Cunningham explores the tensions between chance and choice and between freedom and control that lie at the heart of existential expression.

SUMMARY

Alienation and anxiety were the two principal conditions of the postwar mentality. Pessimists feared the destructive potential of modern technology and anticipated the demise of human freedom. Philosophers and poets lamented the death of God. Existentialism, a humanistic philosophy formulated by Jean-Paul Sartre, emphasized the role of individual choice in a world that lacked moral absolutes. Both secular and Christian existentialism charged human beings with full responsibility for their freely chosen actions.

Twentieth-century writers have given serious attention to the existential condition and to the anguish produced by the freedom to choose. Modern antiheroes—Eliot's Prufrock, Malamud's high school dropout, and the burlesque tramps in Beckett's *Waiting for Godot*—all contend with the despair of making choices in an essentially meaningless universe. Their survival seems to depend only upon an authentic commitment to action. The voices of Asian writers such as Tagore, Iqbal, and Anwar also pursue the quest for meaning in parts of the world where modernism does as much to threaten as to reshape tradition.

In the visual arts, the movement known as abstract expressionism reflects an existential effort at self-actualization through the gestural and often brutal application of paint to canvas. The action paintings of Pollock, the color field paintings of Frankenthaler, and the constructions of David Smith and Alexander Calder explore the dynamic balance between chance and choice even as they seek strategies of simultaneous possibility. While these artists work in an abstract mode, others, such as Hopper, Giacometti, Segal, and Kienholz, employ representational means of exploring the modern condition of alienation. At mid-century, the international style culminated in classic glass-box skyscrapers such as the Seagram Building in New York City, but it also spawned thousands of soulless imitations that reinforced the cold, impersonal nature of urban communities throughout the world. However, the 1950s witnessed a new wave of ferroconcrete architecture, as exemplified in Wright's Guggenheim Museum, that challenged the austerity of the international style.

In the domains of music and dance, as in the visual arts, the postwar generation took the absence of absolutes as the starting point for free experimentation. John Cage, one of the foremost members of the avant-garde, explored the musical possibilities of silence, noise, and chance operations. Merce Cunningham redefined modern dance as movement stripped of thematic and musical associations. While the mood of alienation and anxiety pervaded the postwar decades, artists struggled to sustain their faith in the human capacity for choice, and their hope that, as William Faulkner asserted in his Nobel Prize Address of 1950, "[Man] is immortal, not because he alone among creatures has an inexhaustible voice, but because he has a soul, a spirit of compassion and sacrifice and endurance."

GLOSSARY

aleatory (Latin, *alea*, "dice") any kind of music composed according to chance or random procedures

unprimed lacking the gesso undercoat normally applied to the surface of the canvas

---

SUGGESTIONS FOR READING

Doss, Erika. *Benton, Pollock, and the Politics of Modernism: From Regionalism to Abstract Expressionism.* Chicago: University of Chicago Press, 1991.

Hoffman, Frederick J. *The Mortal No: Death and the Modern Imagination.* Princeton, N.J.: Princeton University Press, 1964.

Jowett, Deborah. *Time and the Dancing Image.* New York: William Morrow, 1990.

Kaufmann, Walter, ed. *Existentialism from Dostoevsky to Sartre.* New York: New American Library, 1975.

Marcuse, H. *One Dimensional Man: Studies in the Ideology of Advanced Industrial Society.* Boston: Beacon Press, 1964.

Policari, Stephen. *Abstract Expressionism and the Modern Experience.* New York: Cambridge University Press, 1991.

Roose-Evans, James. *Experimental Theatre: From Stanislavsky to Today.* New York: Universe Books, 1970.

Rosenberg, Harold. *The Anxious Object.* Chicago: University of Chicago Press, 1966.

Rosenthal, Mark. *Abstraction in the Twentieth Century: Total Risk, Freedom, Discipline.* New York: Abrams, 1996.

Stromberg, Roland N. *After Everything: Western Intellectual History Since 1945.* New York: St. Martin's Press, 1975.

Sypher, Wylie. *Loss of the Self in Modern Literature and Art.* New York: Random House, 1962.

Tomkins, Calvin. *The Bride and the Bachelors: Five Masters of the Avant-Garde.* New York: Viking, 1968.

Wilson, Robert N. *The Writer as Social Seer.* Chapel Hill, N.C.: University of North Carolina Press, 1979.

MUSIC LISTENING SELECTION

Cassette II Selection 18 Cage, *Sonata V*, 1948, excerpt.

PART
II
THE POSTMODERN TURN

The postmodern turn describes a constellation of significant changes in all aspects of the global community. During the postwar era, the nations of the world came to be classified according to their level of economic prosperity: The industrialized capitalistic nations, including the United States, most of Western Europe, Japan, and Canada, constituted the "First World." The less industrialized socialist states of the Soviet Union and Eastern Europe made up the "Second World"; the rest—over one hundred nations located primarily in Africa, Asia, and Latin America—comprised the poor or emerging nations of the "Third World." By mid-century, nations were polarized ideologically between the forces of democratic capitalism and Soviet-style communism. Intense competition for world supremacy in political and military affairs marked the Cold War, a rivalry dominated by the two superpowers, the United States and the Soviet Union. Although internal strife, civil wars within colonial territories, and changing political and economic relationships between and within nations prompted the intervention of First World powers, total war was replaced by local and regional conflict.

Since mid-century, colonial states throughout the world have claimed independence from imperial control; ethnic and racial minorities, and other disenfranchised or oppressed groups, have launched impassioned quests for equality and identity. Ongoing rivalries between religious groups in the Middle East (and elsewhere) and Third World poverty and instability continue to threaten world peace. Hence, while the late twentieth century has been an era of population growth, urbanization, expanding materialism, and progress toward political, economic, and social equality, it has also been an age of acute anxiety. Nevertheless, at the close of the century, a higher quality of life and a more egalitarian social structure exist in more parts of the global village than ever before in history. The dismantling of the Berlin Wall (1989) and the collapse of Soviet communism (1991)—events that marked the end of the Cold War—have fed rising expectations for the future of democracy worldwide and for a new spirit of cooperation between the superpowers.

With regard to the arts and ideas, the postmodern turn involves a shift away from modernism, or what the critic Robert Hughes has called "the Messianic era of modernism," and modernism's impassioned faith in a new world order. The utopianism of Kandinsky and Mondrian, the existential ideal of responsible action, and the heroic celebration of freedom that infused the arts at mid-century have largely disappeared. They have given way to more skeptical claims for human progress—claims shaped by a knowing and often cynical view of the historical past. Some theorists date the end of modernism from the decade of the Holocaust—an episode they perceive as the crime that refuted modernism's utopian agenda. Others identify the new age

(opposite) Nam June Paik, *George Boole*, 1995. 1 old Tektronic computer monitor, 1 old Goodyear Atomic metal cabinet, 15 KEC 9-inch television sets, 1 Samsung 13-inch television set, 2 Pioneer laser disk players, 2 original Paik laser disks, abacus, circuit board, aluminum, 90 × 56 × 30 in. Photo: Courtesy Carl Solway Gallery, Cincinnati, Ohio. Photographer: Chris Gomien.

with a shift in modern morality (linked to the discovery of effective birth control); while still others perceive postmodernism as a product of the information age, an age of high-speed developments in mass communication (television and computers), molecular physics, and the technology of space exploration, all of which have extended human knowledge and power beyond that of any previous era. As the postmodern world approaches the century's end, there has emerged a new framework (or paradigm), that of *globalism*, which reflects the increasing interdependence between all parts of the earth. Globalism appears to be an integrating force in the political, ecological, and cultural future of the planet.

Chapter 36, "Identity and Liberation," treats two of the most urgent themes in twentieth-century history: the modern movements for liberation and self-identity among nations, races, sexes, and ethnic groups. Anticolonialism, the civil rights struggle in the United States, and the international feminist movement, along with representative examples of the artistic expression of each, are the focus of this analysis.

Finally, chapter 37, "The Arts in the Information Age," surveys the plurality of styles in the arts since 1960. The information revolution of the past four decades has produced a thoughtful reassessment of the "debris" of human culture as filtered through the mass media. Electronic technology, computers, and space exploration have made their mark on literature, the visual arts, and music. An astonishing variety of new styles and genres—from pop art to cyberart and from postmodern poetry to electronic music—indicate new directions that, while closely tied to the commercialism and secularism of the late twentieth century, suggest an eagerness to reclaim the spiritual past and a reforming approach to social problems. On the threshold of the twenty-first century, creative minds across the planet are voicing millennial concern for the future of the global village.

36
Identity and Liberation

While the mood of despair pervaded much of the postwar era, a second, more positive spirit fueled movements for liberation in many parts of the world. Movements to reform conditions of oppression and inequality ranged from anticolonial drives for independence from foreign control to crusades for ethnic self-identity, and from fierce demands for racial and gender equality to counterculture attacks on prevailing social norms. The drive toward liberation, one of the most potent themes of the twentieth century, inspired many of its most significant works of art. And while the artistic value of all artworks must, in the long run, be judged without reference to the politics, race, or gender of the artists who created them, their meaning may be better appreciated in the light of the historical circumstances out of which they emerged.

Two major types of liberation movement have marked the second half of the twentieth century: the effort by colonial nations to achieve political, economic, religious, and ethnic independence; and the demand for racial and sexual equality. The first of these—the move toward political and economic independence—resulted from postwar efforts in Third World countries to reduce poverty and raise the standard of living to that of the more highly developed nations. After World War II, the weakened European nations were unable to maintain the military forces necessary to sustain their empires. At the same time, colonial subjects increased their efforts to free themselves of rule by Western nations, which, ironically, had fought for decades to liberate oppressed people from totalitarian dominion.

One of the earliest revolts against colonial rule took place in India. During World War I, the Indian National Congress came under the influence of the devout Hindu Mohandas Gandhi (1869–1948). Gandhi, whose followers called him "Mahatma," or "great soul," led India's struggle for emancipation from Great Britain. Guided by the precepts of Hinduism, as well as by the Sermon on the Mount and the writings of Thoreau and Tolstoy, Gandhi initiated a policy of peaceful protest against colonial oppression. His program of nonviolent resistance, including fasting and peaceful demonstrations, influenced the course of several subsequent liberation movements throughout the world. Gandhi's leadership was crucial to India's emancipation from British control, which occurred only one year before he was assassinated by a Hindu fanatic who opposed his conciliatory gestures toward India's Muslim minority. A related movement for liberation was well under way in India and other parts of Asia even before the end of European domination: The pan-Islamic quest for a modern-day Muslim community on the Indian subcontinent resulted, in 1947, in an independent Pakistan. Similar movements to expand the role of Islam as a worldwide moral and religious force continue to flourish in the late twentieth century.

Between 1944 and 1960, many nations, including Jordan, Burma, Palestine, Sri Lanka, Ghana, Malaya, Cyprus, and Nigeria, freed themselves from British rule; Syria, Lebanon, Cambodia, Laos, North and South Vietnam, Morocco, Tunisia, Cameroon, Mali, and other African states won their independence from France; and still other territories claimed independence from the empires of the United States, Japan, the Netherlands, Belgium, and Italy. In Central America, Southeast Asia, and elsewhere, internal conflicts provoked military intervention by First World powers. For instance, between 1964 and 1973, the United States succeeded France in an unsuccessful effort to defend South Vietnam from communist control. The Vietnam War, the longest war in American history, cost the lives of some fifty thousand Americans and more than fifteen million Vietnamese. More recently, in Eastern Europe the demise of Soviet authority has unleashed age-old ethnic conflicts, producing fragmentation and bloodshed. Sadly, liberation movements often broadcast seeds of tragedy.

Liberation and Literature in Latin America

From the time of Christopher Columbus, the peoples of Latin America have served the political and economic interests of First World countries more powerful than their own. And even after many of the European nations departed from the shores of Argentina, Brazil, Mexico, Peru, and other Latin American states in the early nineteenth century, the conditions that prevailed in the long era of colonialism persisted: The vast majority of Latin Americans, including great masses of peasants of Native American descent, lived in relative poverty, while small, wealthy, land-owning elites held power. These elites maintained their power by virtue of their alliance with the financial and industrial interests of First World nations, including (and especially since the 1890s) the United States.

Spanish-speaking and predominantly Catholic, the rapidly growing populations of the more than two dozen nations of Latin America have suffered repeated social upheaval in their attempt to cope with persistent problems of inequality, exploitation, and underdevelopment. The long and bitter history of the Mexican Revolution, commemorated in the murals of Diego Rivera (see Figure 34.5), provides a vivid example. Since mid-century, from country to country, political and social reformers have struggled to revolutionize the socioeconomic order, to liberate Latin America from economic colonialism, and to bring about a more equitable distribution of the nation's wealth. Support for these essentially socialist movements has come from representatives of the deprived elements of society, including organized labor and, often enough, from the Catholic Church, which has acted on behalf of the masses as an agent of social justice. The "liberation theology" preached by reformist elements in the clergy represents a powerful new rendering of Christian dogma for the twentieth century.

Latin America's artists have tended to support movements for liberation. During the 1960s, the outpouring of exceptionally fine Latin American prose and poetry constituted a literary boom, the influence of which is still being felt worldwide. Among the literary champions of Latin American reform was the Chilean poet Pablo Neruda (1904–1973). Neruda was one of the most prolific and inventive poets in the history of the Spanish language. His poetry, often embellished by violent, surrealist images, endorses a radical, populist ideology. In the poem "The United Fruit Co." (1950) he describes the corruption of justice and freedom in the "Banana Republics" of Latin America. The poem, phrased as a mock Last Judgment, smolders with indignation at American policies of commercial exploitation in the nations south of its borders.

READING 6.18

Neruda's "United Fruit Co."

When the trumpets had sounded and all   1
was in readiness on the face of the earth,
Jehovah divided his universe:
Anaconda, Ford Motors,
Coca-Cola Inc., and similar entities: 5
the most succulent item of all,
The United Fruit Company Incorporated
reserved for itself: the heartland
and coasts of my country,
the delectable waist of America.   10
They rechristened their properties:
the "Banana Republics"—
and over the languishing dead,
the uneasy repose of the heroes
who harried that greatness,   15
their flags and their freedoms,
they established an *opéra bouffe*:
they ravished all enterprise,
awarded the laurels like Caesars,
unleashed all the covetous, and contrived   20
the tyrannical Reign of the Flies—
Trujillo the fly, and Tacho the fly,
the flies called Carias, Martinez,
Ubico[1]—all of them flies, flies
dank with the blood of their marmalade   25
vassalage, flies buzzing drunkenly
on the populous middens:
the fly-circus fly and the scholarly
kind, case-hardened in tyranny.
Then in the bloody domain of the flies   30
The United Fruit Company Incorporated
sailed off with a booty of coffee and fruits
brimming its cargo boats, gliding
like trays with the spoils
of our drowning dominions.   35
And all the while, somewhere in the sugary
hells of our seaports,
smothered by gases, an Indian
fell in the morning:
a body spun off, an anonymous   40
chattel, some numeral tumbling,
a branch with its death running out of it
in the vat of the carrion, fruit laden and foul.

———————————————◆

[1]The twentieth-century dictators of Latin America: Rafael Molina Trujillo brutally dominated the Dominican Republic from 1930 to 1961; "Tacho" was the nickname for Anastasio Somoza, who controlled Nicaragua until his assassination in 1956; Tiburcio Carias, self-styled dictator of Honduras, was supported during the 1930s and 1940s by the United Fruit Company; Maximilian Martinez was the ruthless dictator of El Salvador during the 1930s and 1940s; Jorge Ubico seized power in Guatemala in 1931 and served as a puppet of the United States until 1944.

The Quest for Racial Equality

The most turbulent liberation movement of the twentieth century addressed the issue of racial equality—an issue so dramatically reflected in the African-American* experience that some observers have dubbed this century "The Race Era." Since the days of slavery, millions of black Americans have existed as a Third World minority population living within a First World nation. The Dutch took the first black Africans to America in 1619, and during the late seventeenth and eighteenth centuries, thousands of black slaves were imported to the American colonies, especially those in the South. For 250 years, until the end of the Civil War, slavery was a fact of American life. While the Emancipation Proclamation issued by Abraham Lincoln in 1863 facilitated the liberation of the slaves, it was not until 1865—with the Thirteenth Amendment to the United States Constitution—that all were finally freed. This and other constitutional amendments guaranteed the rights of black people; nevertheless, the lives of African-Americans continued to be harsh and poor by comparison with those of their former white masters. Separation of the races by segregated housing, inferior schools, and exclusion from voting and equal employment were only a few of the inequities suffered by this minority in the post-emancipation United States. It was to these issues and to the more general problem of racism that many African-Americans addressed themselves after World War I.

The Harlem Renaissance

World War I brought a new self-awareness to African-Americans. It also provided new educational and job opportunities. After World War I, over five million African-Americans migrated from the South to the Northern states. Because of frustration over unemployment and crowded ghettos, race riots broke out in over twenty-five cities during the "bloody summer" of 1919 (Figure 36.1). New York City became the center of economic opportunity, as well as the melting pot for black people from other parts of the world. Between 1920 and 1940, the quest for racial equality and a search for self-identity among African-Americans inspired an upsurge of creative expression in the arts. Centered in Harlem—a part of New York City occupied largely by African-Americans—poets, painters, musicians, and dancers forged the movement that came to be called the Harlem Renaissance.

One of the most eloquent voices of the Harlem Renaissance was Langston Hughes (1902–1967). Hughes was born in Missouri and moved to New York in 1921,

where he became the first African-American to support himself as a professional writer. A musician as well as a journalist and a novelist, Hughes became the rare poet whose powerful phrases ("a dream deferred," "a raisin in the sun," and "black like me") have become enshrined in the canon of American literature. His poems, which capture the musical qualities of the African oral tradition, fuse everyday speech with the rhythms of blues and jazz. Hughes, who regarded poets as "lyric historians," drew deeply on his own experience: His "Theme for English B" records his response to the education of blacks in a dominantly white culture. In "Harlem," a meditation on the "bloody summer" of 1919, Hughes looks to the immediate past to presage the angry riots that have recurred regularly since the 1960s in America's black ghettos.

Like the writers of the Harlem Renaissance, the Chicago-born poet Gwendolyn Brooks (b. 1917) draws upon the idioms of jazz and street slang to produce a vivid picture of Chicago's black ghettos. The first African-American to receive the Pulitzer Prize for poetry (1949), Brooks has brought attention to the plight of blacks, especially young black women, in American society. The two poems reproduced below are representative of the early part of her long and productive career.

READING 6.19
The Poems of Hughes and Brooks

Hughes' "Theme for English B"

The instructor said,   1

> Go home and write
> a page tonight.
> And let that page come out of you—
> Then, it will be true.   5

I wonder if it's that simple?

I am twenty-two, colored, born in Winston-Salem.
I went to school there, then Durham, then here
to this college on the hill above Harlem.
I am the only colored student in my class.   10
The steps from the hill lead down into Harlem,
through a park, then I cross St. Nicholas,
Eighth Avenue, Seventh, and I come to the Y,
the Harlem Branch Y, where I take the elevator
up to my room, sit down, and write this page: 15

It's not easy to know what is true for you or me
at twenty-two, my age. But I guess I'm what
I feel and see and hear, Harlem, I hear you:
hear you, hear me—we two—you, me, talk on this page.
(I hear New York, too.) Me—who?   20
Well, I like to eat, sleep, drink, and be in love.
I like to work, read, learn, and understand life.
I like a pipe for a Christmas present,
or records—Bessie, bop, or Bach.
I guess being colored doesn't make me *not* like   25

---

*The current term for an American of African descent, which replaced "Negro," the popular designation of the early twentieth century and, after mid-century, "Black" or "Afro-American."

the same things other folks like who are other races.
So will my page be colored that I write?
Being me, it will not be white.
But it will be
a part of you, instructor.   30
You are white—
yet a part of me, as I am a part of you.
That's American.
Sometimes perhaps you don't want to be a part of me.
Nor do I often want to be a part of you.   35
But we are, that's true!
I guess you learn from me—
although you're older—and white—
and somewhat more free.

This is my page for English B.   40
                                        (1949)

Hughes' "Harlem"

What happens to a dream deferred?   1

   Does it dry up
   like a raisin in the sun?
   Or fester like a sore—
   And then run?   5
   Does it stink like rotten meat?
   Or crust and sugar over—
   like a syrupy sweet?

   Maybe it just sags
   like a heavy load.   10

   Or does it explode?   (1951)

Brooks' "The Mother"

Abortions will not let you forget.   1
You remember the children you got that you did not get,
The damp small pulps with a little or with no hair,
The singers and workers that never handled the air.
You will never neglect or beat   5
Them, or silence or buy with a sweet.
You will never wind up the sucking-thumb
Or scuttle off ghosts that come.
You will never leave them, controlling your luscious sigh,
Return for a snack of them, with gobbling mother-eye.   10

I have heard in the voices of the wind the voices of my
   dim killed children.
I have contracted. I have eased
My dim dears at the breasts they could never suck.
I have said, Sweets, if I sinned, if I seized
Your luck   15
And your lives from your unfinished reach,
If I stole your births and your names,
Your straight baby tears and your games,
Your stilted or lovely loves, your tumults, your marriages,
   aches, and your deaths,

If I poisoned the beginnings of your breaths,   20
Believe that even in my deliberateness I was not deliberate.
Though why should I whine,
Whine that the crime was other than mine?—
Since anyhow you are dead.
Or rather, or instead,   25
You were never made.

Figure 36.1 Jacob Lawrence, "Race riots were numerous. White workers were hostile toward the migrants who had been hired to break strikes." Panel 50 from "The Migration" series, 1940–1941; text and title revised by the artist, 1993. Tempera on gesso on composition board, 18 × 12 in. The Museum of Modern Art, New York. Gift of Mrs. David M. Levy. Photograph © 1997 The Museum of Modern Art, New York.

But that too, I am afraid,
Is faulty: oh, what shall I say, how is the truth to be said?
You were born, you had body, you died.
It is just that you never giggled or planned or cried.   30

Believe me, I loved you all.
Believe me, I knew you, though faintly, and I loved,
   I loved you
All.   (1945)

Brooks' "We Real Cool"

The Pool Players.
Seven at the Golden Shovel.

   We real cool. We
   Left school. We

   Lurk late. We
   Strike straight. We

   Sing sin. We
   Thin gin. We

   Jazz June. We
   Die soon.   (1959)

Richard Wright and the Realities of Racism

Richard Wright (1908–1960) was born on a cotton plantation in Mississippi and came to New York City in 1937, just after the heyday of the Harlem Renaissance. Wright brought to his writings the anger of a man who had known physical punishment and repeated injustice at the hands of whites. In his novel *Native Son* (1940), the nightmarish story of a poor, young black who kills his white employer's daughter, Wright examined the ways in which the frustrated search for identity led some African-Americans to despair, defiance, and even violent crime. The novel won Wright immediate acclaim and was rewritten for the New York stage in 1941.

In the autobiographical sketch *The Ethics of Living Jim Crow, 1937*, Wright records with grim frankness the experience of growing up in a racially segregated community in the American South. "Jim Crow," the stage name of a popular nineteenth-century minstrel performer, Thomas D. Rice, had come to describe anything pertaining to African-Americans, including matters of racial segregation.

READING 6.20

From Wright's *The Ethics of Living Jim Crow, 1937*

I

My first lesson in how to live as a Negro came when I was   1
quite small. We were living in Arkansas. Our house stood
behind the railroad tracks. Its skimpy yard was paved
with black cinders. Nothing green ever grew in that yard.
The only touch of green we could see was far away,
beyond the tracks, over where the white folks lived. But
cinders were good enough for me and I never missed the
green growing things. And anyhow cinders were fine
weapons. You could always have a nice hot war with huge
black cinders. All you had to do was crouch behind the   10
brick pillars of a house with your hands full of gritty
ammunition. And the first woolly black head you saw pop
out from behind another row of pillars was your target.
You tried your very best to knock it off. It was great fun.

I never fully realized the appalling disadvantages of a
cinder environment till one day the gang to which I
belonged found itself engaged in a war with the white
boys who lived beyond the tracks. As usual we laid down
our cinder barrage, thinking that this would wipe the
white boys out. But they replied with a steady   20
bombardment of broken bottles. We doubled our cinder
barrage, but they hid behind trees, hedges, and the
sloping embankment of their lawns. Having no such
fortifications, we retreated to the brick pillars of our homes.
During the retreat a broken milk bottle caught me behind
the ear, opening a deep gash which bled profusely. The
sight of blood pouring over my face completely
demoralized our ranks. My fellow-combatants left me
standing paralyzed in the center of the yard, and scurried
for their homes. A kind neighbor saw me, and rushed me   30
to a doctor, who took three stitches in my neck.

I sat brooding on my front steps, nursing my wound and
waiting for my mother to come from work. I felt that a
grave injustice had been done me. It was all right to
throw cinders. The greatest harm a cinder could do was
leave a bruise. But broken bottles were dangerous; they
left you cut, bleeding, and helpless.

When night fell, my mother came from the white folks'
kitchen. I raced down the street to meet her. I could just
feel in my bones that she would understand. I knew she   40
would tell me exactly what to do next time. I grabbed her
hand and babbled out the whole story. She examined my
wound, then slapped me.

"How come yuh didn't hide?" she asked me. "How
come yuh awways fightin'?"

I was outraged, and bawled. Between sobs I told her
that I didn't have any trees or hedges to hide behind.
There wasn't a thing I could have used as a trench. And
you couldn't throw very far when you were hiding behind
the brick pillars of a house. She grabbed a barrel stave,   50
dragged me home, stripped me naked, and beat me till I
had a fever of one hundred and two. She would smack my
rump with the stave, and, while the skin was still smarting
impart to me gems of Jim Crow wisdom. I was never to
throw cinders any more. I was never to fight any more wars.
I was never, never, under any conditions, to fight *white*
folks again. And they were absolutely right in clouting me
with the broken milk bottle. Didn't I know she was working
hard every day in the hot kitchens of the white folks to
make money to take care of me? When was I ever going to   60
learn to be a good boy? She couldn't be bothered with my
fights. She finished by telling me that I ought to be
thankful to God as long as I lived that they didn't kill me.

All that night I was delirious and could not sleep. Each
time I closed my eyes I saw monstrous white faces
suspended from the ceiling, leering at me.

From that time on, the charm of my cinder yard was
gone. The green trees, the trimmed hedges, the cropped
lawns grew very meaningful, became a symbol. Even today
when I think of white folks, the hard, sharp outlines of   70
white houses surrounded by trees, lawns, and hedges are
present somewhere in the background of my mind. Through
the years they grew into an overreaching symbol of fear.

It was a long time before I came in close contact with
white folks again. We moved from Arkansas to
Mississippi. Here we had the good fortune not to live
behind the railroad tracks, or close to white
neighborhoods. We lived in the very heart of the local
Black Belt. There were black churches and black
preachers; there were black schools and black teachers;   80
black groceries and black clerks. In fact, everything was
so solidly black that for a long time I did not even think
of white folks, save in remote and vague terms. But this
could not last forever. As one grows older one eats more.
One's clothing costs more. When I finished grammar
school I had to go to work. My mother could no longer
feed and clothe me on her cooking job.

There is but one place where a black boy who knows no
trade can get a job, and that's where the houses and
faces are white, where the trees, lawns, and hedges are   90
green. My first job was with an optical company in
Jackson, Mississippi. The morning I applied I stood
straight and neat before the boss, answering all his
questions with sharp yessirs and nosirs. I was very careful

to pronounce my *sirs* distinctly, in order that he might know that I was polite, that I knew where I was, and that I knew he was a *white* man. I wanted that job badly.

He looked me over as though he were examining a prize poodle. He questioned me closely about my schooling, being particularly insistent about how much mathematics 100 I had had. He seemed very pleased when I told him I had had two years of algebra.

"Boy, how would you like to try to learn something around here?" he asked me.

"I'd like it fine, sir," I said, happy. I had visions of "working my way up." Even Negroes have those visions.

"All right," he said. "Come on."

I followed him to the small factory.

"Pease," he said to a white man of about thirty-five, "this is Richard. He's going to work for us." 110

Pease looked at me and nodded.

I was then taken to a white boy of about seventeen.

"Morrie, this is Richard, who's going to work for us."

"Whut yuh sayin' there, boy!" Morrie boomed at me.

"Fine!" I answered.

The boss instructed these two to help me, teach me, give me jobs to do, and let me learn what I could in my spare time.

My wages were five dollars a week.

I worked hard, trying to please. For the first month I 120 got along O.K. Both Pease and Morrie seemed to like me. But one thing was missing. And I kept thinking about it. I was not learning anything and nobody was volunteering to help me. Thinking they had forgotten that I was to learn something about the mechanics of grinding lenses, I asked Morrie one day to tell me about the work. He grew red.

"Whut yuh tryin' t' do, nigger, get smart?" he asked.

"Naw; I ain' tryin' t' git smart," I said.

"Well, don't, if yuh know whut's good for yuh!"

I was puzzled. Maybe he just doesn't want to help me, 130 I thought. I went to Pease.

"Say, are yuh crazy, you black bastard?" Pease asked me, his gray eyes growing hard.

I spoke out, reminding him that the boss had said I was to be given a chance to learn something.

"Nigger, you think you're *white*, don't you?

"Naw, sir!"

"Well, you're acting mighty like it!"

"But, Mr. Pease, the boss said . . ."

Pease shook his fist in my face. 140

"This is a *white* man's work around here, and you better watch yourself!"

From then on they changed toward me. They said good-morning no more. When I was just a bit slow in performing some duty, I was called a lazy black son-of-a-bitch.

Once I thought of reporting all this to the boss. But the mere idea of what would happen to me if Pease and Morrie should learn that I had "snitched" stopped me. And after all the boss was a white man, too. What was the use?

The climax came at noon one summer day. Pease called 150 me to his workbench. To get to him I had to go between two narrow benches and stand with my back against a wall.

"Yes, sir," I said.

"Richard, I want to ask you something," Pease began pleasantly, not looking up from his work.

"Yes, sir," I said again.

Morrie came over, blocking the narrow passage between the benches. He folded his arms, staring at me solemnly.

I looked from one to the other, sensing that something was coming. 160

"Yes, sir," I said for the third time.

Pease looked up and spoke very slowly.

"Richard, *Mr.* Morrie here tells me you called me *Pease*."

I stiffened. A void seemed to open up in me. I knew this was the showdown.

He meant that I had failed to call him Mr. Pease. I looked at Morrie. He was gripping a steel bar in his hands. I opened my mouth to speak, to protest, to assure Pease that I had never called him simply *Pease*, and that I had never had any intentions of doing so, when Morrie grabbed 170 me by the collar, ramming my head against the wall.

"Now be careful, nigger!" snarled Morrie, baring his teeth. "*I* heard yuh call 'im *Pease*! 'N' if yuh say yuh didn't, yuh're callin' me a *lie*, see?" He waved the steel bar threateningly.

If I had said: No, sir, Mr. Pease, I never called you *Pease* I would have been automatically calling Morrie a liar. And if I said: Yes, sir, Mr. Pease, I called you *Pease*, I would have been pleading guilty to having uttered the worst insult that a Negro can utter to a southern white 180 man. I stood hesitating, trying to frame a neutral reply.

"Richard, I asked you a question!" said Pease. Anger was creeping into his voice.

"I don't remember calling you *Pease*, Mr. Pease," I said cautiously. "And if I did, I sure didn't mean . . ."

"You black son-of-a-bitch! You called me *Pease*, then!" he spat, slapping me till I bent sideways over a bench. Morrie was on top of me, demanding:

"Didn't you call 'im *Pease*? If yuh say yuh didn't, I'll rip yo' gut string loose with this bar, yuh black granny 190 dodger! Yuh can't call a white man a lie 'n' git erway with it, you black son-of-a-bitch!"

I wilted. I begged them not to bother me. I knew what they wanted. They wanted me to leave.

"I'll leave," I promised. "I'll leave right *now*."

They gave me a minute to get out of the factory. I was warned not to show up again, or tell the boss.

I went.

When I told the folks at home what had happened, they called me a fool. They told me that I must never again 200 attempt to exceed my boundaries. When you are working for white folks, they said, you got to "stay in your place" if you want to keep working. . . .

————————◆————————

The Civil Rights Movement

Well after World War II, racism remained an undeniable fact of American life. While Americans had fought to oppose Nazi racism in Germany, America itself endured a system of inferior education, restricted jobs, ghetto housing, and generally low living standards for African-Americans. High crime rates, illiteracy, and drug addiction were evidence of affluent America's awesome failure to assimilate a Third World population that suffered in its midst. The fact that African-Americans had served in great numbers in World War II inspired a redoubled effort to end persistent discrimination and segregation in the United States. During the 1950s and 1960s, that effort came to flower in the civil rights movement. Civil rights leaders of the 1950s demanded enforcement of all the provisions for equality promised in the United States Constitution. Their demands led to a landmark Supreme Court decision in 1954 that banned school segregation; by implication, this decision undermined the entire system of legalized segregation in the United States. Desegregation was met with fierce resistance, especially in the American South. In response to that resistance, the so-called Negro Revolt began in 1955 and continued for over a decade. The revolt took the form of nonviolent, direct action protests, including boycotts of segregated lunch counters, peaceful "sit-ins," and protest marches. Leading the revolt was the Reverend Martin Luther King, Jr. (1929–1968), a civil rights activist who modeled his campaign of peaceful protest on the example of Gandhi. As president of the Southern Christian Leadership Conference, King served as an inspiration to African-Americans throughout the United States. The urgency of the African-American cause is conveyed in a letter King wrote while confined to jail for marching without a permit in the city of Birmingham, Alabama. King's measured eloquence and reasoned restraint stand in ironic contrast to the savagery of the opposition: The Birmingham citizenry used guns, hoses, and attack dogs against the demonstrators.

READING 6.21

From King's *Letter from Birmingham Jail*

My dear Fellow Clergymen,
While confined here in the Birmingham City Jail, I came 1
across your recent statement calling our present activities "unwise and untimely." Seldom, if ever, do I pause to answer criticism of my work and ideas. But since I feel that you are men of genuine goodwill and your criticisms are sincerely set forth, I would like to answer your statement in what I hope will be patient and reasonable terms.

I think I should give the reason for my being in Birmingham, since you have been influenced by the argument of "outsiders coming in." Several months ago 10 our local affiliate here in Birmingham invited us to be on call to engage in a nonviolent direct action program if such were deemed necessary. We readily consented and when the hour came we lived up to our promises. So I am here, along with several members of my staff, because we were invited here. Beyond this, I am in Birmingham because injustice is here.

Moreover, I am cognizant of the interrelatedness of all communities and states. I cannot sit idly by in Atlanta and not be concerned about what happens in Birmingham. 20 Injustice anywhere is a threat to justice everywhere. We are caught in an inescapable network of mutuality tied in a single garment of destiny. Never again can we afford to live with the narrow, provincial "outsider agitator" idea.

Anyone who lives inside the United States can never be considered an outsider anywhere in this country.

You deplore the demonstrations that are presently taking place in Birmingham. But I am sorry that your statement did not express a similar concern for the conditions that brought the demonstrations into being. 30 I would not hesitate to say that it is unfortunate that so-called demonstrations are taking place in Birmingham at this time, but I would say in more emphatic terms that it is even more unfortunate that the white power structure of this city left the Negro community with no other alternative.

In any nonviolent campaign there are four basic steps: 1) collection of the facts to determine whether injustices are alive; 2) negotiation; 3) self-purification; and 4) direct action. 40

You may well ask, "Why direct action? Why sit-ins, marches, etc.? Isn't negotiation a better path?" You are exactly right in your call for negotiation. Indeed, this is the purpose of direct action. Nonviolent direct action seeks to create such a crisis and establish such creative tension that a community that has constantly refused to negotiate is forced to confront the issue. So the purpose of the direct action is to create a situation so crisis-packed that it will inevitably open the door to negotiation.

My friends, I must say to you that we have not made a 50
single gain in civil rights without determined legal and nonviolent pressure. History is the long and tragic story of the fact that privileged groups seldom give up their privileges voluntarily. Individuals may see the moral light and voluntarily give up their unjust posture; but as Reinhold Niebuhr[1] has reminded us, groups are more immoral than individuals.

We know through painful experience that freedom is never voluntarily given by the oppressor; it must be demanded by the oppressed. For years now I have heard 60 the word "Wait!" It rings in the ear of every Negro with a piercing familiarity. This "wait" has almost always meant "never." We must come to see with the distinguished jurist of yesterday that "justice too long delayed is justice denied." We have waited for more than three hundred and forty years for our constitutional and God-given rights.

You express a great deal of anxiety over our willingness to break laws. This is certainly a legitimate concern. Since we so diligently urge people to obey the Supreme Court's decision of 1954 outlawing segregation in the 70 public schools, it is rather strange and paradoxical to find us consciously breaking laws. One may well ask, "How can you advocate breaking some laws and obeying others?" The answer is found in the fact that there are two types of laws. There are *just* laws and there are *unjust* laws. One has not only a legal but a moral responsibility to obey just laws. Conversely, one has a moral responsibility to disobey unjust laws.

Now what is the difference between the two? A just law is a man-made code that squares with the moral law or 80 the law of God. An unjust law is a code that is out of harmony with the moral law. Any law that degrades human personality is unjust. All segregation statutes are unjust because segregation distorts the soul and damages

---

[1]An American Protestant theologian (1892–1971) who urged ethical realism in Christian approaches to political debate (see chapter 35).

the personality. It gives the segregator a false sense of superiority and the segregated a false sense of inferiority.

Let us turn to a more concrete example of just and unjust laws. An unjust law is a code that a majority inflicts on a minority that is not binding on itself. This is *difference* made legal. On the other hand a just law is a 90 code that a majority compels a minority to follow and that it is willing to follow itself. This is *sameness* made legal.

I hope you can see the distinction I am trying to point out. In no sense do I advocate evading or defying the law as the rabid segregationist would do. This would lead to anarchy. One who breaks an unjust law *openly, lovingly,* and with a willingness to accept the penalty by staying in jail to arouse the conscience of the community over its injustice, is in reality expressing the very highest respect for law. 100

Of course there is nothing new about this kind of civil disobedience. It was seen sublimely in the refusal of Shadrach, Meshach, and Abednego to obey the laws of Nebuchadnezzar[2] because a higher moral law was involved. It was practiced superbly by the early Christians.

We can never forget that everything Hitler did in Germany was "legal" and everything the Hungarian freedom fighters did in Hungary was "illegal." It was "illegal" to aid and comfort a Jew in Hitler's Germany.

In your statement you asserted that our actions, even 110 though peaceful, must be condemned because they precipitate violence. But can this assertion be logically made? Isn't this like condemning the robbed man because his possession of money precipitated the evil act of robbery? We must come to see, as federal courts have consistently affirmed, that it is immoral to urge an individual to withdraw his efforts to gain his basic constitutional rights because the quest precipitates violence. Society must protect the robbed and punish the robber. 120

Over the last few years I have consistently preached that nonviolence demands that the means we use must be as pure as the ends we seek. So I have tried to make it clear that it is wrong to use immoral means to gain moral ends. But now I must affirm that it is just as wrong, or even more so, to use moral means to preserve immoral ends. T. S. Eliot has said that there is no greater treason than to do the right deed for the wrong reason.

I wish you had commended the Negro sit-inners and demonstrators of Birmingham for their sublime courage, 130 their willingness to suffer, and their amazing discipline in the midst of the most inhuman provocation. One day the South will recognize its real heroes. They will include old, oppressed, battered Negro women, symbolized in a seventy-two-year-old woman of Montgomery, Alabama, who rose up with a sense of dignity and with her people decided not to ride the segregated buses, and responded to one who inquired about her tiredness with ungrammatical profundity: "My feets is tired, but my soul is rested." One day the South will know that when these 140 disinherited children of God sat down at the lunch counters they were in reality standing up for the best in the American dream and the most sacred values in our

Judeo-Christian heritage, and thus carrying our whole nation back to great wells of democracy which were dug deep by the founding fathers in the formulation of the Constitution and the Declaration of Independence.

I hope this letter finds you strong in the faith. I also hope that circumstances will soon make it possible for me to meet each of you, not as an integrationist or a civil 150 rights leader, but as a fellow clergyman and a Christian brother. Let us hope that the dark clouds of racial prejudice will soon pass away and the deep fog of misunderstanding will be lifted from our fear-drenched communities and in some not too distant tomorrow the radiant stars of love and brotherhood will shine over our great nation with all of their scintillating beauty.

Yours for the cause of
Peace and Brotherhood
Martin Luther King, Jr. 160

———————————◆———————————

As the Birmingham Letter suggests, Dr. King practiced tactics of nonviolent protest to achieve the goals of racial integration and civil rights in America. Another black protest leader of the period took a very different tack: Malcolm Little (1925–1965), who called himself "Malcolm X," experienced firsthand the inequities and degradation of life in white America. For a time he turned to crime and drugs as a means of survival. Arrested and sentenced to prison in 1946, he took the opportunity to study history and religion, and most especially the teachings of Islam. By the time he was released in 1952, he had joined the Nation of Islam and was prepared to launch his career as a Muslim minister. Malcolm and other "Black Muslims" despaired over persistent racism in white America, and determined that blacks should pursue a very different course from that of Dr. King and the Southern Christian Leadership Conference. African-Americans, argued Malcolm, should abandon aspirations for integration. Instead, they should separate from American whites in every feasible way; they should create a black nation in which—through hard work and the pursuit of Muslim morality—they might live equally, in dignity, without the daily affronts of white racism. These goals should be achieved by all available means, violent if necessary (armed self-defense was a first step). Only by fighting for black nationalism would African-Americans ever gain power and self-respect in racist America. Little wonder that Malcolm was feared and reviled by whites and deemed a dangerous radical by more moderate blacks as well.

In 1963, Malcolm addressed a conference of black leaders in Detroit, Michigan. His appearance was controversial; it was actually boycotted by many local black dignitaries. In this speech, which later came to be called "Message to the Grass Roots," Malcolm addressed a large (almost entirely black) audience representing a cross-section of the African-American community. The

---

[2]The Chaldean king of the sixth century B.C.E., who, according to the Book of Daniel, demanded that these Hebrew youths worship the Babylonian gods. Nebuchadnezzar cast them into a fiery furnace, but they were delivered unhurt by an angel of God.

power and immediacy of his style is best captured on the tape of the speech published by the African-American Broadcasting and Record Company. Nevertheless, the following brief excerpt provides a glimpse into the ferocious eloquence that Malcolm exhibited throughout his brief career—until his death by assassination in 1965.

READING 6.22

From Malcolm X's *Message to the Grass Roots*

. . . America has a very serious problem. Not only does   1
America have a very serious problem, but our people have
a very serious problem. America's problem is us. We're
her problem. The only reason she has a problem is she
doesn't want us here. And every time you look at yourself,
be you black, brown, red or yellow, a so-called Negro, you
represent a person who poses such a serious problem for
America because you're not wanted. Once you face this
as a fact, then you can start plotting a course that will
make you appear intelligent, instead of unintelligent.   10
     What you and I need to do is learn to forget our
differences. When we come together, we don't come
together as Baptists or Methodists. You don't catch
hell because you're a Baptist, and you don't catch hell
because you're a Methodist. You don't catch hell because
you're a Methodist or Baptist, you don't catch hell
because you're a Democrat or a Republican, you don't
catch hell because you're a Mason or an Elk, and you
sure don't catch hell because you're an American;
because if you were an American, you wouldn't catch   20
hell. You catch hell because you're a black man. You
catch hell, all of us catch hell, for the same reason.
     So we're all black people, so-called Negroes, second-
class citizens, ex-slaves. You're nothing but an ex-slave.
You don't like to be told that. But what else are you? You
are ex-slaves. You didn't come here on the "Mayflower."
You came here on a slave ship. In chains, like a horse, or
a cow, or a chicken. And you were brought here by the
people who came here on the "Mayflower," you were
brought here by the so-called Pilgrims, or Founding   30
Fathers. They were the ones who brought you here.
     We have a common enemy. We have this in common:
We have a common oppressor, a common exploiter, and a
common discriminator. But once we all realize that we
have a common enemy, then we unite—on the basis of
what we have in common. And what we have foremost in
common is that enemy—the white man. . . .
     As long as the white man sent you to Korea, you bled.
He sent you to Germany, you bled. He sent you to the
South Pacific to fight the Japanese, you bled. You bleed   40
for white people, but when it comes to seeing your own
churches being bombed and little black girls murdered,
you haven't got any blood. You bleed when the white man
says bleed; you bite when the white man says bite; and
you bark when the white man says bark. I hate to say this
about us, but it's true. How are you going to be nonviolent
in Mississippi, as violent as you were in Korea? How can
you justify being nonviolent in Mississippi and Alabama,
when your churches are being bombed, and your little
girls are being murdered, and at the same time you are   50

going to get violent with Hitler, and Tojo, and somebody
else you don't even know?
     If violence is wrong in America, violence is wrong
abroad. If it is wrong to be violent defending black
women and black children and black babies and black
men, then it is wrong for America to draft us and make us
violent abroad in defense of her. And if it is right for
America to draft us, and teach us how to be violent in
defense of her, then it is right for you and me to do
whatever is necessary to defend our own people right here   60
in this country. . . .

———————————◆———————————

The Literature of the Black Revolution

The passage of the Civil Rights Act in America in 1964 provided an end to official segregation in public places; but continuing discrimination and the growing militancy of some civil rights groups provoked a more violent phase of the protests during the late 1960s and thereafter. Even before the assassination of Martin Luther King, Jr., in 1968, the black revolution had begun to assume a transnational fervor. American voices joined those of their black neighbors in West India, South Africa, and elsewhere in the world. Fired by **apartheid**, the system of strict racial segregation that prevailed legally in the Union of South Africa until 1994, the Bloke Modisane (b. 1923) lamented:

> it gets awful lonely,
> lonely;
> like screaming,
> screaming lonely
> screaming down dream alley,
> screaming blues, like none can hear*

In *Black Skin, White Masks* (1958)—the handbook for the black revolution—the West Indian essayist and revolutionary Franz Fanon (d. 1961) wrote: "The black man wants to be like the white man. For the black man there is only one destiny. And it is white." In America, where advertising media made clear the disparity between the material comforts of blacks and whites, the black revolution swelled on a tide of rising expectations. LeRoi Jones (b. 1934), who in 1966 adopted the African name Imamu Amiri Baraka, echoed the message of Malcolm X in poems and plays that advocated militant action and pan-Africanism. Attacking the entire white Western literary tradition, Baraka called for "poems that kill"; "Let there be no love poems written," he entreats, "until love can exist freely and cleanly."

     Two luminaries of American black protest literature were James Baldwin (1924–1987) and Ralph Ellison (1914–1994). Baldwin, the oldest of nine children

*From *Poems from Black Africa*, ed. Langston Hughes. Bloomington: Indiana University Press, 1963, 110.

raised in Harlem in conditions of poverty, began writing when he was fourteen years old. Encouraged early in his career by Richard Wright, Baldwin became a formidable preacher of the gospel of equality. For Baldwin, writing was a subversive act. "You write," he insisted, "in order to change the world, knowing perfectly well that you probably can't, but also knowing that literature is indispensable to the world. In some way, your aspirations and concern for a single man in fact do begin to change the world. The world changes according to the way people see it, and if you alter, even by a millimeter, the way a person looks or people look at reality, then you can change it."

In his novels, short stories, and essays, Baldwin stressed the affinity African-Americans felt with other poverty-stricken populations. Yet, as he tried to define the unique differences between blacks and whites, he observed that black people were strangers in the modern world, a world whose traditions were claimed by whites. As he explained in the essay "Stranger in the Village" (1953):

> [European Whites] cannot be, from the point of view of power, strangers anywhere in the world; they have made the modern world, in effect, even if they do not know it. The most illiterate among them is related, in a way that I am not, to Dante, Shakespeare, Michelangelo, Aeschylus, da Vinci, Rembrandt, and Racine; the cathedral at Chartres says something to them which it cannot say to me. . . . Out of their hymns and dances come Beethoven and Bach. Go back a few centuries and they are in their full glory—but I am in Africa, watching the conquerors arrive.

Baldwin nevertheless insisted that black culture has influenced white culture, and especially American culture, in an irreversible manner:

> The time has come to realize that the interracial drama acted out on the American continent has not only created a new black man, it has created a new white man, too. . . . One of the things that distinguishes Americans from other people is that no other people has ever been so deeply involved in the lives of black men, and vice versa. . . . It is precisely this black–white experience which may prove of indispensable value to us in the world we face today. This world is white no longer, and it will never be white again.*

Baldwin's contemporary, Ralph Ellison, a native of Oklahoma and an amateur jazz musician, came to Harlem during the 1930s to study sculpture and musical composition. He was influenced by both Hughes and Wright and soon turned to writing short stories and newspaper reviews. In 1945, he began the novel *Invisible Man*, a fiction masterpiece that probes the black estrangement from white culture. The prologue to the novel, an excerpt of which follows, offers a glimpse into the spiritual odyssey of the "invisible" protagonist. It also broaches, with surrealistic intensity, some of Ellison's most important themes: the nightmarish quality of urban life and the alienation experienced by both blacks and whites in modern American society.

READING 6.23
From Ellison's *Invisible Man*

I am an invisible man. No, I am not a spook like those   1
who haunted Edgar Allan Poe;[1] nor am I one of your
Hollywood-movie ectoplasms. I am a man of substance,
of flesh and bone, fiber and liquids—and I might even be
said to possess a mind. I am invisible, understand, simply
because people refuse to see me. Like the bodiless heads
you see sometimes in circus sideshows, it is as though I
have been surrounded by mirrors of hard, distorting glass.
When they approach me they see only my surroundings,
themselves, or figments of their imagination—indeed,   10
everything and anything except me.

Nor is my invisibility exactly a matter of a bio-chemical
accident to my epidermis. That invisibility to which I refer
occurs because of a peculiar disposition of the eyes of those
with whom I come in contact. A matter of the construction
of their *inner* eyes, those eyes with which they look through
their physical eyes upon reality. I am not complaining, nor
am I protesting either. It is sometimes advantageous to be
unseen, although it is most often rather wearing on the
nerves. Then too, you're constantly being bumped against   20
by those of poor vision. Or again, you often doubt if you
really exist. You wonder whether you aren't simply a phantom
in other people's minds. Say, a figure in a nightmare
which the sleeper tries with all his strength to destroy. It's
when you feel like this that, out of resentment, you begin
to bump people back. And, let me confess, you feel that
way most of the time. You ache with the need to convince
yourself that you do exist in the real world, that you're a
part of all the sound and anguish, and you strike out with
your fists, you curse and you swear to make them   30
recognize you. And, alas, it's seldom successful.

One night I accidentally bumped into a man, and perhaps
because of the near darkness he saw me and called me
an insulting name. I sprang at him, seized his coat lapels
and demanded that he apologize. He was a tall blond
man, and as my face came close to his he looked
insolently out of his blue eyes and cursed me, his breath
hot in my face as he struggled. I pulled his chin down
sharp upon the crown of my head, butting him as I had
seen the West Indians do, and I felt his flesh tear and the   40
blood gush out, and I yelled, "Apologize! Apologize!" But
he continued to curse and struggle, and I butted him

---

*"Stranger in the Village," in James Baldwin, *Notes of a Native Son.* New York: Bantam Press, 1964, 140, 148–149.

[1]A leading American poet, literary critic, and short-story writer (1809–1849), noted for his tales of terror and his clever detective stories.

again and again until he went down heavily, on his knees, profusely bleeding. I kicked him repeatedly, in a frenzy because he still uttered insults though his lips were frothy with blood. Oh yes, I kicked him! And in my outrage I got out my knife and prepared to slit his throat, right there beneath the lamplight in the deserted street, holding him by the collar with one hand, and opening the knife with my teeth—when it occurred to me that the man had not   50
seen me, actually; that he, as far as he knew, was in the midst of a walking nightmare! And I stopped the blade, slicing the air as I pushed him away, letting him fall back to the street. I stared at him hard as the lights of a car stabbed through the darkness. He lay there, moaning on the asphalt; a man almost killed by a phantom. It unnerved me. I was both disgusted and ashamed. I was like a drunken man myself, wavering about on weakened legs. Then I was amused. Something in this man's thick head had sprung out and beaten him within an inch of   60
his life. I began to laugh at this crazy discovery. Would he have awakened at the point of Death? Would Death himself have freed him for wakeful living? But I didn't linger. I ran away into the dark, laughing so hard I feared I might rupture myself. The next day I saw his picture in the *Daily News*, beneath a caption stating that he had been "mugged." Poor fool, poor blind fool, I thought with sincere compassion, mugged by an invisible man! . . .

———————◆———————

In the literature of the black revolution, especially that of that last three decades of the twentieth century, many of the most powerful voices have been female. Succeeding such notable Harlem Renaissance writers as Zora Neale Hurston (1891–1960) and Dorothy West (b. 1912), two contemporary figures—Toni Morrison (b. 1931) and Alice Walker (b. 1944)—have risen to eminence for their courageous and candid characterizations of black women as they have faced the perils of racism, domestic violence, and sexual abuse. Space permits only a short example of the writings of Alice Walker, whose novel *The Color Purple* won the Pulitzer Prize for literature in 1982. As effective as many of Walker's novels and poems, her short story "Elethia" probes the dual issues of identity and liberation as they come to shape the destiny of a young black female.

READING 6.24
Walker's "Elethia"

A certain perverse experience shaped Elethia's life, and   1
made it possible for it to be true that she carried with her at all times a small apothecary jar of ashes.

There was in the town where she was born a man whose ancestors had owned a large plantation on which everything under the sun was made or grown. There had been many slaves, and though slavery no longer existed, this grandson of former slaveowners held a quaint proprietary point of view where colored people were concerned. He adored them, of course. Not in the present—it went   10
without saying—but at that time, stopped, just on the outskirts of his memory: his grandfather's time.

This man, whom Elethia never saw, opened a locally famous restaurant on a busy street near the center of town. He called it "Old Uncle Albert's." In the window of the restaurant was a stuffed likeness of Uncle Albert himself, a small brown dummy of waxen skin and glittery black eyes. His lips were intensely smiling and his false teeth shone. He carried a covered tray in one hand, raised level with his shoulder, and over his other arm was draped   20
a white napkin.

Black people could not eat at Uncle Albert's, though they worked, of course, in the kitchen. But on Saturday afternoons a crowd of them would gather to look at "Uncle Albert" and discuss how near to the real person the dummy looked. Only the very old people remembered Albert Porter, and their eyesight was no better than their memory. Still there was a comfort somehow in knowing that Albert's likeness was here before them daily and that if he smiled as a dummy in a fashion he was not known   30
to do as a man, well, perhaps both memory and eyesight were wrong.

The old people appeared grateful to the rich man who owned the restaurant for giving them a taste of vicarious fame. They could pass by the gleaming window where Uncle Albert stood, seemingly in the act of sprinting forward with his tray, and know that though niggers were not allowed in the front door, ole Albert was already inside, and looking mighty pleased about it, too.

For Elethia the fascination was in Uncle Albert's   40
fingernails. She wondered how his creator had got them on. She wondered also about the white hair that shone so brightly under the lights. One summer she worked as a salad girl in the restaurant's kitchen, and it was she who discovered the truth about Uncle Albert. He was not a dummy; he was stuffed. Like a bird, like a moose's head, like a giant bass. He was stuffed.

One night after the restaurant was closed someone broke in and stole nothing but Uncle Albert. It was Elethia and her friends, boys who were in her class and who called   50
her "Thia." Boys who bought Thunderbird and shared it with her. Boys who laughed at her jokes so much they hardly remembered she was also cute. Her tight buddies. They carefully burned Uncle Albert to ashes in the incinerator of their high school, and each of them kept a bottle of his ashes. And for each of them what they knew and their reaction to what they knew was profound.

The experience undercut whatever solid foundation Elethia had assumed she had. She became secretive, wary, looking over her shoulder at the slightest noise. She   60
haunted the museums of any city in which she found herself, looking, usually, at the remains of Indians, for they were plentiful everywhere she went. She discovered some of the Indian warriors and maidens in the museums were also real, stuffed people, painted and wigged and robed, like figures in the Rue Morgue. There were so many, in fact, that she could not possibly steal and burn them all. Besides, she did not know if these figures—with their valiant glass eyes—would wish to be burned.

About Uncle Albert she felt she knew.   70

What kind of man was Uncle Albert?

Well, the old folks said, he wasn't nobody's uncle and

wouldn't sit still for nobody to call him that, either.

Why, said another old-timer, I recalls the time they hung a boy's privates on a post at the end of the street where all the black folks shopped, just to scare us all, you understand, and Albert Porter was the one took 'em down and buried 'em. Us never did find the rest of the boy though. It was just like always—they would throw you in the river with a big old green log tied to you, and down to 80 the bottom you sunk.

He continued.

Albert was born in slavery and he remembered that his mama and daddy didn't know nothing about slavery'd done ended for near 'bout ten years, the boss man kept them so ignorant of the law, you understand. So he was a mad so-an'-so when he found out. They used to beat him *severe* trying to make him forget the past and grin and act like a nigger. (Whenever you saw somebody acting like a nigger, Albert said, you could be sure he seriously 90 disremembered his past.) But he never would. Never would work in the big house as head servant, neither—always broke up stuff. The master at that time was always going around pinching him too. Looks like he hated Albert more than anything—but he never would let him get a job anywhere else. And Albert never would leave home. Too stubborn.

Stubborn, yes. My land, another one said. That's why it do seem strange to see that dummy that sposed to be old Albert with his mouth open. All them teeth. Hell, all 100 Albert's teeth was knocked out before he was grown.

Elethia went away to college and her friends went into the army because they were poor and that was the way things were. They discovered Uncle Alberts all over the world. Elethia was especially disheartened to find Uncle Alberts in her textbooks, in the newspapers and on t.v.

Everywhere she looked there was an Uncle Albert (and many Aunt Albertas, it goes without saying).

But she had her jar of ashes, the old-timers' memories written down, and her friends who wrote that in the army 110 they were learning skills that would get them through more than a plate glass window.

And she was careful that, no matter how compelling the hype, Uncle Alberts, in her own mind, were not permitted to exist.

◆

African-Americans and the Visual Arts

During the Harlem Renaissance, African-American painters and sculptors made public the social concerns of black poets and writers. In picturing their experience, they drew on African folk idioms and colloquial forms of native expression; but they also absorbed the radically new styles of European modernism. Such was the case with the art of Jacob Lawrence (b. 1917), whose family moved to Harlem in 1930. Lawrence's powerful style features flat, local colors and angular, abstract forms that owe as much to African art as to synthetic cubism and expressionism. His commitment to social and racial issues reflects his esteem for the nineteenth-century artist-critics Goya and Daumier. Painting in tempera on

masonite panels, Lawrence won early acclaim for serial paintings that deal with black history and with the lives of black American heroes and heroines. Among the most famous of these is a series of sixty panels known as *The Migration of the Negro* (1940–1941). For *The Migration*—an expressionistic narrative of the great northward movement of African-Americans after World War I—Lawrence drew on textual sources rather than firsthand visual experience. The drama of each episode (see Figure 36.1) is conveyed by means of powerful, angular rhythms and vigorous, geometric shapes that preserve what Lawrence called "the magic of the picture plane."

Since mid-century, African-American artists have taken increasingly bold and ever more cynical approaches to themes of race discrimination and racial stereotyping. The sculptor Betye Saar (b. 1926) abandoned the African-inspired fetishlike sculptures of her early career and turned to fabricating boxed constructions that attacked the icons of commercial white culture. In the mixed media sculpture entitled *The Liberation of Aunt Jemima*,

Figure 36.2 Betye Saar, *The Liberation of Aunt Jemima*, 1972. Mixed media, 11¾ × 8 × 2¾ in. University Art Museum, University of California at Berkeley. Purchased with the aid of funds from the National Endowment for the Arts. Selected by the Committee for the Acquisition of African-American Art.

Figure 36.3 Robert Colescott, *Les Demoiselles d'Alabama (Vestidas)*, 1985. Acrylic on canvas, 8 ft. × 7 ft. 8 in. Collection of Hanford Yang, New York. Photo courtesy Phyllis Kind Gallery, New York.

Saar transforms the familiar symbol of American pancakes and cozy kitchens into a gun-toting version of the "mammy" stereotype (Figure **36.2**). The satirist-artist Robert Colescott (b. 1925) creates parodies of famous paintings in which whites are recast as cartoon-style, stereotyped blacks. In doing so, Colescott calls attention to the exclusion of blacks from Western art history. His version of Delacroix's *Liberty Leading the People* (1976) features a crew of brashly painted African-American rebels commanded by a black-faced Liberty. Colescott's *Demoiselles d'Alabama* (Figure **36.3**), an obvious funk-art clone of Picasso's seminal painting (see Figure 32.2), slyly challenges contemporary definitions of primitivism and modernism. Colescott observes, "Picasso started with European art and abstracted through African art, producing 'Africanism' but keeping one foot in European art. I began with Picasso's Africanism and moved toward European art, keeping one foot in Africanism. . . . The irony is what most people (including me) know about African conventions comes from Cubist art. Could a knowledge of European art be so derived as well?"*

---

*Lowery S. Sims and M. D. Kahan, *Robert Colescott, A Retrospective, 1975–1986*. San Jose, Calif.: San Jose Museum of Art, 1987, 8.

African-Americans and Jazz

Possibly the most important contribution made by African-Americans to world culture occurred in the area of music, specifically in the birth and development of that unique form of modern music known as *jazz*. Jazz is a synthesis of diverse musical elements that came together in the first decades of the twentieth century, but it was in the interwar era that jazz came to express an exuberant kind of American optimism. Although some music historians insist that jazz is the product of place, not race, the primary role of African-Americans in the origins of jazz is indisputable.

Jazz is a performer's rather than a composer's art. It is dominated by African precepts of rhythm and a wide range of Afro-European concepts of harmony, melody, and tone color. The evolution of jazz has involved a variety of popular musical styles, including that of the marching brass band, the minstrel stage, blues, and ragtime. *Ragtime* music and dance, which featured a syncopated piano style, migrated north after the Civil War and became popular during the 1890s. Its most inspired proponent was the black composer and ragtime pianist Scott Joplin (1868–1917). By the 1920s, ragtime came to feature improvisation (that is, spur-of-the-moment composition) and percussive rhythms. *Blues*, on the other hand, began as a vocal rather than an instrumental form of music. Native to America, but stemming from African traditions, blues is a highly subjective form of expression by which one laments one's troubles, loneliness, and despair. A blues song may recall the wailing cries of plantation slaves; it may describe the anguish of separation and loss or the hope of deliverance from oppression. Often improvised, blues songs like W. C. Handy's "St. Louis Blues"* (1914) begin with a line that states a simple complaint ("I hate to see the evening sun go down"); the complaint is repeated in a second line, and it is "answered" in a third ("It makes me think I'm on my last go-round")—a pattern derived perhaps from African call and response chants (see chapter 19). Musically, blues makes use of a special scale known as a "blues scale," which features the flatted forms of E, G, and B within the standard scale of C.

Both ragtime and blues played a large part in the development of jazz as a generic form of popular music. If jazz has any singular characteristic, it is the exuberant disregard of established forms of Western composition in favor of deviation and variety. Jazz employs a unique variation on rhythm known as **swing**, in which some notes are held for longer or shorter periods or accented in ways that depart from their notated values. Swing gives jazz subtle rhythmic shifts that are virtually impossible to notate with accuracy. Jazz depends on improvisation and on the exploitation of the tone color of various musical instruments. Although syncopated rhythms, improvisation, and variant tonal qualities were not in themselves new, their application, in combination with blues and swing, along with an experimental attitude toward performance style, worked to give jazz a unique sound.

The beginnings of American jazz are found in New Orleans, Louisiana, a melting pot for the rich heritage of Spanish, French, African, Indian, and Black Creole musical traditions. Here, black and white musicians drew on the intricate rhythms of African tribal dance and the European harmonies of traditional marching bands. The street musicians who regularly marched behind funeral or wedding processions, many of whom were neither formally trained nor could read music, might play trumpets, trombones, and clarinets. These musicians made up the "front line" of small groups that also included a rhythm section of drums and other instruments. (The crowd that danced behind them was called the "second line.") Jazz groups also played the kinds of music that were popular in nightclubs and dancehalls. Louis Armstrong (1900–1971), a native of New Orleans who began playing the cornet at the age of twelve, commonly crossed African and local New Orleans street rhythms to produce instrumental jazz pieces often embellished by **scat singing**—an improvised set of

Figure 36.4 King Oliver's Creole Jazz Band, 1923. Honore Dutrey, Warren "Baby" Dodds, Joe Oliver, Louis Armstrong, Lil Hardin, Bill Johnson, and Johnny Dodds. Courtesy Hogan Jazz Archive, Tulane University.

nonsense syllables. Armstrong is widely regarded as having turned jazz into an internationally respected art form. "Hotter Than That"* (1927), a composition by Lillian Hardin (Armstrong's wife), exemplifies the style termed *hot jazz* (Figure **36.4**).

In the 1920s jazz spread north to the urban centers of Chicago, Kansas City, and New York. Armstrong moved to Chicago in 1922. In New York, extraordinary jazz singers like Bessie Smith (1898–1937), known by her fans as the "Empress of the Blues," drew worldwide acclaim through the phenomena of radio and phonograph records. In the so-called Jazz Age, jazz had a major impact on other musical genres. The American composer George Gershwin (1898–1937) incorporated the rhythms of jazz into the mesmerizing *Rhapsody in Blue* (1924), a piece for piano and orchestra. Gershwin's *Porgy and Bess* (1935), a folk opera about the life of Charleston African-Americans, combined jazz, blues, and spiritual and folk idioms to produce a fresh, new style of American musical theater. Popular music of the 1930s and 1940s was closely tied to the popularity of big bands and the danceable rhythms of swing. The white swing bands of Tommy Dorsey, Glenn Miller, and Benny Goodman played a mix of instrumental swing and popular ballads, while black swing bands like that of Bill "Count" Basie leaned more toward blues and a driving jazz sound.

In the years following World War II, jazz took on some of the complex and sophisticated characteristics of "art music." The beguiling suite *Black, Brown, and Beige* (1948) composed by Edward Kennedy "Duke" Ellington

---

*See Music Listening Selections at end of chapter.

*See Music Listening Selections at end of chapter.

(1899–1974) paved the way for concert hall jazz, a form that (reflecting Ellington's influence) is enjoying a revival in the 1990s. On a smaller scale, using groups of five to seven instruments, the jazz of the late 1940s and 1950s engaged the improvisational talents of individual performers. New jazz forms included *bebop* (or *bop*)—a robust musical style characterized by frenzied tempos, complex chord progressions, and dense polyrhythms—and *cool jazz*, a more restrained and gentler style than bop. "Ko-Ko,"[♪] written by Duke Ellington and performed by the saxophonist Charlie Parker (1920–1955) and the trumpeter John "Dizzy" Gillespie (1917–1993), epitomizes the bop style of the 1940s. More recently, the New Orleans composer, trumpet prodigy, and teacher Wynton Marsalis (b. 1961) has reconfirmed the role of jazz as America's classical music. "Jazz is more than the best expression there is of American culture," claims Marsalis, "it is the most democratic of arts." To this day, jazz remains a unique kind of chamber music that combines the best of classical and popular musicianship.

[♪]See Music Listening Selections at end of chapter.

African-Americans and Dance

The African-American impact on twentieth-century dance has rivaled that of music. For centuries, dance served African-Americans as a metaphor of physical freedom. By the late nineteenth century, as all-black theatrical companies and minstrel shows toured the United States, black entertainment styles began to reach white audiences. Popular black dances such as the high-kicking cakewalk became the international fad of the early 1900s, and dance techniques—especially tap dancing—influenced both social and theatrical dance.

With the pioneer African-American choreographer Katherine Dunham (b. 1912), black dance moved beyond the level of stage entertainment. An avid student of Caribbean dance, Dunham drew heavily on Afro-Caribbean and African culture in both choreography and the sets and costumes designed by her husband, John Pratt (Figure **36.5**). Dunham's troupe borrowed from Caribbean music the rhythms of the steel band, an instrumental ensemble consisting entirely of steel drums fashioned from oil containers. Originating in Trinidad,

Figure 36.5 Katherine Dunham in the 1945–1946 production of *Tropical Revue*. The Dance Collection, The New York Public Library for the Performing Arts. Astor, Lenox, and Tilden Foundations.

steel bands provided percussive accompaniment for calypso and other kinds of improvised dance forms. In her book *Dances of Haiti*, Dunham examines the sociological function of dance—for instance, how communal dance captures the spirit of folk celebrations and how African religious dance interacts with European secular dance. Dunham's work inspired others: Pearl Primus (b. 1919) used her studies in anthropology (like Dunham, she earned a doctorate in this field) and choreography to become the world's foremost authority on African dance. Following a trip to Africa in the 1940s, she brought to modern dance the spirit and substance of native tribal rituals. She also choreographed theatrical versions of African-American spirituals and poems, including those of Langston Hughes. In her book *African Dance*, Primus declared: "The dance is strong magic. The dance is a spirit. It turns the body to liquid steel. It makes it vibrate like a guitar. The body can fly without wings. It can sing without voice."

The achievements of Dunham and Primus gave African-American dance theater international stature. Since 1950, such outstanding choreographers as Alvin Ailey (1931–1989), Donald McKayle (b. 1930), and Arthur Mitchell (b. 1934) have graced the history of American dance. Ailey's *Revelations* (1960), a suite that draws on African-American spirituals, song-sermons, and gospel songs, is an enduring tribute to the cultural history of black Americans. Dance compositions of more recent vintage, often driven by jazz or blues tempos, are filled with explosive excitement. Their choreographic themes continue to make powerful use of the black experience in a predominantly white society.

The Quest for Gender Equality

Throughout history and well into modern times, misogyny (the hatred of women) and the perception of the female sex as inferior in intelligence and strength have enforced conditions of gender inequality. While women make up the majority of the population in many cultures, they have exercised little significant political or economic power. Like many ethnic minorities, women have long been relegated to the position of second-class citizens. In 1900, women were permitted to vote in only one country in the world: New Zealand.

1953	biophysicists determine the molecular structure of DNA	
1953	Jonas Salk (American) tests an effective polio vaccine	
1955	an American endocrinologist produces a successful birth control pill	
1982	the fatal immune system disorder AIDS (Acquired Immune Deficiency Syndrome) is diagnosed	

By mid-century, women in most First World countries had gained voting rights; nevertheless, their social and economic status has remained far below that of men. As recently as 1985, the World Conference on Women reported that while women represent fifty percent of the world's population and contribute nearly two-thirds of all working hours, they receive only one-tenth of the world's income and own less than one percent of the world's property. Though female inequality has been a fact of history, it was not until the twentieth century that the quest for female liberation took the form of an international movement.

The Literature of Feminism: Woolf

The history of **feminism** (the principle advocating equal social, political, and economic rights for men and women) reaches back at least to the fourteenth century, when the French poet Christine de Pisan took up the pen in defense of women (see chapter 15). Christine had sporadic followers among Renaissance and Enlightenment humanists. The most notable of these was Mary Wollstonecraft (1759–1797), who published her provocative *Vindication of the Rights of Women* in London in 1792. During the nineteenth century, Condorcet and Mill wrote reasoned pleas for female equality, as did the female novelist George Sand (see chapters 27 and 29). In America, the eloquence of Angelina Grimké (1805–1879) and other suffragettes (women advocating equality for women) was instrumental in winning women the right to vote in 1920.

Among the most impassioned advocates of the feminist movement that flourished in England during the early twentieth century was the novelist Virginia Woolf (1882–1941). Woolf argued that equal opportunity for education and economic advantage were even more important than the right to vote (British women finally gained the vote in 1928). In her novels and essays, Woolf proposed that women might become powerful only by achieving financial and psychological independence from men. Freedom, argued Woolf, is the prerequisite for creativity: For a woman to secure her own creative freedom, she must have money and "a room of her own." In the feminist essay "A Room of One's Own" (1929), Woolf responds to a clergyman's remark that no female could have matched the genius of William Shakespeare. In the excerpt below, Woolf envisions Shakespeare's imaginary sister, Judith, in her sixteenth-century setting. She uses this fictional character to raise some challenging questions concerning the psychological aspects of female creativity.

READING 6.25

From Woolf's "A Room of One's Own"

. . . Let me imagine, since facts are so hard to come by, what would have happened had Shakespeare had a wonderfully gifted sister, called Judith, let us say. Shakespeare himself went, very probably—his mother was an heiress—to the grammar school, where he may have learnt Latin—Ovid, Virgil and Horace—and the elements of grammar and logic. He was, it is well known, a wild boy who poached rabbits, perhaps shot a deer, and had, rather sooner than he should have done, to marry a woman in the neighbourhood, who bore him a child rather quicker than was right. That escapade sent him to seek his fortune in London. He had, it seemed, a taste for the theatre; he began by holding horses at the stage door. Very soon he got work in the theatre, became a successful actor, and lived at the hub of the universe, meeting everybody, knowing everybody, practising his art on the boards, exercising his wits in the streets, and even getting access to the palace of the queen. Meanwhile his extraordinarily gifted sister, let us suppose, remained at home. She was as adventurous, as imaginative, as agog to see the world as he was. But she was not sent to school. She had no chance of learning grammar and logic, let alone of reading Horace and Virgil. She picked up a book now and then, one of her brother's perhaps, and read a few pages. But then her parents came in and told her to mend the stockings or mind the stew and not moon about with books and papers. They would have spoken sharply but kindly, for they were substantial people who knew the conditions of life for a woman and loved their daughter—indeed, more likely than not she was the apple of her father's eye. Perhaps she scribbled some pages up in an apple loft on the sly, but was careful to hide them or set fire to them. Soon, however, before she was out of her teens, she was to be betrothed to the son of a neighbouring wool-stapler. She cried out that marriage was hateful to her, and for that she was severely beaten by her father. Then he ceased to scold her. He begged her instead not to hurt him, not to shame him in this matter of her marriage. He would give her a chain of beads or a fine petticoat, he said; and there were tears in his eyes. How could she disobey him? How could she break his heart? The force of her own gift alone drove her to it. She made up a small parcel of her belongings, let herself down by a rope one summer's night and took the road to London. She was not seventeen. The birds that sang in the hedge were not more musical than she was. She had the quickest fancy, a gift like her brother's, for the tune of words. Like him, she had a taste for the theatre. She stood at the stage door; she wanted to act, she said. Men laughed in her face. The manager—a fat, loose-lipped man—guffawed. He bellowed something about poodles dancing and women acting—no woman, he said, could possibly be an actress. He hinted—you can imagine what. She could get no training in her craft. Could she even seek her dinner in a tavern or roam the streets at midnight? Yet her genius was for fiction and lusted to feed abundantly upon the lives of men and women and the study of their ways. At last—for she was very young,

oddly like Shakespeare the poet in her face, with the same grey eyes and rounded brows—at last Nick Greene the actor-manager took pity on her; she found herself with child by that gentleman and so—who shall measure the heat and violence of the poet's heart when caught and tangled in a woman's body?—killed herself one winter's night and lies buried at some cross-roads where the omnibuses now stop outside the Elephant and Castle.

. . . any woman born with a great gift in the sixteenth century would certainly have gone crazed, shot herself, or ended her days in some lonely cottage outside the village, half witch, half wizard, feared and mocked at. For it needs little skill in psychology to be sure that a highly gifted girl who had tried to use her gift for poetry would have been so thwarted and hindered by other people, so tortured and pulled asunder by her own contrary instincts, that she must have lost her health and sanity to a certainty. No girl could have walked to London and stood at a stage door and forced her way into the presence of actor-managers without doing herself a violence and suffering an anguish which may have been irrational—for chastity may be a fetish invented by certain societies for unknown reasons—but were none the less inevitable. Chastity had then, it has even now, a religious importance in a woman's life, and has so wrapped itself round with nerves and instincts that to cut it free and bring it to the light of day demands courage of the rarest. To have lived a free life in London in the sixteenth century would have meant for a woman who was poet and playwright a nervous stress and dilemma which might well have killed her. Had she survived, whatever she had written would have been twisted and deformed, issuing from a strained and morbid imagination. And undoubtedly, I thought, looking at the shelf where there are no plays by women, her work would have gone unsigned. That refuge she would have sought certainly. It was the relic of the sense of chastity that dictated anonymity to women even so late as the nineteenth century. Currer Bell,[1] George Eliot, George Sand, all the victims of inner strife as their writings prove, sought ineffectively to veil themselves by using the name of a man. Thus they did homage to the convention, which if not implanted by the other sex was liberally encouraged by them (the chief glory of a woman is not to be talked of, said Pericles, himself a much-talked-of man), that publicity in women is detestable. Anonymity runs in their blood. . . .

That woman, then, who was born with a gift of poetry in the sixteenth century, was an unhappy woman, a woman at strife against herself. All the conditions of her life, all her own instincts, were hostile to the state of mind which is needed to set free whatever is in the brain. But what is the state of mind that is most propitious to the act of creation, I asked. Can one come by any notion of the state that furthers and makes possible that strange activity? Here I opened the volume containing the Tragedies of Shakespeare. What was Shakespeare's state of mind, for instance, when he wrote

---

[1] Currer Bell was the pseudonym for the British novelist Charlotte Brontë (1816–1855); for Eliot and Sand, see chapter 28.

Lear and *Antony and Cleopatra*? It was certainly the state of mind most favourable to poetry that there has ever existed. But Shakespeare himself said nothing about it. We only know casually and by chance that he "never blotted a line." Nothing indeed was ever said by the artist himself about his state of mind until the eighteenth century perhaps. Rousseau perhaps began it. At any rate, by the nineteenth century self-consciousness had developed so far that it was the habit for men of letters to describe their minds in confessions and autobiographies. Their lives also were written, and their letters were printed after their deaths. Thus, though we do not know what Shakespeare went through when he wrote *Lear*, we do know what Carlyle went through when he wrote the *French Revolution*: what Flaubert went through when he wrote *Madame Bovary*: what Keats was going through when he tried to write poetry against the coming of death and the indifference of the world.

And one gathers from this enormous modern literature of confession and self-analysis that to write a work of genius is almost always a feat of prodigious difficulty. Everything is against the likelihood that it will come from the writer's mind whole and entire. Generally material circumstances are against it. Dogs will bark; people will interrupt; money must be made; health will break down. Further, accentuating all these difficulties and making them harder to bear is the world's notorious indifference. It does not ask people to write poems and novels and histories; it does not need them. It does not care whether Flaubert finds the right word or whether Carlyle scrupulously verifies this or that fact. Naturally, it will not pay for what it does not want. And so the writer, Keats, Flaubert, Carlyle, suffers, especially in the creative years of youth, every form of distraction and discouragement. A curse, a cry of agony, rises from those books of analysis and confession. "Mighty poets in their misery dead"—that is the burden of their song. If anything comes through in spite of all this, it is a miracle, and probably no book is born entire and uncrippled as it was conceived.

But for women, I thought, looking at the empty shelves, these difficulties were infinitely more formidable. In the first place, to have a room of her own, let alone a quiet room or a sound-proof room, was out of the question, unless her parents were exceptionally rich or very noble, even up to the beginning of the nineteenth century. Since her pin money, which depended on the good will of her father, was only enough to keep her clothed, she was debarred from such alleviations as came even to Keats or Tennyson or Carlyle, all poor men; from a walking tour, a little journey to France, from the separate lodging which, even if it were miserable enough, sheltered them from the claims and tyrannies of their families. Such material difficulties were formidable, but much worse were the immaterial. The indifference of the world which Keats and Flaubert and other men of genius have found so hard to bear was in her case not indifference but hostility. The world did not say to her as it said to them, Write if you choose; it makes no difference to me. The world said with a guffaw, Write? What's the good of your writing? . . .

◆

Postwar Feminism: de Beauvoir

In Western Europe and in America, the two world wars had a positive effect on the position of women. In the absence of men during the wars, women assumed many of the jobs in agriculture and in industry. As Woolf predicted, the newly found financial independence of women gave them a sense of freedom and stimulated their demands for legal and social equality. Women's roles in regions beyond the West were also changing. In the Soviet Union, the communist regime put women to work in industry and on the battlefields. In China, where women had been bought and sold for centuries, the People's Republic in 1949 closed all brothels, forbade arranged marriages, and enforced policies of equal pay for equal work. But the feminist movement in postwar Europe and the United States demanded psychological independence as well as job equality; its goals involved raising the consciousness of *both* sexes.

The new woman must shed her passivity and achieve independence through action; this was the charge of the French novelist, social critic, and existentialist Simone de Beauvoir (1908–1986). In her book *The Second Sex* (1949), de Beauvoir dethroned the "myth of femininity"—the false and disempowering idea of the essentially "clinging" female personality. Reassessing the biological, psychological, and political reasons for women's traditional subordination to men, she charged women with an all too complacent willingness to accept the role of "the Other." De Beauvoir called on women everywhere "to renounce all advantages conferred upon them by their alliance" with men. She pursued this goal (unsuccessfully, according to some critics) in her own life: Her fifty-year association with Jean-Paul Sartre constitutes one of the most intriguing partnerships of the century. Although both enjoyed love affairs with other partners, they shared a lifelong marriage of minds.

In the following brief excerpt from *The Second Sex*, de Beauvoir explores the nature of female dependency upon men and the "metaphysical risk" of liberty.

READING 6.26

From de Beauvoir's *The Second Sex*

If woman seems to be the inessential which never becomes the essential, it is because she herself fails to bring about this change. Proletarians say "We"; Negroes also. Regarding themselves as subjects, they transform the bourgeois, the whites, into "others." But women do not say "We," except at some congress of feminists or similar formal demonstration; men say "women," and women use the same word in referring to themselves. They do not authentically assume a subjective attitude. The proletarians have accomplished the revolution in Russia, the Negroes in Haiti, the Indo-Chinese are battling for it in Indo-China; but the women's effort has never been anything more than a symbolic agitation. They have gained only what men have been willing to grant; they have taken nothing, they have only received.

The reason for this is that women lack concrete means for organizing themselves into a unit which can stand face to face with the correlative unit. They have no past, no history, no religion of their own; and they have no such solidarity of work and interest as that of the proletariat. They are not even promiscuously herded together in the way that creates community feeling among the American Negroes, the ghetto Jews, the workers of Saint-Denis, or the factory hands of Renault. They live dispersed among the males, attached through residence, housework, economic condition, and social standing to certain men—fathers or husbands—more firmly than they are to other women. If they belong to the bourgeoisie, they feel solidarity with men of that class, not with proletarian women; if they are white, their allegiance is to white men, not to Negro women. The proletariat can propose to massacre the ruling class, and a sufficiently fanatical Jew or Negro might dream of getting sole possession of the atomic bomb and making humanity wholly Jewish or black; but woman cannot even dream of exterminating the males. The bond that unites her to her oppressors is not comparable to any other. The division of the sexes is a biological fact, not an event in human history. Male and female stand opposed within a primordial *Mitsein*,[1] and woman has not broken it. The couple is a fundamental unity with two halves riveted together, and the cleavage of society along the line of sex is impossible. Here is to be found the basic trait of woman: she is the *Other* in a totality of which the two components are necessary to one another. . . .

Now, woman has always been man's dependant, if not his slave; the two sexes have never shared the world in equality. And even today woman is heavily handicapped, though her situation is beginning to change. Almost nowhere is her legal status the same as man's, and frequently it is much to her disadvantage. Even when her rights are legally recognized in the abstract, long-standing custom prevents their full expression in the mores. In the economic sphere men and women can almost be said to make up two castes; other things being equal, the former hold the better jobs, get higher wages, and have more opportunity for success than their new competitors. In industry and politics men have a great many more positions and they monopolize the most important posts. In addition to all this, they enjoy a traditional prestige that the education of children tends in every way to support, for the present enshrines the past—and in the past all history has been made by men. At the present time, when women are beginning to take part in the affairs of the world, it is still a world that belongs to men—they have no doubt of it at all and women have scarcely any. To decline to be the Other, to refuse to be a party to the deal—this would be for women to renounce all the advantages conferred upon them by their alliance with the superior caste. Man-the-sovereign will provide woman-the-liege with material protection and will undertake the moral justification of her existence; thus she can evade at once

20

30

40

50

60

70

both economic risk and the metaphysical risk of a liberty in which ends and aims must be contrived without assistance. Indeed, along with the ethical urge of each individual to affirm his subjective existence, there is also the temptation to forego liberty and become a thing. This is an inauspicious road, for he who takes it—passive, lost, ruined—becomes henceforth the creature of another's will, frustrated in his transcendence and deprived of every value. But it is an easy road; on it one avoids the strain involved in undertaking an authentic existence. When man makes of woman the *Other*, he may, then, expect her to manifest deep-seated tendencies toward complicity. Thus, woman may fail to lay claim to the status of subject because she lacks definite resources, because she feels the necessary bond that ties her to man regardless of reciprocity, and because she is often very well pleased with her role as the *Other*. . . .

80

◆

Feminist Poetry

 During the 1960s, and especially in the United States, the struggle for equality between the sexes assumed a militant tone. Continuing discrimination in both education and employment triggered demands for federal legislation on behalf of women. Consciousness-raising literature and protest marches publicized the feminist cause. At the same time, new types of contraceptives gave women control over their reproductive functions and greater sexual freedom. In 1963, Betty Friedan (b. 1921) published *The Feminine Mystique*, which claimed that American society—and commercial advertising in particular—had brainwashed women to prefer the roles of wives and mothers to other positions in life. Friedan was one of the first feminists to attack the theories of Sigmund Freud (see chapter 33), especially Freud's patriarchal view of women as failed men. She challenged women to question the existing order and to seek careers outside the home. With the founding of the National Organization for Women (NOW) in 1966, radical feminists called for a restructuring of all Western institutions.

Since the 1960s, there has been a virtual renaissance of poetry and fiction focused on the twin themes of gender equality and the search for female self-identity. As with the literature of black liberation, feminist writing often seethes with repressed rage and anger. Clearly, not all modern literature written by women addresses exclusively female issues—recent female writers have dealt with subjects as varied as boxing and the plight of the environment. Yet, in postwar literature produced by women, three motifs recur: the victimization of the female, her effort to define her role in a society traditionally dominated by men,

---

[1] German for "coexistence."

and her displacement from her ancient role as goddess and matriarch. In the domain of poetry, the feminist contribution represents some of the most personal and eloquent verse of its time.

Among the many outstanding feminist poets of the last third of the century are Sylvia Plath (1932–1963), Anne Sexton (1928–1975), Sonia Sanchez (b. 1935), and Adrienne Rich (b. 1929). Anne Sexton probed problems related to the socialization of women and the search for female identity. Deeply confessional, her verse often reflects upon her own troubled life, which (like Plath's) ended in suicide—an ironic fulfillment of Woolf's prophecy concerning the fate of Shakespeare's imaginary sister. In the autobiographical poem "Self in 1958," Sexton explores the images that traditionally have defined women: dolls, apparel, kitchens, and, finally, herself as an extension of her mother. Sexton's poem, which contemplates the female struggle for self-identity in modern society, recalls both Nora's plight in Ibsen's *A Doll's House* (see chapter 30) and Woolf's observation that women "think through their mothers."

The African-American poet Sonia Sanchez deals with the interrelated questions of racism and identity. Sanchez's poetry is more colloquial than Sexton's, and (like Baraka's) it is often fiercely confrontational. In the poem "Woman" Sanchez draws on the literary tradition in which eminent (and usually male) writers call upon the classical gods for inspiration: She invokes the spiritual powers of mother earth to infuse her with courage and creative energy.

The poems of Adrienne Rich are among the most challenging in the feminist canon. They are, to a large extent, impassioned responses to her shifting and often conflicting roles as American, Southerner, Jew, wife, mother, teacher, civil rights activist, feminist, and lesbian. Many of Rich's poems explore the complexities of personal and political relationships, especially as they are affected by gender. In the poem "Translations," she draws attention to the ways in which traditional gender roles polarize the sexes and potentially disempower women.

READING 6.27

The Poems of Sexton, Sanchez, and Rich

Sexton's "Self in 1958"

What is reality?	1
I am a plaster doll; I pose	
with eyes that cut open without landfall or nightfall	
upon some shellacked and grinning person,	
eyes that open, blue, steel, and close.	5
Am I approximately an I. Magnin[1] transplant?	
I have hair, black angel,	
black-angel-stuffing to comb,	
nylon legs, luminous arms	
and some advertised clothes.	10

I live in a doll's house	
with four chairs,	
a counterfeit table, a flat roof	
and a big front door.	
Many have come to such a small crossroad.	15
There is an iron bed,	
(Life enlarges, life takes aim)	
a cardboard floor,	
windows that flash open on someone's city,	
and little more.	20
Someone plays with me,	
plants me in the all-electric kitchen,	
Is this what Mrs. Rombauer[2] said?	
Someone pretends with me—	
I am walled in solid by their noise—	25
or puts me upon their straight bed.	
They think I am me!	
Their warmth? Their warmth is not a friend!	
They pry my mouth for their cups of gin	
and their stale bread.	30
What is reality	
to this synthetic doll	
who should smile, who should shift gears,	
should spring the doors open in a wholesome disorder,	
and have no evidence of ruin or fears?	35
But I would cry,	
rooted into the wall that	
was once my mother,	
if I could remember how	
and if I had the tears.	40
	(1966)

Sanchez's "Woman"

Come ride my birth, earth mother	1
tell me how i have become, became	
this woman with razor blades between	
her teeth.	
sing me my history O earth mother	
about tongues multiplying memories	5
about breaths contained in straw.	
pull me from the throat of mankind	
where worms eat, O earth mother.	
come to this Black woman. you.	
rider of earth pilgrimages.	10
tell me how i have held five bodies	
in one large cocktail of love	
and still have the thirst of the beginning sip.	
tell me. tellLLLLLL me. earth mother	
for i want to rediscover me. the secret of me	15
the river of me. the morning ease of me.	
i want my body to carry my words like aqueducts.	
i want to make the world my diary	
and speak rivers.	
rise up earth mother	20
out of rope-strung-trees	
dancing a windless dance	
come phantom mother	
dance me a breakfast of births	
let your mouth spill me forth	25
so i creak with your mornings.	
come old mother, light up my mind	
with a story bright as the sun.	
	(1978)

---

[1] A fashionable department store.

[2] Irma S. Rombauer, author of the popular cookbook, *The Joy of Cooking*.

Rich's "Translations"

You show me the poems of some woman   1
my age, or younger
translated from your language

Certain words occur: *enemy, oven, sorrow*
enough to let me know   5
she's a woman of my time

obsessed

with Love, our subject:
we've trained it like ivy to our walls
baked it like bread in our ovens   10
worn it like lead on our ankles
watched it through binoculars as if
it were a helicopter
bringing food to our famine
or the satellite   15
of a hostile power

I begin so see that woman
doing things: stirring rice
ironing a skirt
typing a manuscript till dawn   20

trying to make a call
from a phonebooth

The phone rings unanswered
in a man's bedroom
she hears him telling someone else   25
Never mind. She'll get tired.
hears him telling her story to her sister

who becomes her enemy
and will in her own time
light her own way to sorrow   30

ignorant of the fact this way of grief
is shared, unnecessary
and political   (1972)

◆

Feminist Art

The history of world art includes only a small number of female artists. Addressing this fact, the British feminist Germaine Greer (b. 1939) explained,

> There is . . . no female Leonardo, no female Titian, no female Poussin, but the reason does not lie in the fact that women have wombs, that they can have babies, that their brains are smaller, that they lack vigor, that they are not sensual. The reason is simply that you cannot make great artists out of egos that have been damaged, with wills that are defective, with libidos that have been driven out of reach and energy diverted into neurotic channels.*

A sure indication of change, however, is the fact that, since the middle of the twentieth century, the number of women in the visual arts (and in music as well) has

The Obstacle Race: The Fortunes of Women Painters and their Work. New York: Farrar, Straus, Giroux, 1979, 327.

been greater than ever before in history. And, as with feminist poetry, much of the painting and sculpture produced by women artists since the 1960s has been driven by feminist concerns. A few examples will suffice to make this point.

Throughout her long and productive career, the Venezuelan artist Marisol Escobar (b. 1930) has used plaster casts, drawings, and prints of her own face, hands, and body to create highly personal life-sized assemblages. Marisol (as she is popularly called) draws inspiration from the folk art of Mexico and pre-Hispanic America, whose brightly painted wooden images of saints and local gods are usually the work of women. She often mixes the traditional media of paint, wood, and plaster with modern synthetics, such as plastic and polyester resin. Marisol's *Women and Dog* (1964) portrays a group of fashionable urban women at leisure

Figure 36.6 Niki de Saint Phalle, *Black Venus*, 1965–1967. Painted polyester, 110 × 35 × 24 in. Collection of Whitney Museum of American Art, New York. Gift of the Howard and Jean Lipman Foundation, Inc. 68.73. Photograph copyright © 1997 Whitney Museum of American Art. Photography by Sandak, Inc./Division of Macmillan Publishing Company. © ADAGP, Paris and DACS, London 1997.

Figure 36.7 Marisol Escobar, *Women and Dog*, 1964. Wood, plaster, synthetic polymer, and miscellaneous items, 72¼ × 73 × 30¹⁵⁄₁₆ in. Collection of the Whitney Museum of American Art, New York.
Purchase, with funds from the Friends of the Whitney Museum of American Art (64.17 a–g).
Photo: Robert E. Mates, N.J. © Marisol Escobar/DACS, London/VAGA, New York 1997.

(Figure **36.7**). The faces of all the figures are self-portraits of the artist.

The internationally acclaimed French sculptor Niki de Saint Phalle (b. 1930) makes gigantic female sculptures that she calls "Nanas." In 1963 Saint Phalle exhibited a monumental 80-foot-long, 20-foot-high, and 30-foot-wide Nana that viewers might enter through a doorway between the figure's legs. Inside was a cinema with Greta Garbo movies, a telephone, a refreshment bar, and taped voices of romantic conversations between a man and a woman. Saint Phalle's *Black Venus* (Figure **36.6**; see also Frontispiece, p.ii), a hugely proportioned polyester "earth mother," wears a symbol of love on her belly and a flower on her breast. This exuberant creature is Saint Phalle's answer to Western stereotypes of female beauty. More closely resembling the ponderous fertility figures of prehistoric cultures (see chapter 1) than the refined marble goddesses of classical antiquity (see chapter 6), Saint Phalle's "Venus" celebrates the joys of sensual freedom. She is the feminist

reproof of the idealized and impassive images of womanhood that glut mainstream Western art history.

The militant American feminist Judy Gerowitz (b. 1939), who in 1969 assumed the surname of her native city (hence, Judy Chicago), has been a lifelong advocate of women's art. Chicago pioneered some of the first art communities in which women worked together to produce, exhibit, and sell art. Her efforts ignited the visual arts with the consciousness-raising politics of the feminist movement. Between 1974 and 1979, Chicago directed a project called *The Dinner Party*, a room-size sculpture consisting of a triangular table with thirty-nine place settings, each symbolizing a famous woman in myth or history. The feminist counterpart of the Last Supper, *The Dinner Party* pays homage to such immortals as Nefertiti, Sappho (Figure **36.8**), Queen Elizabeth I, and Virginia Woolf. To carry out this monumental project, Chicago studied the traditionally female arts of embroidery and china painting, inventing at the same time new techniques for combining such dissimilar materials as ceramics and lace. Over three hundred men and women contributed to this cooperative enterprise, which brought international attention to the cultural contributions of women in world history.

The career of the American photographer Cindy Sherman (b. 1954) addresses one of the more recent concerns of feminist artists: the fact that the *image* of the female in traditional Western art—an image of sweetness, sexiness, and servility—has been shaped by male needs and values. Such images, say contemporary feminists, dominate the world's "great artworks" and reflect the controlling power of the (male) "gaze." Just as Colescott and Saar use art to attack racial stereotypes, so feminists like Sherman make visual assaults on gender stereotypes—those projected by the collective body of "great art" and by the modern-day phenomena of television, "girlie" magazines, and other mass media. Sherman's large, glossy studio photographs of the 1970s feature the artist herself in poses and attire that call attention to the body as political object. In personalized narratives that resemble black-and-white movie stills, Sherman recreates commercial stereotypes that mock the subservient roles that women play: the "little woman," the *femme fatale*, the baby doll, the "pinup," and the lovesick teenager. Since the 1980s, Sherman has used the newest techniques in color photography to assault—often in visceral terms—sexual and historical stereotypes of women. She may replace the male image in a world-famous painting with a female image (often Sherman herself), use artificial body parts to "remake" the traditional nude, or combine contradictory symbols

Figure 36.9 Cindy Sherman, *Untitled #276*, 1993. Color photograph, edition of 6, 6 ft. 8½ in. × 5 ft. 1 in. framed. Courtesy of the artist and Metro Pictures, New York.

Figure 36.8 Judy Chicago, *Sappho*, plate from *The Dinner Party*, 1974–1978. Multimedia, 48 ft. × 48 ft. × 48 ft. Plate 14 in. diameter. © Judy Chicago, 1979. Photo: Donald Woodman.

to recast famous females from Western myth, history, and religion. In Figure **36.9**, a flaxen-haired Cinderella, holding the traditional symbol of purity (the lily), assumes the position and apparel of a prostitute. This vulgar figure Sherman "enshrines" in a manner usually reserved in Western art for images of the Virgin.

Well aware of the extent to which commercialism shapes identity, Barbara Kruger (b. 1945) creates photographs that deftly unite word and image to resemble commercial billboards. "Your Body is a Battleground," insists Kruger; by superimposing the message over the divided (positive and negative) image of a female face, the artist calls attention to the controversial issue of abortion in contemporary society (Figure **36.10**).

The Issue of Sexual Identity

This century's quests for racial and sexual equality have worked to raise public consciousness in matters of gender,* that is, the way in which sex is used as a

---

*Unlike sex (which designates individuals as either male or female), gender (which distinguishes between masculinity and femininity) is culturally, not biologically, prescribed.

Figure 36.10 Barbara Kruger, *Untitled* ("Your body is a battleground"), 1989. Photographic silkscreen on vinyl, 9 ft. 4 in. × 9 ft. 4 in. Courtesy Mary Boone Gallery, New York. Photo: Zindman/Freemont, New York.

structuring principle in human culture and society. Gender, or sexual identity, and sexual freedom are matters that have deeply affected the arts. More so than race, gender determines how people behave and how they are regarded by others. Assumptions concerning gender and, specifically, the sexual and social roles of males and females are rooted in traditions as old as Paleolithic culture and as venerated as the Bible; and, for many, sexual roles are fixed and unchanging. However, these assumptions, like so many others in the cultural history of this century, are now being challenged and reassessed. Gender issues, moreover, have accompanied a demand for equality on the part of those whose sexual orientation is untraditional: homosexuals (gays and lesbians) and other transgendered individuals. In America homosexuals date the birth of their "liberation" to June 1969, when they openly and violently protested a police raid on the Stonewall Inn, a gay bar in New York's Greenwich Village. Since then, the call for protection against harassment has shifted to litigated demands for social equality. While all societies have included a transgendered subculture, it was not until the last decades of this century that sexual and public issues intersected to produce some highly controversial questions: Should homosexuals serve in the armed forces? How does homosexuality affect the future of the traditional family? Should sexually explicit art receive public funding? The resolution of these and other gender-related questions are bound to play a major role in reshaping the humanistic tradition.

There are a number of reasons why issues of human sexuality have become so visible in the culture of the late twentieth century: increasing sexual permissiveness (the consequence of improved pharmaceutical methods for contraception); the activity of the media (especially TV and film) in broadcasting sexually explicit entertainment; and the appearance of the devastating pandemic called AIDS (Acquired Immune Deficiency Syndrome), a life-threatening disease that results from a retrovirus that attacks the blood cells of the body, thus causing a failure of the autoimmune system. Collectively, these phenomena represent an overwhelming challenge to traditional concepts of sexuality, sexual behavior, and (more generally) to conventional morality. They have also generated a provocative blurring of sex roles. And they have complicated the difficulty of distinguishing between forms of expression that have mere shock value and those that represent a substantial creative achievement. The photographs of Robert Mapplethorpe (1946–1989) are significant in this regard. Mapplethorpe's fine-grained silver gelatin prints display exquisitely composed images ranging from still life subjects to classically posed nudes. Although usually lacking explicit narrative, they reflect the artist's preoccupation with physical and sexual themes: male virility, sado-masochism, androgyny, and sexual identity. A sculptor in his early training, Mapplethorpe presents his subjects as pristine objects, occasionally transforming them into erotic symbols. His photographs depict contemporary sexuality in a manner that is at once detached and impassioned, but they often gain added power as gender-bending parodies of sexual stereotypes—witness the masculinity of the female model (herself a weight-lifter) in Figure **36.11** (see also Figure 37.17). Mapplethorpe fulfills the artist's mission to see things (in his words) "like they haven't been seen before."

Themes of human sexuality have also increasingly preoccupied twentieth-century writers. In her provocative science fiction fantasy *The Left Hand of Darkness* (1969), the African-American writer Ursula LeGuin (b. 1929) creates a distant planet, home to creatures with the sexual potential of both males and females. The ambisexuality of the characters in this fictional utopia calls into question human preconceptions about the defined roles of behavior for men and women. Through the device of science fiction, LeGuin suggests a shift in focus from the narrow view of male–female dualities (or opposites) to larger, more urgent matters of interdependence.

While LeGuin examines bisexuality in imaginary settings, others, and in particular gay artists, have dealt with the experience of homosexuality in their day-to-day lives. The past three decades have been especially rich in the production of art that either examines sexual "otherness" or reflects (and celebrates) a "gay sensibility."

Figure 36.11 Robert Mapplethorpe, *Lisa Lyon*, 1982. Silver gelatin print. © 1998 Estate of Robert Mapplethorpe. Courtesy Robert Miller Gallery, New York.

By drawing attention to the ways in which matters of sexuality affect society and its institutions, such art asserts that sexuality and power are as closely related as race and power or gender and power. For example, the Pulitzer Prize-winning play *Angels in America: A Gay Fantasia on National Themes* (written in two parts: *Millennium Approaches*, 1990, and *Perestroika*, 1993) by Tony Kushner (b. 1957) offers a radical vision of American society set against the AIDS epidemic and the politics of conservatism. Kushner urges that the old America—"straight," Protestant, and white—needs to look with greater objectivity at "the fringe" (the variety of ethnic, racial, and sexual minorities) that demands acceptance and its share of power. Kushner's riveting drama represents a movement for body-conscious politics and socially responsible art that animates the last decade of this century (see chapter 37).

Beyond issues of sexual orientation and the struggle against discrimination on the part of the transgendered minority, the more immediate issue of the AIDS pandemic has deeply affected artists of the late twentieth century. Although AIDS has afflicted all segments of the populations throughout the world, the largest group of AIDS victims in the West has been male homosexuals. This group, marginalized by mainstream society, is distinctive, however, in having produced a large number of outstanding artists, many of whom—Mapplethorpe included—have fallen victim to the HIV virus. The loss of so many members of the world arts community has motivated artists like Kushner to view contemporary society through the life-death mirror of AIDS, while at the same time emphasizing the need for compassion and justice. Sympathy for AIDS victims of every race, gender, and sexual orientation has called forth an important body of art. Such works range from hand-crafted folk memorials to sophisticated short stories, dance compositions, and symphonies. The Names Project Quilt, begun in 1985, engaged twenty thousand ordinary individuals, each of whom created a single 6-by 13-foot fabric panel in memory of someone who died of an HIV-related disease. In 1992, AIDS activists assembled the panels in 16-foot squares and took them to Washington, D.C., to protest governmental inaction with regard to the AIDS crisis. Commemorating the deaths of some 150,000 Americans, the Aids Quilt covered 15 acres of ground between the Washington

Figure 36.12 General Idea, *One Day of AZT and One Year of AZT*, March–April 1993. Installation view at The Power Plant, Toronto. Photo: Cheryl O'Brian, Toronto.

Monument and Lincoln Memorial. The Names Project continues: In 1996, the quilt panels numbered forty thousand, that is, double the figure of the original.

The AIDS crisis has been the central allegory in the installation project undertaken by the Canadian artists' group, General Idea. *One Day of AZT and One Year of AZT* (1991), a two-part installation featuring some 1,825 plastic pills, refers to typical daily and annual dosages of the AIDS-retardant medication. Circumscribing five coffinlike tablets that occupy the central space, the mock pills line the gallery walls like tiny tombstones (Figure **36.12**). An equally compelling response to the AIDS epidemic is the Symphony No. 1 (1990) by the American composer John Corigliano (b. 1938). Corigliano, whose contribution to postmodern opera is discussed in chapter 37, wrote the so-called *AIDS Symphony* to express his anger and grief at the loss of his many colleagues and friends to this disease. The union of harsh and tender passages that characterize this musical testament is especially effective in the first movement, appropriately entitled "Apologue:* Rage and Remembrance." One of the most recent monuments to the AIDS crisis is the controversial *Still/Here* (1994), a performance work conceived by the African-American dancer Bill T. Jones (b. 1952). For the piece Jones, who is himself HIV-positive, combined choreography and vocal music with video imagery derived in part from workshops he conducted with AIDS victims. *Still/Here* has provoked heated debate concerning the artistic value of issue-driven art: Does art that showcases sickness and death serve merely to manipulate viewers? This is only one of many questions that probe current efforts to wed art to social action (see chapter 37).

*An allegorical narrative usually intended to convey a moral.

SUMMARY

The quest for liberation from poverty, oppression, and inequality has been a prevailing theme in twentieth-century history. In dozens of countries, movements for decolonization followed World War II. At the same time and even into the last decades of the twentieth century, racial and ethnic minorities in various parts of the world have fought valiantly to oppose discrimination as practiced by the majority culture. These crusades are yet ongoing among the populations of Eastern Europe, Latin America, and elsewhere.

The struggle of African-Americans to achieve freedom from the evils of racism has a long and dramatic history. From the Harlem Renaissance in the early twentieth century through the civil rights movement of the 1960s, the arts have mirrored that history. In the poems of Langston Hughes and Gwendolyn Brooks, and in the novels of Richard Wright, James Baldwin, Ralph Ellison, and Alice Walker, the plight and the identity of the black in white America have been central themes. While the African-American contribution to literature and the visual arts has been significant, the impact of black culture on music and dance has been formidable. Blues and jazz giants from Louis Armstrong to Wynton Marsalis have produced a living body of popular music, while choreographers from Katherine Dunham to Alvin Ailey have inspired generations of dancers to draw on their African heritage.

During the postwar era, women throughout the world worked to gain political, economic, and social equality. The writings of the feminists Virginia Woolf and Simone de Beauvoir influenced women to examine the psychological conditions of their oppression. In America, the feminist movement elicited a virtual golden age in literature. The self-conscious poetry of Anne Sexton, Sonia Sanchez, and Adrienne Rich is representative of this phenomenon. In the visual arts, at least two generations of women have worked to redefine traditional concepts of female identity: first, by celebrating womanhood, and, more recently, by attacking outworn stereotypes. One of the most controversial of the twentieth century's liberation movements has centered on issues of sexual identity. Amidst the AIDS pandemic, artists like Robert Mapplethorpe and Tony Kushner have brought candor and perceptivity to matters of sexuality and sexual behavior. The art inspired by the liberation movements of the twentieth century is the tangible expression of a global search for personal freedom that continues to shape the humanistic tradition.

GLOSSARY

apartheid a policy of strict racial segregation and political and economic discrimination against the black population in the Union of South Africa

feminism the doctrine advocating equal social, political, and economic rights for women

scat singing a jazz performance style in which nonsense syllables replace the lyrics of a song

swing in jazz, a unique variation on rhythm in which some notes are held for longer or shorter periods or accented in ways that depart from their notated values; also, a jazz style featuring danceable rhythms, popular during the age of large dance bands (1932–1942)

MUSIC LISTENING SELECTIONS

Cassette II Selection 19 Handy, "St. Louis Blues," 1914.
Cassette II Selection 20 Hardin/Armstrong, "Hotter than That," 1927.
Cassette II Selection 21 Ellington, "Ko-Ko," Gillespie/Parker, 1945.

SUGGESTIONS FOR READING

Baker, Houston A. *Modernism and the Harlem Renaissance.* Chicago: University of Chicago Press, 1988.
Bechet, Sidney. *Treat It Gentle.* New York: DaCapo Press, 1975.
Broude, Norma, and Mary D. Garrard, eds. *The Power of Feminist Art: The American Movement of the 1970s, History and Impact.* New York: Abrams, 1996.
Chapman, Abraham, ed. *Black Voices: An Anthology of Afro-American Literature.* New York: New American Library, 1968.
Emery, Lynne Fauley. *Black Dance in the United States from 1619 to 1970.* Palo Alto, Calif.: National Press Books, 1972.
Fine, Elsa Honig. *The Afro-American Artist: A Search for Identity.* Reprint. New York: Hacker, 1982.
Lewis, Samella. *Art: African American.* Berkeley: University of California Press, 1994.
Long, Richard A. *The Black Tradition in American Dance.* New York: Rizzoli, 1989.
Oliver, Paul. *The Meaning of the Blues.* New York: Macmillan, 1963.
Parker, Rozsica, and Griselda Pollock. *Old Mistresses: Women, Art, and Ideology.* New York: Pantheon, 1982.
Powell, Richard J. *Black Art and Culture in the 20th Century.* New York: Thames and Hudson, 1995.
Riley, Glenda. *Inventing the American Woman: A Perspective on Women's History 1865 to the Present.* Arlington Heights, Ill.: Harlan Davidson, 1986.
Lucie-Smith, Edward. *Race, Sex, and Gender: Issues in Contemporary Art.* New York: Abrams, 1994.
Watson, Steven. *The Harlem Renaissance: Hub of African American Culture, 1920-1930.* New York: Pantheon, 1996.
Yates, Gayle G. *What Women Want: The Idea of the Movement.* Cambridge, Mass.: Harvard University Press, 1975.

37

The Arts in the Information Age

We are perhaps still too close to events of the past few decades to distinguish major cultural developments from minor and ephemeral ones. Nevertheless, there have been perceptible changes in all forms of cultural life. Two developments may be cited as crucial to these changes: The first is the shift from an industrial to an information age made possible by mass media and electronic means of storing, communicating, and accessing information. The second is the dawn of the space age—an era in which science and technology have propelled humankind beyond planet earth into outer space. These two developments, while not the only significant ones of this age, have worked to make the planet smaller and the universe larger: They have shrunk the distances between the inhabitants of the global community and, at the same time, confirmed our singular role as a human family.

The widespread use of television and computers has worked to effect the shift from an industrial to an information age. In today's First World societies, two-thirds or more of the population are engaged in occupations related to high technology rather than to farming, manufacturing, and service trades. Moreover, the tools of high technology have facilitated an information explosion of immense proportions. While in sixteenth-century Europe it was possible for an intellectual to have read every book ever printed, such a feat would be entirely impossible today. The number of books published between 1945 and 1970 alone equals that issued during the entire five-hundred-year period between the invention of the printing press and the end of World War I. Computer technology has accelerated the process of information production, storage, and retrieval: Multimedia "books" published on floppy discs and on-line electronic bookstores are only two of the newest resources of the information age, an age in which all parts of the global village are linked by the mass phenomenon known as the *information superhighway.*

The Information Explosion

Television and computers—the most pervasive forms of high technology—have altered almost every aspect of life in our time. Television, the wonderchild of electronics and the quintessential example of modern mass media, transmits sound and light by electromagnetic waves that carry information instantaneously into homes across the face of the earth. The very name "television" comes from the Greek word *tele,* meaning "far," and the Latin *videre,* meaning "to see"; hence "to see far." Television did not become a common fixture of middle-class life in First World nations until the 1950s, although it had been invented decades before then. By the 1960s the events of a war in the jungles of Vietnam were relayed via electronic communications satellite into American living rooms. In 1969, in a live telecast, the world saw the first astronauts walk on the surface of the moon. And in the early 1990s, during the Middle Eastern conflict triggered by the Iraqi invasion of Kuwait, Americans and Europeans witnessed the first "prime-time war"—a war that was "processed" by censorship and television newscasting.

The second major technological phenomenon of the information age is the computer. Digital computers, machines that process information in the form of numbers, were first used widely in the 1950s. By the 1960s, computers consisting of electronic circuits were able to perform millions of calculations per second. Smaller and more dependable than earlier models, electronic

1953 the introduction of the first commercially successful computer
1959 American engineers produce the first microchip (made from a silicon wafer)
1960 the first lasers are developed in America
1962 the U.S.A. launches the first commercial communications satellite
1970 fiber optics technology is perfected to carry information thousands of times faster than copper cables
1977 the first international conference on Chaos Theory is organized

computers facilitated various forms of instantaneous communication. More recently, computers have made possible the science of robotics and the creation of so-called artificial forms of intelligence. As more and more information is electronically stored, processed, and dispersed to ever-increasing numbers of individuals, the possibility of a "computopia," that is, a society run by computers, becomes both a promise and a threat; for, while a computerized society can provide its citizens with more leisure time, it might also work to diminish the human capacity for free thought and action.

The electronic media bring more information to more people, but they also alter the way in which information is presented. Communication in the information age is essentially image oriented. Film and television are fundamentally nonverbal modes of communication; they translate words into pictures. In contrast to print, a linear medium, electronic images are generated in diffuse, discontinuous bundles. Moreover, the electronic media tend to homogenize images, that is, to make all images uniform and alike. As information is homogenized, it tends to become devalued; product and message may be sacrificed to process and medium. As the mass media recycle an ill-sorted variety of historical fragments, culture itself becomes what one critic has called "a vast garage sale." Indeed, the electronic processing of information and the rapid diffusion of images via the television screen have worked to blur the differences between the diverse artifacts of the humanistic tradition. In contemporary society, commonplace responses to everyday life—the stuff of "popular culture"— are often indistinguishable from forms of elite or "high" culture. Television has turned all information, from protest marches to breakfast cereals, into marketable commodities. However, the electronic media have created a consumer society that often exercises little critical judgment with regard to the information it receives.

Unlike written and spoken modes of communication, which tend to isolate groups of people from one another, electronically processed visual images bring together the world's population. Reared on television, contemporary society is, according to French sociologist Jacques Ellul (b. 1912), the society of "mass man." Modern technology, explains Ellul, has contributed to producing a "psychological collectivism" that has robbed human beings of freedom and self-esteem. Ellul singles out advertising as the most pernicious factor in the evolution of mass man. According to Ellul, advertising is a form of totalitarian control that—like the process of behavioral conditioning in Huxley's *Brave New World*—subordinates the individual to the technostructure, thus destroying the last vestiges of human freedom and dignity. In his perceptive study of twentieth-century Western civilization, *The Technological Society* (1964), Ellul observed,

Advertising [affects] all people; or at least an overwhelming majority. Its goal is to persuade the masses to buy. . . . The inevitable consequence is the creation of the mass man. As advertising of the most varied products is concentrated, a new type of human being, precise and generalized, emerges. We can get a general impression of this new human type by studying America, where human beings tend clearly to become identified with the ideal of advertising. In America, advertising enjoys universal popular adherence and the American way of life is fashioned by it.*

Late Twentieth-Century Thought

Among the most significant scientific quests of the past three decades has been the search for the universal laws that govern the organization and complexity of matter. Chaos Theory, which had its beginnings in the 1970s, holds that patterns repeat themselves in various phenomena ranging from the formation of snowflakes to the rhythms of the human heart. These patterns, to all appearance random, unstable, and disorderly, are actually self-similar in scale, like the zigs and zags of a lightning bolt, or oscillating, as in electric currents. To Einstein's famous assertion: "God does not play dice with the universe," chaos theorists argue: Not only does God play dice with the universe, but they are loaded. Since the laws of complexity are believed to underlie all aspects of nature, they are being studied by physicists and astronomers, as well as by mathematicians, biologists, and computer scientists.

While science moves optimistically to reveal the underlying natural order, philosophy has entered a phase of radical skepticism that denies the existence of any true or uniform system of philosophy. Contemporary philosophers have fastened on the idea, first popularized by the Austrian philosopher Ludwig Wittgenstein (1889–1951), that all forms of expression, and, indeed, all truths, are dominated by the modes of language used to convey ideas. Wittgenstein, whose life's work was an inquiry into the ways in which language represents the world, argued that sentences (or propositions) were "pictures of reality." Following Wittgenstein, philosophers have tried to unlock the meaning of the *text* (that is, the mode of cultural expression) based on close analysis of its linguistic structure. Language theorists have suggested that one must "deconstruct" or "take apart" discourse in order to "unmask" the many meanings beneath the text. The leaders of *deconstruction*, the French philosophers Jacques Derrida (b. 1930) and

---

*Jacques Ellul, *The Technological Society*, translated by John Wilkinson. New York: Knopf, 1964, 407–408.

Michel Foucault (1926–1984), have been influential in arguing that all human beings are prisoners of the very language they use to think and describe the world. People erroneously believe, notes Foucault, that their language is their servant; they fail to apprehend that they are forever submitting to its demands. Philosophers, he asserts, should abandon the search for absolute truths and concentrate on the discovery of meaning(s). The American philsopher Richard Rorty (b. 1931) is deeply troubled by the limits of both linguistic inquiry and traditional philosophy. Rorty has argued that the great thinkers of the post-philosophical age are not the metaphysicians or the linguists but, rather, those artists whose works provide others with insights into achieving postmodern self-transformation.

Postmodernism

The term "postmodernism" came into use before World War II to describe the reaction to or against modernism, but more recently it has come to designate—quite broadly—the general cultural condition of the last forty years of the twentieth century. Whether seen as a reaction against modernism or as an entirely new form of modernism, postmodernism is a phenomenon that occurred principally in the West. As a style, it is marked by a bemused awareness of a historical past whose "reality" has been processed by mass communication and information technology. Postmodern artists appropriate (or borrow) pre-existing texts and images from history, advertising, and the media. Their playful amalgam of disparate styles and often contradictory ideas mingles the superficial and the profound and tends to dissolve the boundaries between "high" and "low" art. At the same time, their seemingly incongruous "layering" of images calls to mind the fundamentals of Chaos Theory, which uncovers a new geometry of the universe that is "broken up, twisted, tangled, intertwined."*

In contrast with the elitism of modernism, postmodernism is self-consciously populist, even to the point of inviting the active participation of the beholder. Whereas modern artists (consider Eliot or Kandinsky) exalt the artist as visionary and rebel, postmodern artists bring wry skepticism to the creative act. Less preoccupied than the modernists with formal abstraction and its redeeming power, postmodernists acknowledge art as an information system and a commodity. More than any other style in the arts of the last decades, postmodernism embraces the realm of the electronic media, its messages, and its modes of communication. Postmodern artists more closely resemble sign-manipulators than shamans; their stance is more disengaged than

authorial, their message more enigmatic than absolute. They share the contemporary philosopher's disdain for rational structure and the deconstructionist's fascination with the function of language. They offer alternatives to the high seriousness and introversion of modernist expression, and move instead in the direction of parody (burlesque imitation), whimsy, paradox, and irony.

Literature in the Information Age

Information age writers have explored a wide variety of literary styles and genres, the evidence of which is global in scope. Some have pursued the parodic techniques of *postmodernism*, while others have explored the rich ambiguities of *magic realism*. In both of these styles, but more usually as traditional narrative, there has been an uninterrupted outpouring of *social conscience literature*—fiction and non-fiction that addresses such issues as crime, ethnic dislocation, and ecological disaster. In the alternate realm of fantasy, the past few decades have witnessed the growth in popularity of *science fiction*, a genre of futuristic prose that has also inspired some of this century's finest films.

Postmodern Literature

Postmodern writers tend to bypass traditional narrative styles in favor of techniques that test or parody the writer's craft. Prose fiction in this style has been called "metafiction"—fiction about fiction. Such works are filled with fragments of information taken out of their original literary/historical context and juxtaposed with little or no commentary on their meaning. In a single story, a line from a poem by T. S. Eliot or a Shakespeare play may appear alongside a catchy saying or banal slogan from a television commercial, a phrase from a national anthem, or a shopping list, as if the writer were claiming all information as equally valuable. In postmodern fiction, characters undergo little or no development, plots often lack logical direction, and events—whether ordinary, perverse, or fantastic—may be described in the detached tone of a newspaper article. Like the television newscast, the language of postmodern fiction is often diffuse, discontinuous, and filled with innuendo and "commentary." Black humor novelist Kurt Vonnegut (b. 1922) uses clipped sentences framed in the present tense. This technique creates a kind of "videofiction" that seems aimed at readers whose attention spans are linked to television programming and instant intellectual gratification. The Italian writer Italo Calvino (b. 1923) engages the reader in a hunt for meanings that lie in the spaces between the act of writing and the events the words describe. Calvino interrupts the story line of his novel *If On a Winter's Night a Traveler* (1979) to confront the reader, thus:

---

*James Gleick, *Chaos: Making a New Science*. New York: Viking, 1987, 94.

For a couple of pages now you have been reading on, and this would be the time to tell you clearly whether this station where I have got off is a station of the past or a station of today; instead the sentences continue to move in vagueness, grayness, in a kind of no man's land of experience reduced to the lowest kind of denominator. Watch out: it is surely a method of involving you gradually, capturing you in the story before you realize it—a trap. Or perhaps the author still has not made up his mind, just as you, reader, for that matter, are not sure what you would most like to read.*

As with the writers of metafiction, so too among postmodern poets, there has been a preference for verse that has as much reference to language as to that which language describes. Postmodern poets convey the idea that language shapes and articulates the self. The Mexican poet and critic Octavio Paz (b. 1914) expresses this idea in the poem "To Talk," in which he defines language as sacred—a human version of divine power. Others, like the American poet John Ashbery (b. 1927), write verse that may be cryptic, wry, and inscrutable. In the poem "Paradoxes and Oxymorons," Ashbery suggests that both language and life are filled with conditions that are incongruous, contradictory, and intrinsically human. The Irish poet and 1995 Nobel Prize-winner Seamus Heaney (b. 1939) shares with American postmodernists an inclination to conversational and minimal fragments, or "sound bites"; however, he is unsurpassed in lyricism (a gift inherited from fellow Irishman W. B. Yeats) and in his ability to translate the data of everyday experience into transcendent ideas. The poetry of these three postmodernists stands in striking contrast to the self-conscious, anxious (and often moralizing) verse of the modernists.

READING 6.28

Postmodern Poems

Paz's "To Talk"

I read in a poem: 1
to talk is divine.
But gods don't speak:
they create and destroy worlds
while men do the talking,   5
Gods, without words,
play terrifying games.

The spirit descends,
untying tongues,
but it doesn't speak words: 10
it speaks flames.

Language, lit by a god
is a prophecy
of flames and a crash
of burnt syllables: 15
meaningless ash.

Man's word
is the daughter of death.
We talk because we are
mortal: words   20
are not signs, they are years.
Saying what they say,
the names we speak
say time: they say us,
we are the names of time.   25
To talk is human.

(1987)

Ashbery's "Paradoxes and Oxymorons"[1]

This poem is concerned with language on a very plain
  level.   1
Look at it talking to you. You look out a window
Or pretend to fidget. You have it but you don't have it.
You miss it, it misses you. You miss each other.

The poem is sad because it wants to be yours, and
  cannot.   5
What's a plain level? It is that and other things,
Bringing a system of them into play. Play?
Well, actually, yes, but I consider play to be

A deeper outside thing, a dreamed role-pattern,
As in the division of grace these long August days   10
Without proof. Open-ended. And before you know
It gets lost in the steam and chatter of typewriters.

It has been played once more. I think you exist only
To tease me into doing it, on your level, and then you
  aren't there
Or have adopted a different attitude. And the poem   15
Has set me softly down beside you. The poem is you.

(1981)

Heaney's *Squarings*: "I. Lightenings, ii"

Roof it again. Batten down. Dig in.   1
Drink out of tin. Know the scullery cold,
A latch, a door-bar, forged tongs and a grate.

Touch the cross-beam, drive iron in a wall,
Hang a line to verify the plumb   5
From lintel, coping-stone and chimney-breast.

Relocate the bedrock in the threshold.
Take squarings from the recessed gable pane.
Make your study the unregarded floor.

Sink every impulse like a bolt. Secure   10
The bastion of sensation. Do not waver
Into language. Do not waver in it.   (1991)

———————————————◆———————————————

*Italo Calvino, *If On a Winter's Night a Traveler*, translated by William Weaver. New York: Harcourt Brace Jovanovich, 1981, 12.

[1] A paradox is a statement that seems contradictory or absurd, but may actually be true. An oxymoron is a combination of contradictory terms, such as "wise fool" or "cruel kindness" (see Reading 4.23).

Magic Realism

Magic realism (described in chapter 33) is a style that mixes fantasy and realism in ways that evoke a dream-like or mythic reality. This narrative focus characterizes much of the literature of the Latin American "Boom," an explosion of literary virtuosity that began in the late 1960s. It is especially evident in the fiction writings of the Colombian novelist Gabriel García Marquéz (b. 1928) and the Chilean writer Isabel Allende (b. 1943). An experienced journalist, Allende is one of the most hypnotic storytellers of our time: Her short stories begin with a single image that unfolds much like a folk or fairy tale. Allende credits the influence of film and television for the modern tendency to "think in images" and to write in short, tightly packed sentences. She claims, however, that the first sentences of her stories are "dictated" to her in a magical manner. In the story "Two Words," Allende combines terse, straightforward narrative and sensuous allegory to interweave universal themes of language, love, and power.

READING 6.29
Allende's "Two Words"

She went by the name of Belisa Crepusculario, not   1
because she had been baptized with that name or given it
by her mother, but because she herself had searched
until she found the poetry of "beauty" and "twilight" and
cloaked herself in it. She made her living selling words.
She journeyed through the country from the high cold
mountains to the burning coasts, stopping at fairs and in
markets where she set up four poles covered by a canvas
awning under which she took refuge from the sun and rain
to minister to her customers. She did not have to peddle   10
her merchandise because from having wandered far and
near, everyone knew who she was. Some people waited for
her from one year to the next, and when she appeared in
the village with her bundle beneath her arm, they would
form a line in front of her stall. Her prices were fair. For five
centavos she delivered verses from memory; for seven she
improved the quality of dreams; for nine she wrote love
letters; for twelve she invented insults for irreconcilable
enemies. She also sold stories, not fantasies but long, true
stories she recited at one telling, never skipping a word.   20
This is how she carried news from one town to another.
People paid her to add a line or two: our son was born; so-
and-so died; our children got married; the crops burned
in the field. Wherever she went a small crowd gathered
around to listen as she began to speak, and that was how
they learned about each other's doings, about distant
relatives, about what was going on in the civil war. To
anyone who paid her fifty centavos in trade, she gave the
gift of a secret word to drive away melancholy. It was not
the same word for everyone, naturally, because that would   30
have been collective deceit. Each person received his or
her own word, with the assurance that no one else would
use it that way in this universe or the Beyond.

Belisa Crepusculario had been born into a family so poor

they did not even have names to give their children. She
came into the world and grew up in an inhospitable land
where some years the rains became avalanches of water
that bore everything away before them and others when
not a drop fell from the sky and the sun swelled to fill the
horizon and the world became a desert. Until she was   40
twelve, Belisa had no occupation or virtue other than
having withstood hunger and the exhaustion of centuries.
During one interminable drought, it fell to her to bury four
younger brothers and sisters; when she realized that her
turn was next, she decided to set out across the plains in
the direction of the sea, in hopes that she might trick death
along the way. The land was eroded, split with deep cracks,
strewn with rocks, fossils of trees and thorny bushes, and
skeletons of animals bleached by the sun. From time to
time she ran into families who, like her, were heading   50
south, following the mirage of water. Some had begun the
march carrying their belongings on their backs or in small
carts, but they could barely move their own bones, and
after a while they had to abandon their possessions. They
dragged themselves along painfully, their skin turned to
lizard hide and their eyes burned by the reverberating
glare. Belisa greeted them with a wave as she passed, but
she did not stop, because she had no strength to waste in
acts of compassion. Many people fell by the wayside, but
she was so stubborn that she survived to cross through that   60
hell and at long last reach the first trickles of water, fine,
almost invisible threads that fed spindly vegetation and
farther down widened into small streams and marshes.

Belisa Crepusculario saved her life and in the process
accidentally discovered writing. In a village near the
coast, the wind blew a page of newspaper at her feet. She
picked up the brittle yellow paper and stood a long while
looking at it, unable to determine its purpose, until
curiosity overcame her shyness. She walked over to a man
who was washing his horse in the muddy pool where she   70
had quenched her thirst.

"What is this?" she asked.

"The sports page of the newspaper," the man replied,
concealing his surprise at her ignorance.

The answer astounded the girl, but she did not want to
seem rude, so she merely inquired about the significance
of the fly tracks scattered across the page.

"Those are words, child. Here it says that Fulgencio
Barba knocked out El Negro Tiznao in the third round."

That was the day Belisa Crepusculario found out that   80
words make their way in the world without a master, and
that anyone with a little cleverness can appropriate them
and do business with them. She made a quick assessment
of her situation and concluded that aside from becoming a
prostitute or working as a servant in the kitchens of the
rich there were few occupations she was qualified for. It
seemed to her that selling words would be an honorable
alternative. From that moment on, she worked at that
profession, and was never tempted by any other. At the
beginning, she offered her merchandise unaware that   90
words could be written outside of newspapers. When she
learned otherwise, she calculated the infinite possibilities
of her trade and with her savings paid a priest twenty pesos
to teach her to read and write; with her three remaining
coins she bought a dictionary. She pored over it from A to
Z and then threw it into the sea, because it was not her
intention to defraud her customers with packaged words.

One August morning several years later, Belisa Crepusculario was sitting in her tent in the middle of a plaza, surrounded by the uproar of market day, selling 100 legal arguments to an old man who had been trying for sixteen years to get his pension. Suddenly she heard yelling and thudding hoofbeats. She looked up from her writing and saw, first, a cloud of dust, and then a band of horsemen come galloping into the plaza. They were the Colonel's men, sent under orders of El Mulato, a giant known throughout the land for the speed of his knife and his loyalty to his chief. Both the Colonel and El Mulato had spent their lives fighting in the civil war, and their names were ineradicably linked to devastation and 110 calamity. The rebels swept into town like a stampeding herd, wrapped in noise, bathed in sweat, and leaving a hurricane of fear in their trail. Chickens took wing, dogs ran for their lives, women and children scurried out of sight, until the only living soul left in the market was Belisa Crepusculario. She had never seen El Mulato and was surprised to see him walking toward her.

"I'm looking for you," he shouted, pointing his coiled whip at her; even before the words were out, two men rushed her—knocking over her canopy and shattering 120 her inkwell—bound her hand and foot, and threw her like a sea bag across the rump of El Mulato's mount. Then they thundered off toward the hills.

Hours later, just as Belisa Crepusculario was near death, her heart ground to sand by the pounding of the horse, they stopped, and four strong hands set her down. She tried to stand on her feet and hold her head high, but her strength failed her and she slumped to the ground, sinking into a confused dream. She awakened several hours later to the murmur of night in the camp, but 130 before she had time to sort out the sounds, she opened her eyes and found herself staring into the impatient glare of El Mulato, kneeling beside her.

"Well, woman, at last you've come to," he said. To speed her to her senses, he tipped his canteen and offered her a sip of liquor laced with gunpowder.

She demanded to know the reason for such rough treatment, and El Mulato explained that the Colonel needed her services. He allowed her to splash water on her face, and then led her to the far end of the camp 140 where the most feared man in all the land was lazing in a hammock strung between two trees. She could not see his face, because he lay in the deceptive shadow of the leaves and the indelible shadow of all his years as a bandit, but she imagined from the way his gigantic aide addressed him with such humility that he must have a very menacing expression. She was surprised by the Colonel's voice, as soft and well-modulated as a professor's.

"Are you the woman who sells words?" he asked.

"At your service," she stammered, peering into the 150 dark and trying to see him better.

The Colonel stood up, and turned straight toward her. She saw dark skin and the eyes of a ferocious puma, and she knew immediately that she was standing before the loneliest man in the world.

"I want to be President," he announced.

The Colonel was weary of riding across that godforsaken land, waging useless wars and suffering defeats that no subterfuge could transform into victories. For years he had been sleeping in the open air, bitten by mosquitoes, 160 eating iguanas and snake soup, but those minor inconveniences were not why he wanted to change his destiny. What truly troubled him was the terror he saw in people's eyes. He longed to ride into a town beneath a triumphal arch with bright flags and flowers everywhere; he wanted to be cheered, and be given newly laid eggs and freshly baked bread. Men fled at the sight of him, children trembled, and women miscarried from fright; he had had enough, and so he had decided to become President. El Mulato had suggested that they ride to the 170 capital, gallop up to the Palace, and take over the government, the way they had taken so many other things without anyone's permission. The Colonel, however, did not want to be just another tyrant; there had been enough of those before him and, besides, if he did that, he would never win people's hearts. It was his aspiration to win the popular vote in the December elections.

"To do that, I have to talk like a candidate. Can you sell me the words for a speech?" the Colonel asked Belisa Crepusculario. 180

She had accepted many assignments, but none like this. She did not dare refuse, fearing that El Mulato would shoot her between the eyes, or worse still, that the Colonel would burst into tears. There was more to it than that, however; she felt the urge to help him because she felt a throbbing warmth beneath her skin, a powerful desire to touch that man, to fondle him, to clasp him in her arms.

All night and a good part of the following day, Belisa Crepusculario searched her repertory for words adequate 190 for a presidential speech, closely watched by El Mulato, who could not take his eyes from her firm wanderer's legs and virginal breasts. She discarded harsh, cold words, words that were too flowery, words worn from abuse, words that offered improbable promises, untruthful and confusing words, until all she had left were words sure to touch the minds of men and women's intuition. Calling upon the knowledge she had purchased from the priest for twenty pesos, she wrote the speech on a sheet of paper and then signaled El Mulato to untie the rope that 200 bound her ankles to a tree. He led her once more to the Colonel, and again she felt the throbbing anxiety that had seized her when she first saw him. She handed him the paper and waited while he looked at it, holding it gingerly between thumbs and fingertips.

"What the shit does this say?" he asked finally.

"Don't you know how to read?"

"War's what I know," he replied.

She read the speech aloud. She read it three times, so her client could engrave it on his memory. When she 210 finished, she saw the emotion in the faces of the soldiers who had gathered round to listen, and saw that the Colonel's eyes glittered with enthusiasm, convinced that with those words the presidential chair would be his.

"If after they've heard it three times, the boys are still standing there with their mouths hanging open, it must mean the thing's damn good, Colonel" was El Mulato's approval.

"All right, woman. How much do I owe you?" the leader asked. 220

"One peso, Colonel."

"That's not much," he said, opening the pouch he wore at his belt, heavy with proceeds from the last foray.

"The peso entitles you to a bonus. I'm going to give you two secret words," said Belisa Crepusculario.

"What for?"

She explained that for every fifty centavos a client paid, she gave him the gift of a word for his exclusive use. The Colonel shrugged. He had no interest at all in her offer, but he did not want to be impolite to someone who had   230 served him so well. She walked slowly to the leather stool where he was sitting, and bent down to give him her gift. The man smelled the scent of a mountain cat issuing from the woman, a fiery heat radiating from her hips, he heard the terrible whisper of her hair, and a breath of sweetmint murmured into his ear the two secret words that were his alone.

"They are yours, Colonel," she said as she stepped back. "You may use them as much as you please."

El Mulato accompanied Belisa to the roadside, his eyes   240 as entreating as a stray dog's, but when he reached out to touch her, he was stopped by an avalanche of words he had never heard before; believing them to be an irrevocable curse, the flame of his desire was extinguished.

During the months of September, October, and November the Colonel delivered his speech so many times that had it not been crafted from glowing and durable words it would have turned to ash as he spoke. He traveled up and down and across the country, riding into cities with a triumphal air, stopping in even the most forgotten   250 villages where only the dump heap betrayed a human presence, to convince his fellow citizens to vote for him. While he spoke from a platform erected in the middle of the plaza, El Mulato and his men handed out sweets and painted his name on all the walls in gold frost. No one paid the least attention to those advertising ploys; they were dazzled by the clarity of the Colonel's proposals and the poetic lucidity of his arguments, infected by his powerful wish to right the wrongs of history, happy for the first time in their lives. When the Candidate had finished   260 his speech, his soldiers would fire their pistols into the air and set off firecrackers, and when finally they rode off, they left behind a wake of hope that lingered for days on the air, like the splendid memory of a comet's tail. Soon the Colonel was the favorite. No one had ever witnessed such a phenomenon: a man who surfaced from the civil war, covered with scars and speaking like a professor, a man whose fame spread to every corner of the land and captured the nation's heart. The press focused their attention on him. Newspapermen came from far away to   270 interview him and repeat his phrases, and the number of his followers and enemies continued to grow.

"We're doing great, Colonel," said El Mulato, after twelve successful weeks of campaigning.

But the Candidate did not hear. He was repeating his secret words, as he did more and more obsessively. He said them when he was mellow with nostalgia; he murmured them in his sleep; he carried them with him on horseback; he thought them before delivering his famous speech; and he caught himself savoring them in his   280 leisure time. And every time he thought of those two words, he thought of Belisa Crepusculario, and his senses were inflamed with the memory of her feral scent, her fiery heat, the whisper of her hair, and her sweetmint breath in his ear, until he began to go around like a sleepwalker,

and his men realized that he might die before he ever sat in the presidential chair.

"What's got hold of you, Colonel?" El Mulato asked so often that finally one day his chief broke down and told him the source of his befuddlement: those two words   290 that were buried like two daggers in his gut.

"Tell me what they are and maybe they'll lose their magic," his faithful aide suggested.

"I can't tell them, they're for me alone," the Colonel replied.

Saddened by watching his chief decline like a man with a death sentence on his head, El Mulato slung his rifle over his shoulder and set out to find Belisa Crepusculario. He followed her trail through all that vast country, until he found her in a village in the far south, sitting under   300 her tent reciting her rosary of news. He planted himself, spraddle-legged, before her, weapon in hand.

"You! You're coming with me," he ordered.

She had been waiting. She picked up her inkwell, folded the canvas of her small stall, arranged her shawl around her shoulders, and without a word took her place behind El Mulato's saddle. They did not exchange so much as a word in all the trip; El Mulato's desire for her had turned into rage, and only his fear of her tongue prevented his cutting her to shreds with his whip. Nor was he inclined   310 to tell her that the Colonel was in a fog, and that a spell whispered into his ear had done what years of battle had not been able to do. Three days later they arrived at the encampment, and immediately, in view of all the troops, El Mulato led his prisoner before the Candidate.

"I brought this witch here so you can give her back her words, Colonel," El Mulato said, pointing the barrel of his rifle at the woman's head. "And then she can give you back your manhood."

The Colonel and Belisa Crepusculario stared at each   320 other, measuring one another from a distance. The men knew then that their leader would never undo the witchcraft of those accursed words, because the whole world could see the voracious-puma eyes soften as the woman walked to him and took his hand in hers.

———————◆———————

The Literature of Social Conscience: Poetry

Since the 1950s writers have become especially attentive to issues and themes that are products of our age, and, at the same time, are global in reach. Urban violence, ethnic and racial division, homelessness, and the search for spiritual renewal in a commodity-driven world are major themes in the literature of the late twentieth century. Writers of the past few decades have also explored the effects of modern scientific and electronic technology upon the environment and its inhabitants. In the chapter "A Look at the Year 2000" from Ellul's *Technological Society,* the sociologist predicts that a wide variety of devices, from tranquilizers to artificial insemination, may be used to shape and control the society of the future. **Ecologists** (those who study the interrelationships between organisms and their environments) observe that while modern technology has brought vast benefits to millions of people, it has also worked to violate the global environment. The technology of any one country or region potentially affects the entire global village. For instance, sulphur dioxide and other industrial by-products emitted in one area cause acid rain that damages forests, lakes, and soil in another part of the world. Industrial pollution poisons rivers and oceans. And leaks in nuclear reactors endanger populations thousands of miles from their sites. Such realities, all of which threaten our global environment, have inspired a more holistic regard for the destiny of planet earth.

Contemporary writers have expressed increasing concern over the possibility of ecological disaster. None, however, has spoken for the survival of the planet so passionately as the American poet Gary Snyder (b. 1930). Snyder grew up on a small farm in the Pacific Northwest. His affection for the Native American populations of that region, his travels throughout Asia, and his keen appreciation of Daoism and Zen Buddhism give shape to his pantheistic credo that all creatures (indeed, all living forms) constitute a single whole—the whole of nature. This notion, often associated with the Gaia hypothesis, holds that the earth is a single, purposeful, living whole and the ecosystem an obvious model for global integration. In his poetry Snyder tries to achieve a balance between "the world of people and language and society" and "the nonhuman, nonverbal world, which is nature as nature in itself." In the "Smokey the Bear Sutra," a poem humorously styled on a Buddhist instructional discourse (see chapter 8), Snyder combines Eastern ritual and Western pop culture to warn that the human race is destroying the planet. The American folk hero Smokey the Bear becomes the counterpart of the Great Sun Buddha, who, in the poem, preaches the truth of universal survival.

While ecological disaster poses a slow, insidious threat to the global community, political terrorism wears the face of immediate, overt violence. Terrorist bombs threaten the safety and freedom of human beings in public places throughout the world, victimizing the innocent and creating a climate of insecurity and fear. The Polish poet and winner of the Nobel Prize for poetry in 1996, Wislawa Szymborska (b. 1923), comments on these aspects of contemporary life in the poem "The Terrorist, He Watches." Like Snyder, Szymborska

1962 Rachel Carson's *Silent Spring* argues that manmade chemicals are damaging the earth's ecosystem

1967 Christian Barnard (South African) performs the first human heart transplant

1973 American biochemists isolate genes to make genetic engineering possible

1974 American scientists demonstrate that chlorofluorocarbons (CFCs) are eroding the earth's ozone layer

(pronounced "sheem-BOR-ska") prefers straightforward, conversational speech to the verbal complexities of postmodern poets. Her poems convey a humane and moral urgency that is both universal and personal. In the nervous, yet nonchalant, "voice" of this poet, one detects the gentle apprehension of somebody who has lived most of her life in communist-controlled Poland—a country that lost nearly one-fifth of its population during World War II.

READING 6.30

The Poems of Snyder and Szymborska

Snyder's "Smokey the Bear Sutra"[1]

Once in the Jurassic, about 150 million years ago,   1
the Great Sun Buddha in this corner of the Infinite
Void gave a great Discourse to all the assembled elements
and energies: to the standing beings, the walking beings,
the flying beings, and the sitting beings—even grasses,   5
to the number of thirteen billion, each one born from a
seed, were assembled there: a Discourse concerning
Enlightenment on the planet Earth.

"In some future time, there will be a continent called
America. It will have great centers of power called   10
such as Pyramid Lake, Walden Pond, Mt. Rainier, Big Sur,
Everglades, and so forth; and powerful nerves and
          channels
such as Columbia River, Mississippi River, and Grand
          Canyon.
The human race in that era will get into troubles all over
its head, and practically wreck everything in spite of   15
its own strong intelligent Buddha-nature."

"The twisting strata of the great mountains and the
          pulsings
of great volcanoes are my love burning deep in the earth.
My obstinate compassion is schist and basalt and
granite, to be mountains, to bring down the rain. In that   20
future American Era I shall enter a new form: to cure
the world of loveless knowledge that seeks with blind
          hunger;
and mindless rage eating food that will not fill it."

And he showed himself in his true form of
          SMOKEY THE BEAR   25
A handsome smokey-colored brown bear standing on
his hind legs, showing that he is aroused and watchful.
Bearing in his right paw the Shovel that digs to the
truth beneath appearances; cuts the roots of useless
attachments, and flings damp sand on the fires of greed
          and war;   30
His left paw in the Mudra[2] of Comradely Display—
          indicating
that all creatures have the full right to live to their limits
and that deer, rabbits, chipmunks, snakes, dandelions,
and lizards all grow in the realm of the Dharma;[3]
          Wearing the blue work overalls symbolic of slaves and   35

---

[1]Gary Snyder, "Smokey the Bear Sutra" (may be reproduced free forever).
[2]A hand gesture in Indian yoga and classical dance.
[3]The Law, or basic universal principles, according to Hindu and Buddhist doctrine.

laborers, the countless men oppressed by a civilization
that claims to save but only destroys;

Wearing the broad-brimmed hat of the West, symbolic of
the forces that guard the Wilderness, which is the Natural
State of the Dharma and the True Path of man on earth;   40
all true paths lead through mountains—

With a halo of smoke and flame behind, the forest fires
of the kali-yuga,[4] fires caused by the stupidity of those who
think things can be gained and lost whereas in truth all is
contained vast and free in the Blue Sky and Green Earth   45
of One Mind;

Round-bellied to show his kind nature and that the great
earth has food enough for everyone who loves her and
trusts her;

Trampling underfoot wasteful freeways and needless   50
suburbs; smashing the worms of capitalism and
        totalitarianism;

Indicating the Task: his followers, becoming free of cars,
houses, canned food, universities, and shoes, master the
Three Mysteries of their own Body, Speech, and Mind; and
fearlessly chop down the rotten trees and prune out the   55
sick lambs of this country America and then burn the
leftover trash.

Wrathful but Calm, Austere but Comic, Smokey the Bear will
Illuminate those who would help him; but for those who would
hinder or slander him,   60
        HE WILL PUT THEM OUT
Thus his great Mantra:[5]
        Namah samanta vajranam chanda maharoshana
        Sphataya hum traka ham mam
        "I DEDICATE MYSELF TO THE UNIVERSAL DIAMOND   65
        BE THIS RAGING FURY DESTROYED"
And he will protect those who love woods and rivers,
Gods and animals, hobos and madmen, prisoners and sick
people, musicians, playful women, and hopeful children;
And if anyone is threatened by advertising, air pollution,   70
or the police, they should chant SMOKEY THE BEAR'S
        WAR SPELL:
        DROWN THEIR BUTTS
        CRUSH THEIR BUTTS
        DROWN THEIR BUTTS   75
        CRUSH THEIR BUTTS
And SMOKEY THE BEAR will surely appear to put the
        enemy out with his vajra[6]—shovel.

Now those who recite this Sutra and then try to put it in
        practice will accumulate merit as countless as the
        sands of Arizona and Nevada,   80
Will help save the planet Earth from total oil slick,
Will enter the age of harmony of man and nature,
Will win the tender love and caresses of men, women,
        and beasts
Will always have ripe blackberries to eat and a sunny spot
        under a pine tree to sit at,   85
AND IN THE END WILL WIN HIGHEST PERFECT
        ENLIGHTENMENT thus have we heard.   (1969)

---

[4]In Indian thought, the last and most evil phase of the four cycles
of creation.
[5]A mystical formula recited by Hindus and Buddhists.
[6]A Sanskrit word meaning "thunderbolt."

Szymborska's "The Terrorist, He Watches"

The bomb will explode in the bar at twenty past one.   1
Now it's only sixteen minutes past.
Some will still have time to enter,
some to leave.

The terrorist's already on the other side.   5
That distance protects him from all harm
and, well, it's like the pictures:

A woman in a yellow jacket, she enters.
A man in dark glasses, he leaves.
Boys in jeans, they're talking.   10
Sixteen minutes past and four seconds.
The smaller one, he's lucky, mounts his scooter,
but that taller chap, he walks in.

Seventeen minutes and forty seconds.
A girl, she walks by, a green ribbon in her hair.   15
But that bus suddenly hides her.
Eighteen minutes past.
The girl's disappeared.
Was she stupid enough to go in, or wasn't she.
We shall see when they bring out the bodies.   20

Nineteen minutes past.
No one else appears to be going in.
On the other hand, a fat bald man leaves.
But seems to seach his pockets and
at ten seconds to twenty past one   25
he returns to look for his wretched gloves.

It's twenty past one.
Time, how it drags.
Surely, it's now.
No, not quite.   30
Yes, now.
The bomb, it explodes.   (1976)

————————◆————————

The Literature of Social Conscience: Prose Fiction

Issues that drive social conscience—racial violence, political terrorism, drugs, and street crime, for instance—have occupied the literary generation of our time. Writers have found that while the visual images of film and TV reveal human values only superficially, narrative prose still performs an invaluable function. Among the leading voices in the domain of contemporary fiction are Chinua Achebe and Joyce Carol Oates. Their work, examples of which are reproduced below, provides some insight into the literature of social conscience. "Dead Men's Path" by Chinua Achebe (b. 1930), Africa's leading English-language writer, deals with present-day bicultural conflicts that plague many parts of black Africa; at the same time the story probes larger, more universal tensions—those between tradition and innovation, between spiritual and secular allegiances, and between faith and reason—tensions which continue to affect and shape human values.

READING 6.31
Achebe's "Dead Men's Path"

Michael Obi's hopes were fulfilled much earlier than he had expected. He was appointed headmaster of Ndume Central School in January 1949. It had always been an unprogressive school, so the Mission authorities decided to send a young and energetic man to run it. Obi accepted this responsibility with enthusiasm. He had many wonderful ideas and this was an opportunity to put them into practice. He had had sound secondary school education which designated him a "pivotal teacher" in the official records and set him apart from the other headmasters in the mission field. He was outspoken in his condemnation of the narrow views of these older and often less-educated ones.

"We shall make a good job of it, shan't we?" he asked his young wife when they first heard the joyful news of his promotion.

"We shall do our best," she replied. "We shall have such beautiful gardens and everything will be just *modern* and delightful. . . ." In their two years of married life she had become completely infected by his passion for "modern methods" and his denigration of "these old and superannuated people in the teaching field who would be better employed as traders in the Onitsha market." She began to see herself already as the admired wife of the young headmaster, the queen of the school.

The wives of the other teachers would envy her position. She would set the fashion in everything. . . . Then, suddenly, it occurred to her that there might not be other wives. Wavering between hope and fear, she asked her husband, looking anxiously at him.

"All our colleagues are young and unmarried," he said with enthusiasm which for once she did not share. "Which is a good thing," he continued.

"Why?"

"Why? They will give all their time and energy to the school."

Nancy was downcast. For a few minutes she became sceptical about the new school; but it was only for a few minutes. Her little personal misfortune could not blind her to her husband's happy prospects. She looked at him as he sat folded up in a chair. He was stoop-shouldered and looked frail. But he sometimes surprised people with sudden bursts of physical energy. In his present posture, however, all his bodily strength seemed to have retired behind his deep-set eyes, giving them an extraordinary power of penetration. He was only twenty-six, but looked thirty or more. On the whole, he was not unhandsome.

"A penny for your thoughts, Mike," said Nancy after a while, imitating the woman's magazine she read.

"I was thinking what a grand opportunity we've got at last to show these people how a school should be run."

Ndume School was backward in every sense of the word. Mr. Obi put his whole life into the work, and his wife hers too. He had two aims. A high standard of teaching was insisted upon, and the school compound was to be turned into a place of beauty. Nancy's dream-gardens came to life with the coming of the rains, and blossomed. Beautiful hibiscus and allamanda hedges in brilliant red and yellow marked out the carefully tended school compound from the rank neighbourhood bushes.

One evening as Obi was admiring his work he was scandalized to see an old woman from the village hobble right across the compound, through a marigold flowerbed and the hedges. On going up there he found faint signs of an almost disused path from the village across the school compound to the bush on the other side.

"It amazes me," said Obi to one of his teachers who had been three years in the school, "that you people allowed the villagers to make use of this footpath. It is simply incredible." He shook his head.

"The path," said the teacher apologetically, "appears to be very important to them. Although it is hardly used, it connects the village shrine with their place of burial."

"And what has that got to do with the school?" asked the headmaster.

"Well, I don't know," replied the other with a shrug of the shoulders. "But I remember there was a big row some time ago when we attempted to close it."

"That was some time ago. But it will not be used now," said Obi as he walked away. "What will the Government Education Officer think of this when he comes to inspect the school next week? The villagers might, for all I know, decide to use the schoolroom for a pagan ritual during the inspection."

Heavy sticks were planted closely across the path at the two places where it entered and left the school premises. These were further strengthened with barbed wire.

Three days later the village priest of *Ani* called on the headmaster. He was an old man and walked with a slight stoop. He carried a stout walking-stick which he usually tapped on the floor, by way of emphasis, each time he made a new point in his argument.

"I have heard," he said after the usual exchange of cordialities, "that our ancestral footpath has recently been closed. . . ."

"Yes," replied Mr. Obi. "We cannot allow people to make a highway of our school compound."

"Look here, my son," said the priest bringing down his walking-stick, "this path was here before you were born and before your father was born. The whole life of this village depends on it. Our dead relatives depart by it and our ancestors visit us by it. But most important, it is the path of children coming in to be born. . . ."

Mr. Obi listened with a satisfied smile on his face.

"The whole purpose of our school," he said finally, "is to eradicate just such beliefs as that. Dead men do not require footpaths. The whole idea is just fantastic. Our duty is to teach your children to laugh at such ideas."

"What you say may be true," replied the priest, "but we follow the practices of our fathers. If you re-open the path we shall have nothing to quarrel about. What I always say is: let the hawk perch and let the eagle perch." He rose to go.

"I am sorry," said the young headmaster. "But the school compound cannot be a thoroughfare. It is against our regulations. I would suggest your constructing another path, skirting our premises. We can even get our boys to help in building it. I don't suppose the ancestors will find the little detour too burdensome."

"I have no more words to say," said the old priest, already outside.

Two days later a young woman in the village died in childbed. A diviner was immediately consulted and he prescribed heavy sacrifices to propitiate ancestors insulted by the fence.

Obi woke up next morning among the ruins of his work. The beautiful hedges were torn up not just near the path but right round the school, the flowers trampled to death and one of the school buildings pulled down.   130
. . . That day, the white Supervisor came to inspect the school and wrote a nasty report on the state of the premises but more seriously about the "tribal-war situation developing between the school and the village, arising in part from the misguided zeal of the new headmaster."

———————◆———————

Joyce Carol Oates (b. 1938) deals with the violent underlayer of contemporary society. The story "Ace" is a highly concentrated kind of prose fiction that Oates calls the "miniature narrative." Its tale of random violence—the familiar fare of the daily broadcast television news—unfolds with cinematic intensity, an effect embellished by powerful present-tense narrative and vivid characterization.

READING 6.32

Oates' "Ace"

A gang of overgrown boys, aged eighteen to twenty-five,   1
has taken over the northeast corner of our park again this summer. Early evenings they start arriving, hang out until the park closes at midnight. Nothing to do but get high on beer and dope, the police leave them alone as long as they mind their own business, don't hassle people too much. Now and then there's fighting but nothing serious—nobody shot or stabbed.

Of course no girl or woman in her right mind would go anywhere near them, if she didn't have a boyfriend there.   10

Ace is the leader, a big boy in his twenties with a mean baby-face, pouty mouth, and cheeks so red they look fresh-slapped, sly little steely eyes curling up at the corners like he's laughing or getting ready to laugh. He's six foot two weighing maybe two hundred twenty pounds—lifts weights at the gym—but there's some loose flabby flesh around his middle, straining against his belt. He goes bare-chested in the heat, likes to sweat in the open air, muscles bunched and gleaming, and he can show off his weird tattoos—ace of spades on his   20
right bicep, inky-black octopus on his left. Long shaggy hair the color of dirty sand and he wears a red sweatband for looks.

Nobody notices anything special about a car circling the park, lots of traffic on summer nights and nobody's watching then there's this popping noise like a firecracker and right away Ace screams and claps his

hand to his eye and it's streaming blood—what the hell? Did somebody shoot him? His buddies just freeze not knowing what to do. There's a long terrible minute when   30
everybody stands there staring at Ace not knowing what to do—then the boys run and duck for cover, scattering like pigeons. And Ace is left alone standing there, crouched, his hand to his left eye screaming, Help, Jesus, hey, help, my eye—Standing there crouched at the knee like he's waiting for a second shot to finish him off.

The bullet must have come at an angle, skimmed the side of Ace's face, otherwise he'd be flat-out dead lying in the scrubby grass. He's panicked though, breathing   40
loud through his mouth saying, O Jesus, O Jesus, and after a minute people start yelling, word's out there's been a shooting and somebody's hurt. Ace wheels around like he's been hit again but it's only to get away, suddenly he's walking fast stooped over dripping blood, could be he's embarrassed, doesn't want people to see him, red headband and tattoos, and now he's dripping blood down his big beefy forearm, in a hurry to get home.

Some young girls have started screaming. Nobody   50
knows what has happened for sure and where Ace is headed people clear out of his way. There's blood running down his chest, soaking into his jeans, splashing onto the sidewalk. His friends are scared following along after him asking where he's going, is he going to the hospital, but Ace glares up out of his one good eye like a crazy man, saying, Get the fuck away! Don't touch me! and nobody wants to come near.

On the street the cops stop him and there's a call put in for an ambulance. Ace stands there dazed and   60
shamed and the cops ask him questions as if he's to blame for what happened, was he in a fight, where's he coming from, is that a bullet wound?—all the while a crowd's gathering, excitement in the air you can feel. It's an August night, late, eighty-nine degrees and no breeze. The crowd is all strangers, Ace's friends have disappeared. He'd beg the cops to let him go but his heart is beating so hard he can't get his breath. Starts swaying like a drunk man, his knees so weak the cops have to steady him. They can smell the panic sweat on   70
him, running in rivulets down his sides.

In the ambulance he's held in place and a black orderly tells him he's O.K., he's going to be O.K., goin' to be at the hospital in two minutes flat. He talks to Ace the way you'd talk to a small child, or an animal. They give him some quick first aid trying to stop the bleeding but Ace can't control himself can't hold still, he's crazy with fear, his heart gives a half-dozen kicks then it's off and going—like a drum tattoo right in his chest. The ambulance is tearing along the street, siren going, Ace   80
says O God O God O God his terrible heartbeat carrying him away.

He's never been in a hospital in his life—knows he's going to die there.

Then he's being hauled out of the ambulance. Stumbling through automatic-eye doors not knowing where he is. Jaws so tight he could grind his teeth away and he can't get his breath and he's ashamed how people are looking at him, right there in the lights in the

hallway people staring at his face like they'd never seen 90
anything so terrible. He can't keep up with the
attendants, knees buckling and his heart beating so hard
but they don't notice, trying to make him walk faster,
Come on man they're saying, you ain't hurt that bad, Ace
just can't keep up and he'd fall if they weren't gripping
him under the arms then he's in the emergency room
and lying on a table, filmy white curtains yanked closed
around him and there's a doctor, two nurses, What seems
to be the trouble here the doctor asks squinting at Ace
through his glasses, takes away the bloody gauze and 100
doesn't flinch at what he sees. He warns Ace to lie still,
he sounds tired and annoyed as if Ace is to blame, how
did this happen he asks but doesn't wait for any answer
and Ace lies there stiff and shivering with fear clutching
at the underside of the table so hard his nails are digging
through the tissue-paper covering into the vinyl, he can't
see out of his left eye, nothing there but pain, pain
throbbing and pounding everywhere in his head and the
nurses—are there two? three?—look down at him with
sympathy he thinks, with pity he thinks, they're 110
attending to him, touching him, nobody has ever touched
him so tenderly in all his life Ace thinks and how
shamed he is hauled in here like this flat on his back
like this bleeding like a stuck pig and sweating bare-
chested and his big gut exposed quivering there in the
light for everybody to see—

The doctor puts eight stitches in Ace's forehead, tells
him he's damned lucky he didn't lose his eye, the bullet
missed it by about two inches and it's going to be
swollen and blackened for a while, next time you might 120
not be so lucky he says but Ace doesn't catch this, his
heart's going so hard. They wrap gauze around his head
tight then hook him up to a machine to monitor his
heartbeat, the doctor's whistling under his breath like
he's surprised, lays the flat of his hand against Ace's
chest to feel the weird loud rocking beat. Ace is broken
out in sweat but it's cold clammy sick sweat, he knows
he's going to die. The machine is going bleep-bleep-
bleep high-pitched and fast and how fast can it go before
his heart bursts?—he sees the nurses looking down at 130
him, one of the nurses just staring at him, Don't let me
die Ace wants to beg but he'd be too ashamed. The
doctor is listening to Ace's heartbeat with his
stethoscope, asks does he have any pain in his chest,
has he ever had an attack like this before, Ace whispers
no but too soft to be heard, all the blood has drained
from his face and his skin is dead-white, mouth gone
slack like a fish's and toes like ice where Death is
creeping up his feet: he can feel it.

The heart isn't Ace's heart but just something inside 140
him gone angry and mean pounding like a hammer
pounding pounding pounding against his ribs making his
body rock so he's panicked suddenly and wants to get
loose, tries to push his way off the table—he isn't
thinking but if he could think he'd say he wanted to
leave behind what's happening to him here as if it was
only happening in the emergency room, there on that
table. But they don't let him go. There's an outcry in the
place and two orderlies hold him down and he gives up,
all the strength drained out of him and he gives up, 150
there's no need to strap him down the way they do, he's

finished. They hook him up to the heart monitor again
and the terrible high-pitched bleeping starts again and
he lies there shamed knowing he's going to die he's
forgotten about the gunshot, his eye, who did it and was
it on purpose meant for him and how can he get revenge,
he's forgotten all that covered in sick clammy sweat his
nipples puckered and the kinky hairs on his chest wet,
even his belly button showing exposed from the struggle
and how silly and sad his tattoos must look under these 160
lights where they were never meant to be seen.

One of the nurses sinks a long needle in his arm, and
there's another needle in the soft thin flesh of the back
of his hand, takes him by surprise, they've got a tube in
there, and something coming in hot and stinging
dripping into his vein the doctor's telling him something
he can't follow, This is to bring the heartbeat down the
doctor says, just a tachycardia attack and it isn't fatal try
to relax but Ace knows he's going to die, he can feel
Death creeping up his feet up his legs like stepping out 170
into cold water and suddenly he's so tired he can't lift
his head, couldn't get up from the table if they
unstrapped him. And he dies—it's that easy. Like
slipping off into the water, pushing out, letting the water
take you. It's that easy.

They're asking Ace if he saw who shot him and Ace says,
Naw, didn't see nobody. They ask does he have any
enemies and he says, Naw, no more than anybody else.
They ask can he think of anybody who might have
wanted to shoot him and he says, embarrassed, looking 180
down at the floor with his one good eye, Naw, can't think
of nobody right now. So they let him go.

Next night Ace is back in the park out of pride but
there's a feeling to him he isn't real or isn't the same
person he'd been. One eye bandaged shut and everything
looks flat, people staring at him like he's a freak, wanting
to know What about the eye and Ace shrugs and tells
them he's O.K., the bullet just got his forehead.
Everybody wants to speculate who fired the shot, whose
car it was, but Ace stands sullen and quiet thinking his 190
own thoughts. Say he'd been standing just a little to one
side the bullet would have got him square in the
forehead or plowed right into his eye, killed him dead,
it's something to think about and he tries to keep it in
mind so he'll feel good. But he doesn't feel good. He
doesn't feel like he'd ever felt before. His secret is
something that happened to him in the hospital he can't
remember except to know it happened and it happened
to him. And he's in a mean mood his head half-
bandaged like a mummy, weird-looking in the dark, 200
picking up on how people look at him and say things
behind his back calling him Ace which goes through him
like a razor because it's a punk name and not really his.

Mostly it's O.K. He hides how he feels. He's got a
sense of humor. He doesn't mind them clowning around
pretending they hear gunshots and got to duck for cover,
nobody's going to remember it for long, except once Ace
stops laughing and backhands this guy in the belly, low
below the belt, says in his old jeering voice, What do you
know?—you don't know shit. 210

◆

Science Fiction and Film

Science fiction is the most popular vehicle of the contemporary concern for the future of the planet. During the twentieth century, a virtual golden age of science fiction, futurist writers have contemplated how scientific control over genetic makeup might affect society (see chapters 35 and 36), whether it is possible and desirable to abolish death, how humans might interact with other forms of life, and what life might be like following a nuclear disaster. Despite the large number of "schlock" fantasy novels and films of recent decades, the best examples of the genre of science fiction reveal a profound sense of moral responsibility for resolving human problems in the twenty-first century.

The beginnings of modern science fiction may be traced to the French novelist Jules Verne (1828–1905) and the British writer H. G. Wells (1866–1946). But the more recent flowering of the genre dates from the nativity of space exploration—specifically the Soviet Union's historic launching of an artificial earth satellite (*Sputnik 1*) in 1957 and the American moon landing of 1969. These events triggered an energetic outpouring of fiction related to the adventure of space exploration. In 1950, Arthur C. Clarke (b. 1917), one of Britain's most successful writers, produced the intriguing science fiction story "The Sentinel," which in turn became the basis for an extraordinary cinematic conceptualization of the Space Age, *2001: A Space Odyssey* (1968). Directed by the American filmmaker Stanley Kubrick (b. 1928), the film builds on the intriguing hypothesis that intelligent life exists in outer space. The plot involves a quest prompted by the discovery of a mysterious four-million-year-old crystal monolith that appears to be emitting powerful radio waves in the direction of the planet Jupiter. Outfitted with a state-of-the-art spaceship called *Discovery*, which is engineered by a super computer named HAL-9000, the fictional heroes of the space odyssey set out for the planet Jupiter. Their adventures include a contest of wills between the astronauts and the ruthless and deviant HAL, a breathtaking encounter with the mysteries of outer space, and a shattering revelation of regeneration and rebirth. Kubrick's *2001* is the modern counterpart of the *Epic of Gilgamesh*, Homer's *Odyssey*, and Dante's *Commedia*. The similarities between the film and such epics are not accidental: "We set out with the deliberate intention of creating a myth," explained Clarke. "The Odyssean parallel was in our minds from the beginning, long before the film's title was chosen."

Like all epics, the film *2001* celebrates the adventures of a hero who challenges the unknown by force of wit and imagination. The vast, mysterious realm of outer space is the twentieth-century equivalent of Gilgamesh's untamed wilderness, Odysseus' wine-dark Aegean, and Dante's Christian cosmos. Just as the lands beyond the sea represented to ancient peoples the earth's outermost reaches, so extraterrestrial space constitutes for moderns the unprobed celestial fringe of the universe. Kubrick and Clarke pose questions that are timely and profound: Is there intelligent life in outer space? Are computers actually paradigms of human intelligence? Is it possible for humankind to map all parts of the universe, and, if so, at what cost? Is the cause-and-effect world of science and technology the only meaningful world accessible to human experience? The answer to the last question—a resounding no—is one of the many revelations of *2001*. Both the film and the short story achieve what science fiction at its best can offer: the sense of awe and a spirit of intellectual curiosity in the face of the unknown.

The Visual Arts in the Information Age

Since 1960, the visual arts have been overwhelmingly diverse in styles and techniques. Collectively, however, they are characterized by an indebtedness to mass media and high technology, by an emphasis on process and medium at the expense of product and message, and by such typically postmodern features as parody and playfulness. Postmodern artists frequently appropriate, or borrow, visual imagery from the "junk heap" of high and popular culture. They may rework and reassemble familiar images with dispassionate disregard for their original meaning. Since 1960, such materials as fiberglass, Plexiglas, stainless steel, and polyester resin have become as commonplace in the art world as tempera, clay, and oil paints were in past centuries. The experimental mixing of media initiated by Picasso and Duchamp at the beginning of the century has assumed eclectic breadth that now includes the electronic media of film, television, and computers.

The artists of the information age have joined rock musicians and athletes in becoming the superstars of contemporary society. The art of some prominent living painters and sculptors commands fortunes comparable to those of industrial barons. Critics and gallery owners now play a more active role than ever before in marketing and commercializing art, so that (for better or for worse) artists have become celebrities and art has become "big business."

1957	the first artificial satellite (*Sputnik 1*) is put in orbit by the Soviet Union	
1961	a Soviet astronaut becomes the first person to orbit the earth	
1969	an American astronaut is the first person to walk on the moon	

Pop Art

The term *pop art* was coined in England in the 1950s, but the movement came to fruition in New York City in the following decade. Pop artists made art that glorified commonplace objects and popular personalities. They rejected the postwar trends in gestural abstraction and action painting in favor of realism—a move that gave new life to the Western representational tradition. One of the pioneers of American pop art was Andy Warhol (1931–1987). Trained as a commercial artist, Warhol took as his subject matter familiar and banal supermarket products such as Brillo, Campbell's soup, and Coca-Cola (Figure **37.1**), American superstars like Elvis Presley and Marilyn Monroe (Figure **37.2**), and media-documented episodes of social violence (such as the civil rights riots of the 1960s). Warhol depersonalized images by enlarging them or by reproducing them in monotonous, postage-stamp rows that resemble supermarket displays. He employed the slick advertising techniques of **silkscreen** and airbrush, thus flouting distinctions between fine and applied art. Warhol's

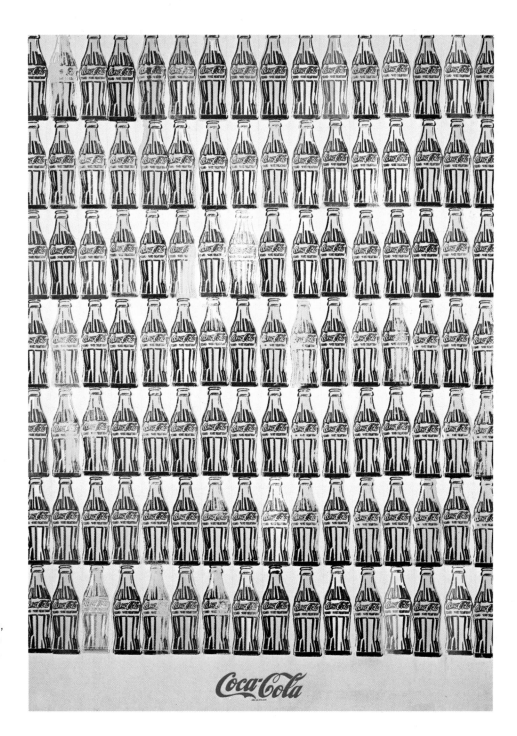

Figure 37.1 Andy Warhol, *Green Coca-Cola Bottles*, 1962. Oil on canvas, 6 ft. 10½ in. × 4 ft. 9 in. Collection of Whitney Museum of American Art, New York. Purchase, with funds from the Friends of the Whitney Museum of American Art. 68.25. Photograph copyright © 1997 Whitney Museum of American Art. © ARS, New York and DACS, London 1997.

Figure 37.2 Andy Warhol, *"Mint Marilyn Monroe,"* 1962. Oil and silkscreen enamel on canvas, 20½ × 16½ in. Jasper Johns Collection © 1997 and the Estate and Foundation of Andy Warhol/ARS, New York and DACS, London 1997.

Coke bottles and soup cans exalt the commercialism of contemporary life even as they mock the consumer mentality of Ellul's "mass society."

Jasper Johns (b. 1930), an artist whose career has spanned half a century, shared Warhol's interest in manipulating commonplace objects in ways that pose questions about the imitative power of art and the growing commercialism of the art object. When Willem de Kooning quipped that Johns' art dealer could sell anything—even two beer cans—Johns created *Painted Bronze* (1960), a set of bronze-cast, hand-painted cans of ale (Figure 37.3). Johns' beer cans, like his flags and targets, are at once neo-dada tributes to Marcel Duchamp (see Figure 33.5), whom Johns knew personally, and postmodern parodies of the cherished icons of contemporary life. But they are also mock-heroic commentaries on the fact that art, like beer, is a marketable commodity.

Among the most intriguing vehicles of pop parody are the monumental soft vinyl sculptures of Claes Oldenburg (b. 1929)—gigantic versions of such everyday items as clothespins, hot dogs, table fans, typewriter erasers, and toilets (Figure 37.4). Often enlarged ten to twenty times their natural size, these objects assume a comic vulgarity that shatters our complacent acceptance of their presence in our daily lives. With similar bravado, the oversized paintings of Roy Lichtenstein (b. 1923), modeled on comic-book cartoons, bring attention to familiar clichés and stereotypes of popular entertainment. Violence and romance are trivialized in the fictional lives of Lichtenstein's comic-book stereotypes—superheroes and helpless women (Figure 37.5). Like other pop artists, Lichtenstein employs

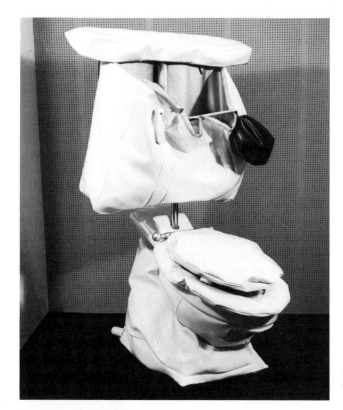

commercial techniques, including stencil and airbrush; he even imitates the Benday dots used in advertising design to achieve tonal gradation. The resulting canvases, with their slickly finished surfaces and flat, bold shapes, are burlesque versions of mass media advertisements. With tongue-in-cheek humor, however, the commercial world of the 1990s has "reclaimed" pop art: Just as Warhol and Lichtenstein appropriated the images of popular culture, so the popular media now "quote" from the works of these two artists.

Figure 37.6 Robert Rauschenberg, *Buffalo II*, 1964. Oil on canvas with silkscreen, 8 ft. × 6 ft.
The Robert B. Mayer Family Collection, Chicago, Illinois. © Robert Rauschenberg/DACS, London/VAGA, New York 1997.

Assemblage

Art that freely combines two- and three-dimensional elements has a history that reaches back to the early twentieth century—recall Picasso's collages and Duchamp's modified ready-mades. Since mid-century, however, the American artist Robert Rauschenberg (b. 1925) has monumentalized the art of *assemblage* in works that incorporate what he refers to as "the excess of the world." In creating bold, large-scale art objects out of old car tires, street signs, broken furniture, and other debris, he fathered "combines" (as he calls them) that eliminate the boundary between painting and sculpture and force us to reexamine ordinary objects in extraordinary new guises. Rauschenberg is a talented printmaker as well as a daring sculptor. He has experimented with a wide variety of transfer techniques, including collage and silkscreen, to produce provocative two-dimensional kaleidoscopes of contemporary culture (Figure 37.6). These bits and pieces of cultural debris appear thrown together, as if all were equally valuable (or equally useless).

Many contemporary artists have used assemblage to bring attention to the random and violent aspects of contemporary society. John Chamberlain (b. 1927) makes seductive sculptures out of junked automobiles, whose corroded sheet-metal bodies and twisted steel bumpers suggest the transience of high-tech products and the dangers inherent in their misuse (Figure 37.7). Louise Nevelson (1900–1988) collected wooden boxes, filled

Figure 37.7 John Chamberlain, *Debonaire Apache*, 1991. Painted and chromium plated steel, 7 ft. 10 in. × 4 ft. 6¾ in. × 4 ft. 2½ in. Photo: Peter Foe/Fotoworks. Photograph courtesy of the Pace Gallery, New York. © ARS, New York and DACS, London 1997.

them with discarded fragments of found and machine-made objects, and painted them a uniform black, white, or gold. Like decaying altarpieces, these structures enshrine the vaguely familiar and haunting objects of modern materialist culture (Figure **37.8**).

Geometric Abstraction, Op, Minimal, Neon, and Kinetic Art

Not all contemporary artists have embraced the ironic stance of pop and assemblage art. Some artists have remained loyal to the nonobjective mode of *geometric abstraction*, first initiated in painting by Malevich and Mondrian (see chapter 32). Obedient to the credo of the Bauhaus architect Mies van der Rohe that "less is more," these artists have strived for the machinelike purity of elemental forms and colors, occasionally enlarging such forms to colossal sizes. The American artist Frank Stella (b. 1936) has painted huge canvases consisting of brightly colored, hard-edged geometric patterns that look as though they are made with a giant protractor (Figure **37.9**). In place of the traditional square or rectangular canvas, Stella and others of the geometric abstract school have constructed canvases shaped like chevrons or triangles, which may be fastened together or assembled into groups. Stella, who

Figure 37.8 (above) Louise Nevelson, *Black Wall*, 1959. Gilded wood, 112 × 85¼ × 25½ in. Tate Gallery, London.

Figure 37.9 Frank Stella, *Agbatana III*, 1968. Fluorescent acrylic on canvas, 10 ft. × 15 ft. Allen Memorial Art Gallery, Oberlin College. Ruth C. Roush Fund for Contemporary Art and National Foundation for the Arts and Humanities Grant, 1968. © ARS, New York and DACS, London 1997.

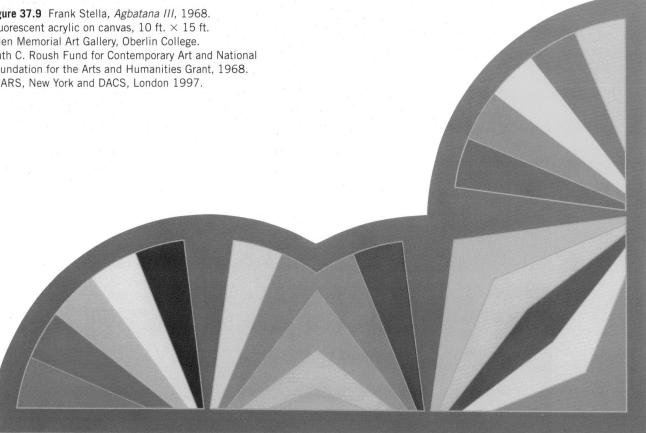

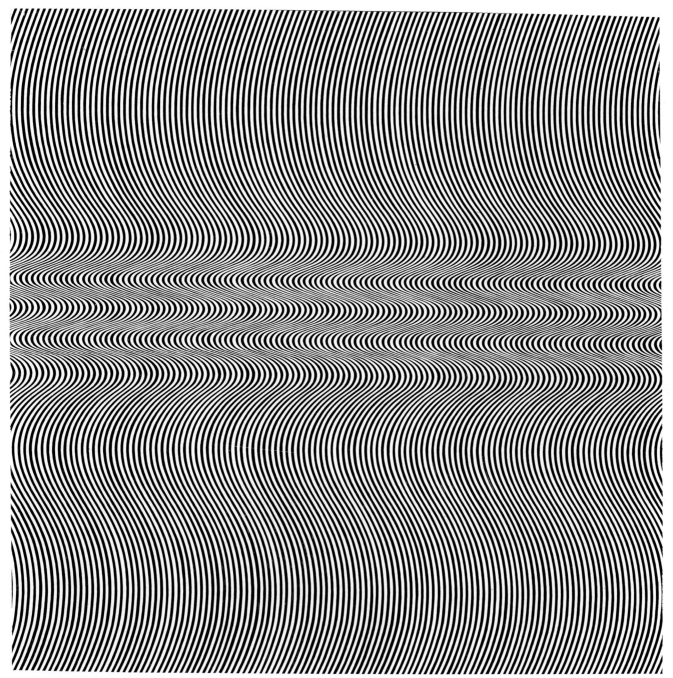

Figure 37.10 Bridget Riley, *Current*, 1964. Synthetic polymer paint on composition board, 4 ft. 10⅜ in. × 4 ft. 10⅞ in. The Museum of Modern Art, New York. Philip Johnson Fund. Photograph © 1997 The Museum of Modern Art, New York.

self-consciously rejects value-oriented art, makes art that is neutral and impersonal—features that dominate even his more recent flamboyant three-dimensional pieces. "All I want anyone to get out of my paintings, and all I ever get out of them, is the fact that you can see the whole thing without confusion," explains Stella: "What you see is what you see."

The idea that what one sees is determined by *how* one sees has been central to the work of Hungarian-born Victor Vasarely (b. 1908) and Britain's Bridget Riley (b. 1931). Both Vasarely and Riley explore the operation of conflicting visual cues and the elemental effects of colors and shapes on the faculties of the human retina—a style known as *optical art*, or *op art*. In Riley's *Current* (Figure **37.10**), a series of curved black lines painted on a white surface creates the illusion of vibrating movement and elusive color—look for yellow by staring hard at the painting for a few minutes.

While Europeans pioneered optical abstractionism, Americans have led the way in the development of *minimalism*. Minimalist sculptors developed a highly refined industrial aesthetic that featured elemental forms made of high-tech materials, including anodized aluminum, laminated wood, fiberglass, Plexiglas, and neon. The geometric components of minimalist artworks are usually factory produced and assembled according to the artist's instructions. The untitled stainless steel and Plexiglas boxes of Donald Judd (1928–1994) protrude from the wall with mathematical clarity and perfect regularity (Figure 37.11). They resemble a stack of shelves, yet they neither contain nor support anything. The visual rhythms of Judd's serial forms create a "dialogue" between space and volume, between flat, bright enamel colors and dull or reflective metal grays, and between subtly textured and smooth surfaces. More monumental in scale are the primal forms of the Japanese-American sculptor Isamu Noguchi (b. 1904). Poised on one corner of its steel and aluminum frame, Noguchi's gigantic *Cube* (Figure 37.12) shares the purity of form and the mysterious resonance of such monuments as the Egyptian pyramids and the jade discs of ancient China.

Minimalists have enthusiastically embraced the tools of modern electronic technology. The Greek artist Chryssa (b. 1933) transforms fluorescent lights into powerful shapes inspired by commercial lettering and industrial neon signs (Figure 37.13). Others design stainless steel or aluminum sculptures that move in response to currents of electricity or

Figure 37.12 Isamu Noguchi, *Cube*, 1968. Steel subframe with aluminum panels, height 28 ft. Marine Midland Building, New York. Photo: Gloria Fiero.

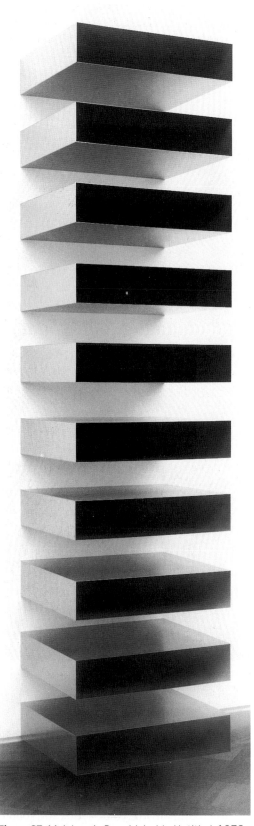

Figure 37.11 (above) Donald Judd, *Untitled*, 1973. Stainless steel and oil enamel on Plexiglas, 114 × 27 × 24 in. San Francisco Museum of Modern Art. Purchased with the aid of funds from the National Endowment for the Arts and Friends of the Museum.

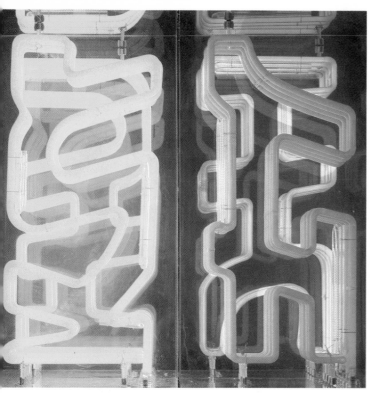

to the natural rhythms of wind and water. Constructed on the principle of movement, *kinetic* art looks back to the innovative mobiles of Alexander Calder (see Figure 35.13).

New Realism

During the 1970s, there emerged a new version of realism that emphasized the stop-action stillness and sharp-focus immediacy of the photograph. *New realism* (also called *neorealism, hyperrealism,* and *photorealism*) differs from previous realist strategies (including social realism and pop art) in its disavowal of narrative content and its indifference to moral, social, and political issues. Although decidedly representational, new realism is as impersonal as minimal art. New realist artists do not imitate natural phenomena; rather, they recreate the artificially processed view of reality captured by the photographic image. Richard Estes (b. 1936), for instance, paints urban still lifes based on fragments of the photographs that he himself makes (Figure **37.14**). A virtuoso painter, Estes tantalizes the eye with details refracted by polished aluminum surfaces and plate-glass windows. Chuck Close (b. 1940) uses an opaque

Figure 37.13 Chryssa, *Fragment for "The Gates to Times Square,"* 1966. Neon, Plexiglas, steel, and painted wood, 75¼ × 34⅞ × 27⅝ in. Collection of Whitney Museum of American Art, New York. Purchase, with funds from Howard and Jean Lipman. 66.135a–b. Photograph copyright © 1997 Whitney Museum of American Art.

Figure 37.14 Richard Estes, *Helene's Florist*, 1971. Oil on canvas, 4 ft. × 6 ft. The Toledo Museum of Art, Toledo, Ohio. Purchased with funds from the Libbey Endowment. Gift of Edward Drummond Libbey.

Figure 37.16 (right) Duane Hanson, *Tourists*, 1970. Fiberglass and polyester polychromed, 5 ft. 4 in. × 5 ft. 5 in. × 3 ft. 11 in. Scottish National Gallery of Modern Art, Edinburgh.

projector to transfer the photographic image to canvas after both photograph and canvas have been ruled to resemble graph paper; he then fills each square of the canvas with tiny gradations of color that resemble the pixels of a television screen (Figure **37.15**). The brutally impersonal tabloid quality of Close's oversized "mugshots" is reinforced by his monochromatic palette.

High-tech materials and techniques have made possible the fabrication of new realist sculptures that are shockingly lifelike. Duane Hanson (1925–1996) used fiberglass-reinforced polyester resin to recreate the appearance of ordinary and often lower-class individuals in their everyday occupations (Figure **37.16**). Hanson cast his polyester molds from live models, then added wigs, clothing, and accessories. By comparison with George Segal's melancholic figures (see Figure 35.10), Hanson's "living dead" are symbolic of modern life at its most prosaic.

Figure 37.15 Chuck Close, *Self-Portrait*, 1968. Acrylic on canvas, 8 ft. 11½ in. × 6 ft. 11½ in. Walker Art Center, Minneapolis.

Camp and New Expressionism

More pointedly anti-elitist and anti-bourgeois, *camp art* makes popular imagery the fuel for sophisticated ridicule. Camp artists operate with the bravado of the black humor novelist and the biting cynicism of the pop painter. Typically postmodern, camp art renders art and life—the sublime and the banal—with a tongue-in-cheek neutrality that creates clichés of both. In the work entitled simply *Portrait (Twins)*, for example, the Japanese painter Yasumasa Morimura (b. 1945) turns Manet's *Olympia* (see chapter 30) into a drag queen decked out in a blond wig and rhinestone-trimmed slippers (Figure **37.17**). By "updating" Manet's *Olympia*, itself an "update" of Titian, Morimura questions the authority of these historical icons and mocks the classic stereotypes of gender. *Portrait* is a color photograph produced from a studio setup—a popular postmodern technique appropriated from fashion advertising.

The paintings of the American artist David Salle (b. 1952) share some of the features of camp art, but are patently expressionistic. Salle's elusive canvases resemble a computer screen on which is juxtaposed an assortment of seemingly unrelated motifs, including cartoon graffiti, provocatively posed nudes, and 1950s furniture. Rendered in lurid colors, these images may be layered so that the final composition has the appearance of a double-exposure photograph or film still (Figure **37.18**). Quintessentially postmodern, Salle wrenches images from their historical context, then combines them with an ironic detachment that evokes a sense of melancholy.

Figure 37.17 Yasumasa Morimura, *Portrait (Twins)*, 1988. Color photograph, clear medium, 6 ft. 10½ in. × 9 ft. 10 in. NW House, Tokyo. Courtesy Luhring Augustine, New York.

Figure 37.18 David Salle, *Yellow Bread*, 1987. Acrylic and oil on canvas, 9 ft. 4 in. × 8 ft. Courtesy Gagosian Gallery, New York.
© David Salle/DACS, London/VAGA, New York 1997.

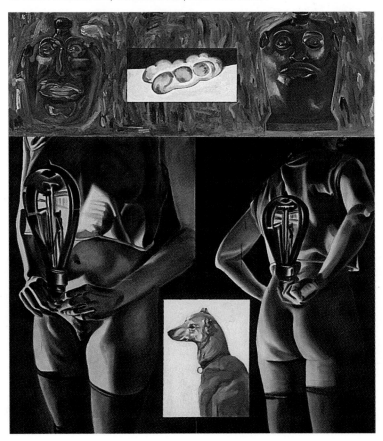

Social Conscience Art

While all art may be said to offer a perspective on the social scene, some of the art of this century's final decade has assumed a socially committed, even missionary stance. Not overtly political nor even necessarily critical of the status quo, *social conscience art* seeks to transform society by awakening its visionary potential. Such art works holistically to reclaim the spiritual power that art once held in ancient societies: the power to integrate individual and communal needs. Social conscience art rejects the art for art's sake heroism of modernism, as well as the ironic skepticism of postmodernism. Issue-driven art, like the literature of social conscience, draws attention to ecological ruin and widespread disease (see Figure 36.12), to the threat of nuclear terrorism and the plight of marginalized populations, to the decay in the quality of urban life and the erosion of moral values. Social conscience artists use a variety of different styles and media to achieve their ends.

The Cuban-born Luis Cruz Azaceta (b. 1942) combines figurative and expressionistic techniques to address the realities of arson, street crime, AIDS, and drug addiction (Figure **37.19**)—the evidence of a universal social disorder. His huge canvases are often splotched with harshly colored paint, their surfaces blistered, burned, cut, or collaged with wire and debris. In the tradition of American comedians like Richard Pryor and Woody Allen—masters of an often brutal brand of black humor—Azaceta conceives grotesque and macabre images that deliver a message of decay and the need for reform.

Figure 37.19 Luis Cruz Azaceta, *Coke Heads VIII*, 1991. Synthetic polymer paint on canvas, 8 ft. 11 in. × 10 ft. 2 in. Courtesy Frederick Snitzer Gallery, Coral Gables, Florida.

Figure 37.20 Magdalena Abakanowicz, detail of *Crowd 1*, 1986–1987. Burlap and resin, 50 standing life-sized figures, each 66⅞ × 23⅝ × 11¾ in. Courtesy Marlborough Gallery, New York. 1997 © Magdalena Abakanowicz. Photography © Artur Starewicz.

In contrast with the aggressive canvases of Azaceta, the social conscience artworks that come from postwar Eastern Europe are subtle, understated, and three-dimensional. Of the Eastern European countries, Poland in particular has enjoyed a renaissance in the arts (see Reading 6.30). The Polish sculptor Magdalena Abakanowicz (b. 1930) draws on traditional methods of weaving and modeling to cast hulking, monumental figures that stage the drama of the human condition (Figure 37.20). Sisal, jute, and burlap make up the substance of these figures, whose scarred and patched surfaces call to mind earth, mud, and the dusty origins of primordial creatures. Abakanowicz installs her headless, sexless figures in groups that evoke a sense of collective anonymity and vulnerability, but at the same time underscore the kinship between human and natural forms. Abakanowicz, who regards art as potentially transformative and redeeming, brings to these highly concentrated works her talents as a weaver and her experience as a survivor of World War II (and Poland's repressive communist regime).

In Russia, revolutionary political changes accompanying the collapse of the communist regime in 1991 ended the Cold War and relaxed totalitarian restrictions of free expression. At liberty to travel to the West, and increasingly familiar with the broad range of modern and postmodern styles, contemporary Russian artists have flooded the world market with intellectually and aesthetically provocative art. These artworks are typically postmodern in that they are not uniform in style but, rather, pluralistic, with strong leanings toward recognizable visual subjects. Some Russian artists look back to native traditions of folk art, while others draw on the sacred imagery of the Russian Orthodox Church. In general, however, they demonstrate a high level of technical sophistication derived from decades of training in Soviet art academies. They have accommodated, as well, the dual heritage of suprematist abstraction (see chapter 32) and socialist realism (see chapter 33).

The Moscow artist Olga Bulgakova (b. 1951) transforms the characters of Russian fairytales into icons of magic realism: *The Magician* (Figure **37.21**) depicts a blind sorcerer engaged in a ritual that recalls the mythic ceremonies of the Minoan snake-priestess (see chapter 4). Her arms form the sign associated in ancient Asian culture with the power of the sun; on her head and arm, she balances the vessels and geometric tokens of some occult rite. A bird, an ancient symbol of spiritual rebirth, stands on a table that doubles as her gown. Paradoxically, *The Magician* is brightly colored, yet darkly ambiguous. Since it is possible to read the main figure as a priestess or regenerative agent, the painting may be taken as an allegory of the artist's magical power to transform reality, or to foretell the future. (Asian and Mediterranean mythic traditions link blindness and prophetic power.) Regeneration and metamorphosis—key motifs in contemporary Russian culture—are the resonant themes in Bulgakova's art.

Official state art in the People's Republic of China has served the precepts of communism with little interruption for almost a century. Following the death of Mao Zedong in 1976, shifts in China's leadership led to a climate of uncertainty for the arts. Despite communist efforts to modernize culture, Chinese officials tightened control over intellectual and artistic expression: Resolving in 1983 to eradicate "spiritual pollution," the

Figure 37.21 Olga Bulgakova, *The Magician*, 1995. Oil on canvas, 4 ft. 8 in. × 3 ft. 3½ in. © Zalman Gallery, New York.

Figure 37.22 Feng Mengbo, *The Video Endgame Series: Street Fighter I*, 1995. Oil on canvas, 4 ft. 11 in. × 6 ft. 6¾ in. Courtesy of Hanart TZ Gallery, Hong Kong.

Figure 37.23 Feng Mengbo, *The Video Endgame Series: Street Fighter II*, 1995. Oil on canvas, 4 ft. 11 in. × 6 ft. 6¾ in. Courtesy of Hanart TZ Gallery, Hong Kong.

state forbade all artworks that propagated religion, embraced "bourgeois" humanist values, or included pornographic material. Despite the repressive measures, young Chinese artists, imbued with a keen sense of mission and historical consciousness, continued to write and paint, either in exile or at their own peril. In June of 1989, at Tiananmen Square in Beijing, thousands of student activists demonstrated in support of democratic reform. With Beethoven's Ninth Symphony blaring from loudspeakers, demonstrators raised a plaster figure of the Goddess of Democracy modeled on the *Statue of Liberty*. The official response to this overt display of freedom resulted in the massacre of some protesters and the imprisonment of others. Since Tiananmen Square, literary publication has remained under the watchful eye of the state, but efforts to control music and the visual arts have been less successful. Chinese artists continue to pursue the traditional crafts of jade and porcelain, along with that favorite of Chinese genres, landscape painting. Others, however, have absorbed the styles of the Western avant-garde that continue to challenge the aesthetic mandates of the People's Republic.

The last decades of the twentieth century have generated a rich variety of painting styles, some of which deliberately mock the conformist ideals of China's socialist society. Particularly popular among young Chinese artists is *cynical realism*—a style that employs academic and commercial painting techniques to draw attention to current social and political contradictions. Cynical realism reflects the sentiments of post-Tienanmen artists who, having abandoned the idealism of the 1980s, use roguish humor to register a sense of powerlessness. Cynical realists share the humorously subversive tone of China's *political pop* painters, who seize on Western icons to glamorize the mundane aspects of contemporary Chinese life. Painters of political pop art

are involved in a search for a new cultural rationale that might resolve the contradictions between ancient (Confucian) values and modern (communist) ideals, between Chinese holism and Western materialism, and between socialist realism and other, less conventional, modes of expression. The Beijing artist Feng Mengbo (b. 1966) borrows the imagery and the colors of the electronic amusement arcade to create artworks that resemble video-game screens. In the past decades he has painted warplanes bombarding Tiananmen Square with cases of Coca-Cola, and has transformed Madonna into the star of a Chinese revolutionary opera. *The Video Endgame Series: Street Fighter I* (Figure **37.22**) is based on a popular multilevel video game. Feng appropriates several characters from the game, adding others of his own devising. The character "Guile" is an ex-member of the United States elite Special Forces, while "Wang" belongs to China's Red Guard. In one painting from the series, the Chinese hero opposes the blond-haired American muscleman in martial arts combat (Figure **37.23**). The contests between Wang and an assortment of international characters take place before carefully chosen cultural symbols: a reclining golden Buddha, a Chinese marketplace, a jet fighter plane, and so on. Borrowing

1981	lasers are utilized for the study of matter
1986	development of high-temperature superconductors
1990	the internationally-linked computer network (the internet) becomes accessible to personal computers
1995	the Hubble Space Telescope confirms the existence of extra-solar planets and fifty billion galaxies
1996	NASA scientists produce strong meteorological evidence of life on Mars

popular Chinese and American motifs in a typically postmodern manner, Feng alludes to the similarities between the two cultures: Video game-playing is as much the rage in China's urban centers as it has been in the United States. The prevailing combat theme suggests the ongoing rivalry between communist and democratic ideologies. In the broader sense, however, *Street Fighter* is a subtle commentary on the uneasy union of commercial and political motives driving the more serious games played among the competing nations of the late twentieth century.

Social Conscience Film

In the past two decades, a golden age of cinematic creativity, the films of two men—one Chinese, the other American—have testified to the vitality of this versatile medium. China's leading filmmaker and cinematographer Zhang Yimou (b. 1951) has crafted visually compelling movies that focus on China's disenfranchised rural population (*The Story of Qiu Ju*, 1992) and in particular its women, many of whom remain hostage to feudal and patriarchal traditions (*Raise the Red Lantern*, 1991). An admirer of Ingmar Berman and Akira Kurasawa (see chapter 35), Zhang rejected the socialist realism of the communist era in favor of a cinematic style that combines purity of vision and fierce honesty. His films, at least three of which have been banned in China, are noted for their sensuous use of color and their engaging insights into moral and cultural issues. Although issue-driven subjects are common fare in the history of American film, they have rarely been treated as powerfully as in Steven Spielberg's *Schindler's List* (1993), a story of the Holocaust adapted from Thomas Keneally's prize-winning 1982 nonfiction novel. A virtuoso filmmaker, Spielberg makes brilliant use of the techniques of documentary newscasting to create visually shattering effects that are retained in the mind long after historical fact.

Total Art

The postmodern era has witnessed a great outpouring of *total art*, that is, art that integrates a variety of conventional and unconventional forms of expression. Somewhat like the Roman Catholic Mass or the African funeral, total art involves planned (though usually not rehearsed) performance that may engage the spectator. Such art deliberately embraces chance and theatrical effect; hence it makes little distinction between art and life. The beginnings of total art are found in the mixed-media, aleatory enterprises of John Cage and Merce Cunningham (see chapter 35)—artists who, in turn, influenced Allan Kaprow (b. 1927), the American pioneer of *happenings*. Kaprow called the "happening" a

Figure 37.24 Yves Klein, *Anthropometry ANT 49*, 1960. © Harry Shunk, New York.

performance occurring "in a given time and space." That space might be a city street, a beach, a studio, or a private home. During the 1960s Kaprow wrote and orchestrated over fifty happenings, most of which engaged dozens of ordinary people in the dual roles of performers and spectators. *Fluids*, a happening staged in Pasadena, California, in 1967, called for a group of individuals to construct a house of ice blocks and then witness the melting process that followed. As in most happenings, the performance was itself the work of art.

In contrast to happenings, *performance art* usually involves only the artist (with perhaps one or two assistants). The French performance artist Yves Klein (1928–1962) used nude women as "human brushes" in his notorious piece entitled *Anthropometry* (Figure **37.24**). Klein's contemporary Jean Tinguely (1925–1991) made a distinctive comment on twentieth-century technology with a series of machines he programmed to self-destruct amidst a spectacle of noise, fire, and smoke. Happenings and performance pieces have influenced our way of looking at the semiritualized events of contemporary life—political demonstrations, street riots, and rock concerts, for instance, all of which are reorchestrated by the mass media. Since both happenings and performance art are ephemeral, the only lasting "product" may be a photographic or videotaped record of the occasion.

Like "happenings," *environmental art* involves the inventive modification of a designated space. The mixed-media sculptures of George Segal and Edward Kienholz (see Figures 35.10 and 35.11) anticipated this type of total art. More recently, however, mixed-media installations have come to incorporate the physical presence of the spectator. Examples of such installations include a "walk-in infinity chamber" consisting of mirrors studded with thousands of miniature lights or filled with menacing, fur-covered furniture and floors.

Figure 37.25 Robert Smithson, *Spiral Jetty*, Great Salt Lake, Utah, 1970. Rock, salt crystals, earth, algae; coil 1,500 ft.

Figure 37.26 Christo and Jeanne-Claude, *Running Fence*, Sonoma and Marin counties, California, 1972–1976. Fabric fence, height 18 ft., length 24½ miles. © Christo 1976. Photo: Jeanne-Claude, New York.

Perhaps the most monumental type of total art is *earth sculpture*, a kind of sculpture that takes the natural landscape as both its medium and its subject. Earth sculptures are usually colossal, heroic, and temporary. Among the most impressive examples of this genre was the piece called *Spiral Jetty*, built in 1970 by Robert Smithson (1938–1973) at the edge of the Great Salt Lake of Utah (Figure 37.25). Smithson's spiral—the snail-like symbol of eternity in ancient art—was 1,500 feet wide and consisted of over 6,000 tons of black basalt, limestone, and earth—materials which are virtually identical with the surrounding area. A conscious reference to ancient earthworks, such as those found among the Native American cultures of South America (see chapter 1), Smithson's project brought attention to the role of the artist in reconstructing the environment and its ecology. Earthworks like *Spiral Jetty*, however, which moved art out of the gallery and into nature, were often best appreciated from the air. Tragically, it was in the crash of a plane surveying one such sculpture that Smithson was killed. Smithson's heroic earthwork also disappeared; a part of nature, it fell subject to processes of dissolution and submersion beneath the waters of the Great Salt Lake. But Smithson's documentary drawings, photographs, and films of this and other earthworks have heightened public awareness of the fragile ecological balance between culture and nature.

The environmental sculptures of the American artists Christo and Jeanne-Claude (both b. 1935) are among the most inventive examples of total art. The Christos have magically transformed natural and human sites by enveloping them with huge amounts of fabric. They have wrapped monumental public structures, such as the Pont-Neuf in Paris and the Reichstag in Berlin, and they have reshaped nature, wrapping part of the coast of Australia, for instance, and surrounding eleven islands in Miami's Biscayne Bay with over six million square feet of pink woven polypropylene fabric. One of the Christos' earlier projects, *Running Fence*, 1972–1976 (Figure 37.26), involved the construction of a nylon "fence" 24½ miles long and 18 feet high. The nylon panels were hung on cables and steel poles and ran through Sonoma and Marin Counties, California, to the Pacific Ocean. The fascinating history of this visually breathtaking piece, which cost the artists over three million dollars and mobilized the efforts of a large crew of workers, is documented in films, photographs, and books. The fence itself, meandering along the California hills like a modern-day version of the Great Wall of China, remained on site for two weeks. Unlike Smithson, the Christos do not seek to remake the natural landscape; rather they modify it temporarily in order to dramatize the difference between the natural world and the increasingly artificial domain of postmodern society.

Total art is essentially conceptual, since it is driven by ideas rather than by purely visual or formal concerns. Perhaps the purest kinds of *conceptual art*, however, are those that consist only of words. Since the 1960s, a variety of artists have created artworks that feature definitions, directions, or messages devoid of other visual images. Barbara Kruger's billboard-style posters (see Figure 36.10) combine photographic images and words that make cryptic comment on social and political issues. The superstar of conceptual art is the American sculptor Jenny Holzer (b. 1950). Holzer carves paradoxical and often subversive messages in stone or broadcasts them electronically on public billboards. She often transmits her slogans by way of light-emitting diodes, a favorite medium of commercial advertising. In language that is at once banal and acerbic, Holzer informs us that "Lack of charisma can

Figure 37.27 Nam June Paik, *Megatron*, 1995. 215 monitors, 8-channel color video and 2-channel sound, left side 142½ × 270 × 23½ in.; right side 128 × 128 × 23½ in. Guggenheim Soho. Courtesy the artist and Holly Solomon Gallery, New York.

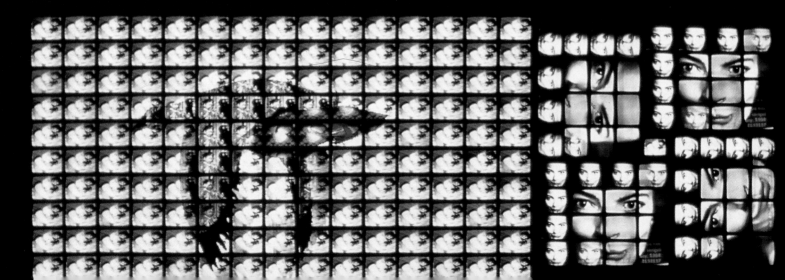

be fatal," "Myths make reality more intelligible," "Humanism is obsolete," "Decency is a relative thing," and "Ambivalence can ruin your life." Holzer's typically postmodern word-art wryly tests the authority of public information, particularly information as dispersed by contemporary electronic media.

In the expanding realm of total art, the electronic media have come to play an increasingly important role. As early as the 1960s, the Korean artist and acclaimed father of video art, Nam June Paik (b. 1932), asserted that the television cathode ray would replace the canvas as the postmodern artist's most effective medium. Paik, a musician and composer, began his career by creating performance pieces and multiscreen television robots (see Part Opener, p. 96). More recently, he has assembled entire walls of video monitors programmed to dazzle viewers with a kaleidoscopic barrage of images whose fast-paced editing imitates mainstream television. Paik's *Megatron* (1995) consists of 215 monitors programmed with a rapid-fire assortment of animated and live-video images drawn from East and West: The Seoul Olympic Games and Korean drummers, rock concert clips, girlie-magazine nudes, and quick-cuts of Paik's favorite artists alternate with the national flags of various countries and other global logos (Figure **37.27**). The animated contour of a bird flying gracefully across the wall of screens brings magical unity to this visual blitz, while a two-channel audio track adds booming syncopated sound to the visual rhythms.

Performances and video installations, which often double as political theater, have become increasingly elaborate: They frequently feature holograms, laser beams, moving pictures, television images, and computer-generated special effects, all of which may be projected onto screens and walls to the accompaniment of electronically recorded sounds. The leading American performance artist, Laurie Anderson (b. 1947), appropriates images from classic movies, newsreels, and other video resources and combines them with tape-recorded and live music. In one recent performance she played an electric violin with a neon-lit bow, waving the bow in the air to create not only sounds, but computer-generated images. For artists like Anderson, the computer has become a "metamedium"—a medium that transcends and transforms all other forms of media.

Cyberart

Not only in multimedia performance, but in dozens of traditional forms of expression, computers are transforming the way in which art is made and experienced. New software programs allow artists to draw and paint electronically. At the same time, the use of the computer to manipulate old images and generate new ones—a specialty known as *digital imaging*—is revolutionizing

Figure 37.28 Charley Murphy (computer graphics), Hames Williams (photography), and Leonardo da Vinci (painting), *Cover for Utne Reader*, 34, July/August 1989.

the world of film, television, video, holography, and photography (Figure **37.28**). Digital imaging is of two varieties: One involves combining photographic material to create new images with the aid of a special computer "paintbrush" program; the other generates entirely new photo-realistic imagery by mathematical means. In the second approach, the artist gives the computer a set of instructions about the "look" of an image, which is then simulated by the computer. Such digital imaging techniques, currently popular among American photographers and filmmakers, raise questions concerning differences between "originals" and "replicas," and between live-action documentation and synthetic imitations. More profoundly, they empower images to mask distinctions between objective reality and electronic illusion.

The use of the computer in making art is no longer exclusive to artists, however. *Interactive art* programs, available both in the art gallery and on the home computer screen, invite the viewer to become a partner in the creative act. In the interactive *Piano* (1995) designed by the Japanese media artist Toshio Iwai (b. 1962), the viewer creates a musical "score" by manipulating a trackball that triggers star-shaped points of light that travel along a scroll until they "strike" a piano keyboard; both visual and aural patterns are generated by the viewer—within limits predetermined by Iwai. And in *Electronic Eve* (1997), an interactive project conceived by Jenny Marketou (b. 1944), "image consumers" create their own multimedia environment by selecting (through direct touch on the computer screen) from a database of video sequences, still images, computer graphics, texts, and sounds.

The computer has also put at everyman's disposal the entire history of art, as well as a vast assortment of electronic information on the arts. Sophisticated telecommunication systems facilitate collaborative electronic artworks and electronic art galleries, while the *internet*, a global interconnection of computer networks, provides access to the contents of more than three thousand museums in the world.

Postmodernism's most intriguing fusion of media, often called *hypermedia*, is a powerful combination of high technology tools—computers, videotape, and photography—used to generate a form of **virtual reality**. By means of optical discs, high-powered computers simulate artificial environments that are flashed onto a huge screen or onto the inside of a head-shaped helmet. Donning the helmet, the spectator enters hyperspace and interacts with the simulated environment. Like a giant video game, virtual reality combines visual illusion, sound, and spoken texts. A synthesis of all retrievable informational forms, hypermedia offers an image-saturated playground for the mind. While virtual reality technology is still somewhat crude, the artistic possibilities of this artform are as vast as they are explosive. On the internet, for instance, one can create an on-line identity by selecting components from a vast software database.* The virtual self then interacts with others in a computer-mediated electronic community.

The Visual Arts and the Global Paradigm

The emerging new framework for contemporary culture, known as the global paradigm, involves the reality of interdependence among cultures throughout the world. This new sense of cultural and communal collectivity is apparent in most social conscience artworks, but it is especially evident in the Japanese art environment. One example of such a project is by the Japanese artist Yukinori Yanagi (b. 1959). Yanagi's imaginative installation *The World Flag Ant Farm* (Figure **37.29**) involves a series of sand-poured flags representing many different nations. The physical appearance of each flag is altered owing to the activity of hundreds of ants who carry grains of colored sand from box to box (thus flag to flag). Yanagi identifies the ant as a natural "trickster" which defies the artificial rules and boundaries of geographic place. His *World Flag Ant Farm* offers an intriguing metaphor for the internationalism of the global village. At the same time, it subscribes to the typically Japanese respect for nature, and the Japanese philosophy of symbiosis, by which nature and culture thrive in a mutually beneficial relationship.

---

*Research in cyber communities is under way at various schools, such as the University of Art and Design in Helsinki, Finland.

Figure 37.29 Yukinori Yanagi, *The World Flag Ant Farm*, 1990. Ants, colored sand, plastic boxes and plastic tubes. 170 boxes, each 8 × 12 in. Photo: William Murray, London.

Architecture in the Information Age

Contemporary critics often attribute the birth of post-modernism to the architecture of the 1960s and, specifically, to the efforts of those architects who turned their backs on the international style. Robert Venturi (b. 1925), who first introduced architectural postmodernism in his book *Complexity and Contradiction in Architecture* (1966), countered Mies van der Rohe's dictum "less is more" with the claim "less is a bore." Venturi and others shunned the anonymity and austerity of the glass and steel skyscraper (see Figure 35.15) and the concrete high rise (see Figure 35.14), along with the progressive utopianism of modernists who hoped to transform society through functional form. Instead, postmodernists opted for an architecture that emphasized visual complexity, individuality, and outright fun. In contrast to the machine-like purity of the international style structure, the postmodern building is a playful assortment of fragments "quoted" from architectural traditions as ill-mated as a fast-food stand and a Hellenistic temple. Postmodern architecture, like postmodern fiction, engages a colorful mix of fragments in a whimsical and often witty manner.

The Sony Building in New York City (formerly the American Telephone and Telegraph Building) was designed by Philip Johnson (b. 1906), the former high priest of modernism. It provides an example of the postmodern aesthetic (Figure **37.30**): The base of the building looks like Brunelleschi's Pazzi Chapel (see chapter 17), its cornice recalls the contours of an eighteenth-century highboy (a chest of drawers), and its lobby resembles a Romanesque nave. The rose granite-clad building, with its punning references to the past, is a study in elegance and irony.

Equally witty is the Piazza d'Italia in New Orleans, designed by Charles Moore (1925–1993). The plaza, which serves as an Italian cultural center, is a burlesque yet elegant combination of motifs borrowed from Pompeii, Palladio, and Italian baroque architecture (Figure **37.31**). Its brightly colored colonnaded portico—looking every bit like a gaudy stage set—is adorned with fountains, neon lights, and polished aluminum balustrades. Moore's parodic grab bag appropriation of the Italian heritage culminates in an apron (shaped like a map of Italy) that floats in the central pool of the piazza.

Postmodernism has embraced numerous architectural experiments in **geodesic** and modular design. One of the most inventive of these is the extraordinary glass pyramid that serves as the formal entrance to the Louvre Museum in Paris (Figure **37.32**). Built in 1988 by the Chinese-born American I. M. Pei (b. 1917), this monumental cage of stainless steel and Plexiglas opens up vast areas of interior space in the greenhouse style

Figure 37.30 Philip Johnson and John Burgee, with Simmons Architects, Sony Building, New York, 1978–1983. Photo: © Peter Mauss/Esto.

Figure 37.31 Perez Associates with Charles Moore, Ron Filson, Urban Innovations, Inc., Piazza d'Italia, New Orleans, 1976–1979. © Norman McGrath, New York.

initiated by Paxton's Crystal Palace (see chapter 30). Pei has transcended national styles and periods by synthesizing the techniques of modern technology (including the glass-and-steel vocabulary of the international style) with the designs of seventeenth-century French landscape architects and the geometry of the Great Pyramid at Giza. His pyramid complex, despite its references to the historic past, is futuristic—a kind of space station for the arts.

Deconstructivism, a typically postmodern architectural style, first emerged in the 1980s. Deconstructivist architects—somewhat like the literary theorists who "deconstruct" verbal texts in search of multiple meanings—design buildings that call attention to the eclectic and chaotic quality of contemporary life. Just as there is, according to postmodern philosophers, no single text for the whole of our experience, so in any single piece of deconstructivist architecture, there is no dominant, unifying design. Deconstructivists have added daring and humor to the utilitarian modernism of those "pioneer-engineers," the Russian constructivists (see

chapter 32). In the buildings designed by the American architect Frank Gehry (b. 1930), facades tilt, columns lean, and interior spaces are skewed rather than squared. Gehry, who favors such humble materials as plywood, corrugated zinc, stainless steel, and chainlink fence, assembles his buildings as a series of separate but interdependent units, each of which may serve a distinct function. He has replaced the classical principles of symmetry and stability with an architecture of undulating contours and oscillating rooflines inspired by *fractals*, that is, lines or surfaces formed by an infinite number of similarly irregular sections. Gehry's Weisman Museum in Minneapolis, Minnesota, for instance, consists of curved and flaring stainless steel facets that shimmer like mercury (Figure **37.33**). Such architecture, which consciously embraces recent cosmological hypotheses in Complexity Theory and Chaos Theory, may be thought of as "cosmogenic." Gehry's debt to postmodern science does not mean that his architecture is devoid of humanist values; as Gehry himself insists, "Just being an architect is an act of social responsibility."

Figure 37.32 I. M. Pei & Associates, Louvre Pyramid, Paris, 1988. Photo: © R.M.N., Paris.

Figure 37.33 Frank Gehry, Weisman Museum, Minneapolis, Minnesota, completed 1993. North and west sides clad in panels of brushed stainless steel, east side clad in terra-cotta colored brick, south side brick with dyed mortar; museum 47,300 sq. ft. with approx. 11,000 sq. ft. of exhibition space. Photo: Warren Bruland.

Music in the Information Age

As with the visual arts and architecture, music since 1960 has been boldly experimental, stylistically diverse, and (with the exception of popular music) largely impersonal. Some late twentieth-century composers have imitated the random style of John Cage (see chapter 35), while others have moved in the opposite direction, writing highly structured music that extends Schoenberg's serial techniques to pitch, counterpoint, and other aspects of composition. In a field that has been dominated by men for centuries, women composers and conductors have become increasingly visible—witness the Pulitzer Prize-winning American composer Ellen Taaffe Zwilich (b. 1938). Jazz, a style that habitually "quotes" and parodies other music, may best represent the postmodern sensibility, but contemporary opera has also experimented with postmodern techniques. In general, hard-and-fast lines between art music and popular music are beginning to blur, as each adapts to the availability of world-musical forms and electronic manipulation.

The music of the late twentieth century is distinctly multicultural. Employing Western genres such as the string quartet, the versatile Japanese composer Toru Takemitsu (1930–1996) interwove silence and sound to approximate the effects of *haiku* poetry. His almost one hundred film scores reflect a synthesis of Eastern and Western instruments, forms, and techniques. In the West, many composers have rejected the European emphasis on harmony and form in favor of experimentation with the rhythms, textures, and inflections of African and Caribbean music. They have revived ancient and non-Western traditions of oral and instrumental improvisation, thereby breaking with the European dependence on the score instead of the ears.

In the last decades of the twentieth century, Western composers have been particularly responsive to the influence of Chinese, Japanese, and Cambodian musical practices. Some have abandoned the Western harmonic system of dividing the octave into twelve equal parts in favor of **microtonality**—the use of musical intervals smaller than the semitones of traditional European and American music. In the microtonal works of the Hungarian-born composer György Ligeti (b. 1923), melody gives way to dense clusters of sound—subtle, shimmering currents that murmur in a continuous, hypnotic flow. Ligeti's choral *Lux Eterna* and his instrumental piece entitled *Atmospheres*,♮ both of which are featured on the soundtrack of the film *2001*, achieve a new sonority that, as the composer explains, "is so dense that the individual interwoven instrumental voices are absorbed into the general texture and completely lose their individuality." While Ligeti's pieces are composed for traditional instruments, the microtonal works of other composers may depend on electronic apparatus that is capable of producing an infinite number of microtones.

Electronic technology has shaped the sound of both popular music and music written for the concert hall. Indeed, electronics has affected all aspects of music, from its composition to its performance and distribution. Just as television has democratized the reception of visual images, so long-playing records, tapes, and digital recordings have brought the history of sound into every living room. At the same time, the cheap and ready availability of electronically reproduced music has worked to virtually eliminate the patronage system that governed musical composition in former eras. More recently, electronic synthesizers, which make possible the simultaneous fusion of composition, performance, and recording, are facilitating new forms of musical production.

Electronic Music

Quite apart from the electronic technology used to record musical performance, there exists the phenomenon of electronic music. Unique to the twentieth century, electronic music is not a style in itself; rather, it is a medium for creating new types of sound. While traditional instruments produce only seventy to eighty pitches and a limited range of dynamic intensities, electronic devices offer a range of frequencies from fifty to fifteen thousand cycles per second. This capacity provides the potential for almost unlimited variability of pitch. Further, electronic instruments can execute rhythms at speeds and in complex patterns that are beyond the capability of live performers. Because such features defy traditional notation, electronic music is often graphed in acoustical diagrams that serve as "scores."

Much like digital imaging (see "Cyberart," p. 157), electronic music may be created in two main ways: either by the electronic modification of pre-existing sound or by the purely electronic generation of sound. In the first method, electronic equipment is used to modify a wide variety of natural, instrumental, and mechanically contrived sounds, either while or after they are performed. In the late 1950s, John Cage and other avant-garde composers began to employ magnetic tape to record and manipulate sound. By means of such techniques as splicing and reversing the taped sounds of various kinds of environmental noise—thunder, human voices, bird calls, train whistles, and ticking clocks—they produced a kind of music known as *musique concrète* (concrete music).

♮See Music Listening Selections at end of chapter.

The second method of creating electronic music involves the use of special equipment to generate sound itself. "Pure" electronic music differs from *musique concrète* in its reliance on oscillators, wave generators, and other electronic devices. The pioneer in this type of music was the German composer Karlheinz Stockhausen (b. 1928). As musical director of the Studio for Electronic Music in Cologne, Germany, Stockhausen employed electronic devices both by themselves and to manipulate and combine pretaped sounds, including music generated by traditional instruments and voices. Stockhausen's compositions—atonal patterns of sounds and silence that lack any controlling frame of reference—renounce all traditional rules of rhythm and harmony. Editing taped sounds as a filmmaker edits footage, Stockhausen may dispense with a written score and compose directly on tape, thus assuming simultaneously the roles of composer and performer. Like a Kaprow "happening," a Christo environmental sculpture, or a jazz improvisation, a Stockhausen composition is an artform in which process becomes identical with product.

The most revolutionary musical invention of the late 1960s was the computerized **synthesizer**, an integrated system of electronic components designed for both the production and manipulation of sound. Stockhausen's American contemporary Milton Babbitt (b. 1916) was the first composer to use the RCA Synthesizer to control the texture, timbre, and intensity of electronic sound.[♭] Since the 1970s, more sophisticated and portable digital synthesizers have been attached to individual instruments. The digital synthesizer allows the musician to manipulate the pitch, duration, and dynamics of sound even as the music is being performed. While some musical instruments have been computerized, computers themselves have become "musical instruments." Equipped with a miniature keyboard, faders, and foot pedals, the contemporary computer is not only capable of producing a full range of sounds but is also able to produce and reproduce sounds more subtle and complex than any emitted by human voices or traditional musical instruments. For better or for worse, such devices have now begun to replace musicians in the studio and in staged musical performances. Among some artists, synthesizers have become an indispensable aid to composition: The American composer Barton McLean (b. 1938), for instance, composes music with a Lightpen that draws the contours of sound waves on the video screen of a sophisticated computer. His short piece *Etunytude*[♭] is the product of such a procedure.

Minimal Music and Dance

Minimal music, like minimal art, reduces the vocabulary of expression to elemental or primary components. In the "stripped down" compositions of American minimalists such as Philip Glass, Steve Reich, and John Adams, melodic fragments are repeated in subtly shifting patterns. In the instrumental and choral works of the Polish composer Henryk Gorecki (b. 1933) and the so-called "mystical minimalists" of Eastern Europe, these fragments look back to folk songs and chantlike hymns. Minimal music is simple in tonality and melody, but it is often complex and innovative in its rhythms and textures.

Philip Glass (b. 1937) received his early training in the fundamentals of Western musical composition. In the 1970s, however, after touring Asia and studying with the Indian sitar master Ravi Shankar (b. 1920), Glass began writing music that embraced the rhythmic structures of Indian *ragas*, progressive jazz, and rock and roll. The musical drama *Einstein on the Beach*[♭] (1976), which Glass produced in collaboration with the designer/director Robert Wilson (b. 1941), was the first opera performed at the Metropolitan Opera House in New York City to feature electronically amplified instruments. Like traditional opera, *Einstein on the Beach* combines instrumental and vocal music, as well as recitation, mime, and dance. But it departs radically from operatic tradition in its lack of a narrative story line and character development, as well as in its instrumentation. The opera, which is performed with no intermissions over a period of four-and-a-half hours, is not the story of Albert Einstein's life or work but, rather, an extended poetic statement honoring the twentieth century's greatest scientist. The music for the piece consists of novel yet simple melodic lines that are layered and repeated in seemingly endless permutations. Mesmerizing and seductive, Glass' music recalls the texture of Gregorian chant, the "stuck-record" sound of electronic tape loops, and the subtle rhythms of the Indian *raga*. Harmonic changes occur so slowly that one must, as Glass explains, learn to listen at "a different speed," a feat that closely resembles an act of meditation.

The choreography for *Einstein on the Beach*, written and danced in the original performance by Lucinda Childs (b. 1940), complements the hypnotic quality of the music. It consists of ritualized gestures and robotlike movements that are repeated serially. Childs' choreography takes the dance style of Merce Cunningham to its logical conclusion: It obeys Cunningham's credo of pure movement by reducing body motions to patterns that

---

[♭]See Music Listening Selections at end of chapter.

[♭]See Music Listening Selections at end of chapter.

are geometric, recurrent, and—for some critics—unspeakably boring.

Historical themes continue to inspire the music of Glass. In 1980, he composed the opera *Satyagraha*, which celebrates the achievements of India's pacifist hero Mohandas Gandhi (see chapter 36). Sung in Sanskrit and English, the opera uses a text drawn from the *Bhagavad-Gita*, the sacred book of the Hindu religion. For the quincentennial commemoration of the Columbian voyage to the Americas, the composer wrote an imaginative modern-day analogue (*The Voyage*, 1992) that links the idea of great exploration to the theme of interplanetary travel.

Postmodern Opera

One would think that the electronic media might have displaced opera as the form of expression that, for centuries, had most successfully integrated all of the arts. However, at the close of the twentieth century, opera not only continues to flourish, but is renewed by current events such as international hijacking (John Adams' *Death of Klinghofer*), black nationalism (Anthony Davis' *X*), gay rights (Stewart Wallace's *Harvey Milk*), and culture icons—witness Ezra Laderman's *Marilyn* (Monroe), John Adams' *Nixon*, and Robert Xavier Rodriguez's *Frida* (Kahlo). Few of these operas offer memorable music and even fewer attain the compositional sophistication of the century's first typically postmodern opera: John Corigliano's *The Ghosts of Versailles* (1992). Scored for orchestra and synthesizer and cast in the style of a comic opera, *Ghosts of Versailles* takes place in three different (and interlayered) worlds: the eighteenth-century court of Versailles, the scenario of a Mozartean opera, and the realm of the afterlife—a place peopled by the ghosts of Marie Antoinette and her court. Corigliano, whose *AIDS Symphony* was discussed in chapter 36, mixes traditional and contemporary musical styles, alternating modern dissonance and pseudo-Mozartean lyricism in a bold and inventive (although often astonishingly disjunctive) manner. In the spirit of postmodernism, Corigliano makes historical style itself the subject; he creates a multivalent allegory and tests his text against past texts by having one of his characters in the opera suddenly exclaim, "This is not opera; Wagner is opera."

Rock Music

The musical style called *rock* has dominated popular culture since the mid-1950s. The words "rocking" and "rolling," originally used to describe sexual activity, came to identify an uninhibited musical style that drew on a broad combination of popular American and African-American music, including country, swing, gospel, and rhythm and blues. Although no one musician is responsible for the birth of rock, the style gained popularity with such performers as Bill Haley, Little Richard, and Elvis Presley. In the hands of these musicians, rock came to be characterized by a high dynamic level of sound, fast and hard rhythms, a strong beat, and earthy, colloquial lyrics.

From its inception, rock music has been an expression of a youth culture: The rock sound, associated with dancing, sexual freedom, and rebellion against restrictive parental and cultural norms, also mirrored the new consumerism of the postwar era. While 1950s rock and roll often featured superficial, "bubble-gum" lyrics, 1960s rock became more sophisticated—the aural counterpart of Western-style pop art. With the success of the Beatles, a British group of the 1960s, rock also became (like pop art) an international phenomenon, uniting young people across the globe. The Beatles absorbed the music of Little Richard and the rhythms and instrumentation of Indian classical music. They made imaginative use of electronic effects, such as feedback and splicing. Their compositions, which reflected the spirit of the Western counterculture, reached a creative peak in the album *Sergeant Pepper's Lonely Hearts Club Band* (1967). Although the electric guitar was in use well before the Beatles, it was with this group that the instrument became the hallmark of rock music, and it has remained the principal instrument of the rock musician.

During the 1960s, "establishment" America faced the protests of a youthful counterculture that was disenchanted with middle-class values, mindless consumerism, and bureaucratic authority. Counterculture "hippies"—the word derives from "hipster," an admirer of jazz and its subculture—exalted a neoromantic lifestyle that called for peaceful coexistence, a return to natural and communal habitation, more relaxed sexual standards, and experimentation with mind-altering drugs such as marijuana and lysergic acid diethylamide (LSD). The use of psychedelic drugs among members of the counterculture became associated with the emergence of a number of British and West Coast acid rock (or hard rock) groups, such as The Who and The Jefferson Airplane. The music of these groups often featured ear-splitting, electronically amplified sound and sexually provocative lyrics. The decade produced a few superb virtuoso performers, like the guitarist Jimi Hendrix (1942–1970). The 1960s also spawned the folk rock hero Bob Dylan (b. 1941), whose songs gave voice to the anger and despair of the American counterculture. Dylan's lyrics, filled with scathing references to modern materialism, hypocrisy, greed, and warfare—specifically, the American involvement in Vietnam—attacked the moral detachment of contemporary authority figures.

Music and the Global Paradigm

The music of the 1990s, in its multicultural character, anticipates the extension of cultural interdependence in the global village. The rhythms of the African griot (storyteller) resound in rap music; snippets of Arabic chant and Indian *ragas* embellish jazz compositions; and Cuban brass punctuates rock sounds. While some critics lament that the Western music world has bifurcated irresolvably into two cultures—art music and popular music—the fact is that art and popular music are becoming more alike or, more exactly, that they share various aspects of the world's musical menu. Evidence of this phenomenon lies in the concert jazz compositions of Wynton Marsalis (*Citi Movement,* 1991) and Marcus Roberts (*Portraits in Blue,* 1995). In what Roberts calls "semi-classical form" and with full orchestra, the jazz pianist assembles a "personal listening mix" that includes Beethoven, John Coltrane, Chopin, Little Richard, Billie Holliday, and George Gershwin. Other musicians create a musical pastiche in instrumentation, achieving unique textures from combinations of electronic gadgetry, ancient musical devices such as the *balafon* (an African version of the xylophone), and traditional Western instruments.

The democratic character of contemporary music is also evident in its protest or issue-driven lyrics, often chanted in multiple languages. The Jamaican musician Bob Marley (1945–1981) brought to the international scene the lyrics of a socially conscious popular culture and the music known as *reggae*—an eclectic style that draws on a wide variety of black Jamaican musical forms, including African religious music and Christian revival songs. The following lines from Marley's "Them Belly Full" offer some idea of how he used reggae as a vehicle of complaint:

> Them belly full but we hungry.
> A hungry mob is an angry mob.
> A rain a-fall but the dirt it tough;
> A pot a-cook but the food no 'nough.
> We're gonna chuck to Jah music, chuckin'
> We're chuckin' to Jah music, we're chuckin'.

SUMMARY

On the threshold of the twenty-first century, the arts have become multicultural, globally oriented, and deeply responsive to contemporary uncertainties. In literature, as in all of the arts, there has been a turn from the anxious subjectivity, the idealism, and the high seriousness of modernism toward skepticism, parody, and dispassionate play. Postmodern poets explore the self-referential function of language and its role in shaping human understanding. The magic realism of Isabel Allende and the social conscience fiction of Achebe and Oates explore the contradictory and violent aspects of contemporary life. Social conscience writers manifest concern for the ecological future of this planet; while writers of science fiction weave the futuristic mythology of outer space.

As with literature, the visual arts of the information age do not assume any single, unifying style. Rather, they are pluralistic, rapidly changing, and deeply indebted to the materials and processes of high technology. For pop artists, the art object is a kind of information that parodies contemporary values in a commodity-driven society. Minimal art, kinetic art, the permutations of cyberart, and multimedia performance call attention to the impersonal world of high technology, even as they embrace new electronic methods of processing information. Photorealists, camp artists, new expressionists, and other postmodernists artificially process images they have borrowed from the historical dustbin. In architecture, the international style has given way to postmodern pastiche and playfulness, the zany, piecemeal designs of the deconstructivists, and the fractal inventions of the futurists.

Electronic technology has had a massive effect on all phases of contemporary culture, including the composition, performance, and dissemination of music. Electronically generated music constitutes an entirely new sound experience. At the same time, contemporary music reflects the global paradigm, as composers deviate from traditional European modes of harmony and meter to explore microtonality, improvisation, and various non-Western techniques and instruments. The minimal operas of Philip Glass feature hypnotic aural and visual effects inspired by Eastern forms of meditation. Contemporary issues mingle with historical motifs in postmodern opera. As the line between art and popular music continues to blur, concert jazz commands sophisticated audiences. Like the new jazz, rock music and its distinctive substyles have become increasingly multicultural, while retaining their improvisational vigor.

EPILOGUE

On the Threshold of the Millennium

The arts of the information age eagerly embrace the twin realities of globalism and multiculturalism. As all facets of culture from blue jeans to blues become more readily accessible to all parts of planet earth, culture itself grows ever more homogeneous. While Western democracy and Western products are absorbed and imitated in the East, the Asian notion that mind and body are inseparable forms of information and energy are shaping Western thought. On the threshold of the twenty-first century, as the planet remains threatened by ecological and nuclear disaster, a holistic view of nature and a respect for the universality of the human condition seem ever more essential to ensuring the salvation of humankind. The arts of our time remind us that beneath the cool dispassion of an information age society, there lies a troubled awareness of the human responsibility for safeguarding the earth, ourselves, and the humanistic tradition. To be sure, the violence and the fragility of contemporary life offer sobering arguments for efforts toward preserving the humanistic tradition, which, despite recent evidence of the possibility of life on other planets, still belongs to the population of the earth alone.

Any epilogue for a book that looks back on the twentieth century must also be a prologue. If one were to use a broad "futuristic" brush to paint the outlines of the next century, what might the contours contain? Consider the following random *possibilities* for the year 2010 (and then add your own speculations):

- Interactive forms of artistic expression feature telepathic forms of virtual reality (in which, for instance, electrodes attached to parts of the body produce computer images).
- An information superhighway, utilizing television, telephone, and computer, makes accessible a vast resource of multimedia data.
- The electronic arts, especially video and computer graphics, become the leading artforms.
- Intuitive, perceptual, and auditory modes of human experience overtake the logical.
- Options for genetic engineering and the cloning of humans generate international moral debate.
- The confirmation of life in outer space is the revolutionary turning point for a new age.
- Russia and America establish stations in outer space.
- The information explosion passes the critical mass, producing cultural fatigue and a return to traditional religious and ethnic values.

GLOSSARY

ecologist one who studies the interrelationships between organisms and their environments

geodesic a type of space-frame employing light straight-sided polygons in tension

microtonality the use of musical intervals smaller than the semitones of traditional European and American music

musique concrète (French, "concrete music") a kind of music based on real or "concrete" sounds, such as street noises, human voices, bird calls, and thunder, that are recorded, altered, and assembled on magnetic tape

silkscreen a printmaking technique employing the use of a stenciled image cut and attached to finely meshed silk, through which printing ink is forced so as to transfer the image to paper or cloth; also called "seriography"

synthesizer an integrated system of electronic components designed for the production and control of sound; it may be used in combination with a computer and with most musical instruments

virtual reality the computer-generated simulation of three-dimensional imagery with which the viewer may interact (by means of special electronic equipment) in a seemingly physical way

MUSIC LISTENING SELECTIONS

Cassette II Selection 22 Ligeti, *Atmospheres*, 1961, excerpt.
Cassette II Selection 23 Babbitt, *Ensembles for Synthesizer*, 1951, excerpt.
Cassette II Selection 24 McLean, *Etunytude*, 1982.
Cassette II Selection 25 Glass, *Einstein on the Beach*, "Knee 1," 1977.

SUGGESTIONS FOR READING

Carr, C. *On Edge: Performance at the End of the Twentieth Century*. Hanover, N.H.: Wesleyan University Press, 1993.
Danto, Arthur C. *After the End of Art: Contemporary Art and the Pale of History*. Princeton, N.J.: Princeton University Press, 1997.
Foster, Hall. *The Return of the Real: The Avant-Garde at the End of the Century*. Cambridge, Mass.: MIT Press, 1996.
Felshin, Nina, ed. *But Is It Art? The Spirit of Art as Activism*. Seattle: Bay Press, 1994.
Fineberg, John. *Strategies of Being: Art Since 1945*. Englewood Cliffs, N.J.: Prentice-Hall, 1995.
Gablik, Suzi. *The Reenchantment of Art*. London: Thames and Hudson, 1991.
Glass, Philip, and R. T. Jones. *Music by Philip Glass*. New York: Harper, 1987.
Hassan, Ihab. *The Postmodern Turn: Essays in Postmodern Theory and Culture*. Columbus, Ohio: Ohio State University Press, 1987.
Henri, Adrian. *Total Art: Environments, Happenings, and Performance*. New York: Oxford University Press, 1974.
Jencks, Charles. *The Architecture of the Jumping Universe*. London: Academy Editions, 1995.
Lovejoy, Margot. *Postmodern Currents: Art and Artists in the Age of Electronic Media*. Ann Arbor, Mich.: UMI Press, 1989.
Loveless, Richard L., ed. *The Computer Revolution and the Arts*. Tampa, Fla.: South Florida Press, 1989.
Lucie-Smith, Edward. *Late Modern: The Visual Arts Since 1945*. New York: Praeger, 1976.
Norman, Philip. *Shout: The Beatles in Their Generation*. New York: Simon and Schuster, 1981.
Shapiro, Gary, ed. *After the Future: Postmodern Times and Places*. Albany, N.Y.: State University of New York Press, 1990.
Tomkins, Calvin. *Post to Neo: The Art World of the 1980s*. New York: Holt, 1988.

Selected
General Bibliography

Anderson, Bonnie S., and Judith P. Zinsser. *A History of Their Own. Women in Europe from Prehistory to the Present*. Vol. 2. New York: Harper, 1988.

Arnason, H. H. *History of Modern Art: Painting, Sculpture, Architecture, Photography*, 3rd ed. Englewood Cliffs, N.J.: Prentice-Hall, 1986.

Ashton, Dore. *Twentieth-Century Artists on Art*. New York: Pantheon, 1985.

Beaver, Frank E. *On Film: A History of the Motion Picture*. New York: McGraw-Hill, 1983.

Bridenthal, Renate, and Claudia Koonz, eds. *Becoming Visible: Women in European History*. Boston: Houghton Mifflin, 1977.

Brown, Calvin S. *Music and Literature: A Comparison of the Arts*. Hanover, N.H.: University Press of New England, 1987.

Bullock, Alan, and Stephen Trombley. *The Harper Dictionary of Modern Thought*. New York: Harper, 1988.

——, and R. B. Woodbridge, eds. *Modern Culture: A Biographical Companion*. New York: Harper, 1984.

Canaday, John. *Mainstreams of Modern Art*, 2nd ed. New York: Holt, Rinehart and Winston, 1981.

Chadwick, Whitney. *Women, Art and Society*. New York: Norton, 1991.

Chang, H. C. *Chinese Literature: Popular Fiction and Drama*. New York: Columbia University Press, 1973.

Clarke, Mary, and Clement Crisp. *The History of Dance*. New York: Crown, 1981.

Copland, Aaron. *What to Listen For in Music*, rev. ed. New York: New American Library, 1963.

Danto, Arthur C. *Beyond the Brillo Box: The Visual Arts in Post-Historical Perspective*. New York: Farrar, Strauss, and Giroux, 1992.

Dunning, William V. *The Roots of Postmodernism*. Englewood Cliffs, N.J.: Prentice-Hall, 1995.

Esposito, John L. *Islam: The Straight Path*. New York: Oxford University Press, 1988.

Fitzgerald, C. P. *The Horizon History of China*. New York: American Heritage, 1969.

Fleming, William. *Concerts of the Arts: Their Interplay and Modes of Relationship*. Gainesville, Fla.: University of West Florida Press, 1990.

——. *Musical Arts and Styles*. Gainesville, Fla.: University of West Florida Press, 1990.

Golding, John. *Visions of the Modern*. Berkeley, Calif.: University of California Press, 1994.

Harbison, O. B. *Disappearing Through the Skylight: Technology in the Twentieth Century*. New York: Penguin, 1989.

Harman, Carter. *A Popular History of Music*, rev. ed. New York: Dell, 1973.

Henderson, Harry. *A History of African-American Artists: From 1792 to the Present*. New York: Pantheon, 1996.

Honour, Hugh. *The Image of the Black in Western Art*. Vol. 4, *From the American Revolution to World War I*: Part 1, "Slaves and Liberators"; Part 2, "Black Models and White Myths." Cambridge, Mass.: Harvard University Press, 1989.

Kaufmann, Walter. *Discovering the Mind*. 3 vols. New York: McGraw-Hill, 1980.

Kostoff, Spiro. *A History of Architecture: Settings and Rituals*. New York: Oxford University Press, 1985.

Lees, Gene. *Cats of any Color: Jazz Black and White*. New York: Oxford University Press, 1996.

Levin, David M., ed. *Modernity and the Hegemony of Vision*. Berkeley, Calif.: University of California Press, 1993.

Lippard, Lucy R., ed. *The Pink Glass Swan: Selected Feminist Essays on Art*. New York: The New Press, 1995.

Maybury-Lewis, David. *Millennium: Tribal Wisdom and the Modern World*. New York: Viking, 1992.

McLuhan, Marshall. *Understanding Media: The Extensions of Man*. New York: McGraw-Hill, 1965.

——, and Quentin Fiore. *War and Peace in the Global Village*. New York: Bantam, 1968.

Nelson, Lynn H., and Patrick Peebles, eds. *Classics of Eastern Thought*. San Diego: Harcourt, 1991.

Newhall, Beaumont. *The History of Photography: From 1839 to the Present*, rev. ed. New York: Museum of Modern Art, 1982.

Orrey, Leslie. *Opera: A Concise History*. London: Thames and Hudson, 1968.

Richards, J. M. *An Introduction to Modern Architecture*. Baltimore, Md.: Penguin, 1962.

Sadie, Stanley, ed. *The New Grove Dictionary of Music and Musicians*. New York: Macmillan, 1980.

Shlain, Leonard. *Art and Physics: Parallel Visions in Space, Time, and Light*. New York: William Morrow, 1991.

Solomon, Robert C., and Kathleen M. Higgens, eds. *From Africa to Zen: An Invitation to World Philosophy*. Boston: Rowman and Littlefield, 1993.

Sorrell, Walter. *The Dance Through the Ages*. New York: Grosset and Dunlap, 1967.

Spence, Jonathan D. *The Search for Modern China*. New York: Norton, 1990.

Sullivan, Michael. *Art and Artists of the Twentieth Century*. Berkeley, Calif.: University of California Press, 1996.

Sypher, Wylie. *Rococo to Cubism in Art and Literature*. New York: Random House, 1960.

Taylor, Charles. *The Ethics of Authenticity*. Cambridge, Mass.: Harvard University Press, 1992.

Walker, John A. *Glossary of Art, Architecture and Design Since 1945*. Riverside, N.J.: G. K. Hall, 1992.

Weiss, Piero, and Richard Taruskin. *Music in the Western World. A History in Documents*. New York: Schirmer, 1984.

Wiener, Philip P., ed. *Dictionary of the History of Ideas*. New York: Scribners, 1973.

BOOKS IN SERIES

Great Ages of Man. A History of the World's Cultures. New York: Time, 1965–1969.

Library of Art Series. New York: Time-Life Books, 1967.

Heritage of Music. 4 vols. New York: Oxford University Press, 1989.

This Fabulous Century: Sixty Years of American Life. 8 vols. New York: Time-Life Books, 1969–1970.

Time-Frame. 25 vols. (projected). New York: Time-Life Books, 1990–.

Credits

The author and publishers wish to thank the following for permission to use copyright material. Every effort has been made to trace the copyright holders but if any have been inadvertently overlooked the publishers will be pleased to make the necessary arrangement at the first opportunity.

Reading 6.1 (p. 5) Ezra Pound, "In a Station of the Metro" and "The Bathtub" from *Personae*. Copyright © 1926 by Ezra Pound, by permission of New Directions Publishing Corporation

Reading 6.3 (p. 28) Excerpts from Sigmund Freud, *Civilization and Its Discontents*, trs. James Strachey. Translation copyright © 1961 by James Strachey, renewed 1989 by Alix Strachey, by permission of W. W. Norton & Company, Inc., and Random House UK Ltd. on behalf of Sigmund Freud Copyrights, The Institute of Psycho-Analysis and The Hogarth Press

Reading 6.4 (p. 31) Excerpts from Marcel Proust, "Swann's Way" from *Remembrance of Things Past*, trs. C. K. Scott Moncrieff. Translation copyright © 1981 by Random House, Inc., and Chatto & Windus, by permission of Random House, Inc., and Random House UK Ltd. on behalf of the Estate of C. K. Scott Moncrieff and Chatto & Windus

Reading 6.6 (p. 36) E. E. Cummings, "she being Brand" from *Complete Poems: 1904–1962*, ed. George J. Firmage. Copyright © 1926, 1954, 1991 by the Trustees for the E. E. Cummings Trust, copyright © 1985 by George J. Firmage, by permission of Liveright Publishing Corporation

Reading 6.8 (p. 53) Excerpts from Erich Maria Remarque, *All Quiet on the Western Front*. Copyright © 1929, 1930 by Little, Brown and Company, renewed © 1957, 1958 by Erich Maria Remarque [as *Im Westen Nichts Neues*, copyright © 1928, renewed 1956 by Erich Maria Remarque], by permission of Pryor, Cashman, Sherman & Flynn on behalf of the Estate of Paulette Goddard Remarque

Reading 6.9 (p. 62) Randall Jarrell, "The Death of the Ball Turret Gunner" from *The Complete Poems*. Copyright © 1969 by Mrs. Randall Jarrell, by permission of Farrar, Straus & Giroux, Inc.; Kato Shuson, three *haikus*, from *Modern Japanese Literature*, ed. Donald Keene. Copyright © 1956 by Grove Press, Inc., by permission of Grove/Atlantic, Inc.

Reading 6.10 (p. 63) Excerpt from Elie Wiesel, *Night*, trs. Stella Rodway. Copyright © 1960 by MacGibbon & Kee, renewed © 1988 by The Collins Publishing Group, by permission of Hill and Wang, a division of Farrar, Straus & Giroux, Inc.

Reading 6.11 (p. 71) Excerpts from Jean-Paul Sartre, *Existentialism*, trs. Bernard Friedman. Copyright © Philosophical Library [as *L'Existentialisme est un humanisme*. Copyright © Editions Gallimard, Paris 1996], by permission of Philosophical Library and Editions Gallimard

Reading 6.12 (p. 74) Bernard Malamud, "A Summer's Reading" from *The Magic Barrel*. Copyright © 1958, renewed © 1986 by Bernard Malamud, by permission of Farrar, Straus & Giroux, Inc., and A. M. Heath & Company, Ltd., on behalf of the author

Reading 6.13 (p. 77) T. S. Eliot, "The Love Song of J. Alfred Prufrock" from *Collected Poems 1909–1962*, by permission of Faber & Faber Ltd.

Reading 6.14 (p. 79) Dylan Thomas, "Do Not Go Gentle Into That Good Night" from *The Poems of Dylan Thomas*. Copyright © 1952 by Dylan Thomas, by permission of New Directions Publishing Corporation and David Higham Associates on behalf of the Estate of the author

Reading 6.15 (p. 80) Excerpt from Rabindranath Tagore, "The Man Had No Useful Work" from *The Fugitive and Other Poems*. Copyright © 1921 by Macmillan Publishing Company, renewed 1949 by Rabindranath Tagore, by permission of Simon & Schuster and Macmillan General Books

Reading 6.16 (p. 81) Excerpts from Iqbal, "Revolution" and "Europe and Syria" from *Poems from Iqbal*, trs. V. Kiernan, by permission of John Murray (Publishers) Ltd.; Chairil Anwar, "At the Mosque" from *The Voice of the Night: Complete Poetry and Prose of Chairil Anwar*, trs. Burton Raffel, by permission of Ohio University Press/Swallow Press, Athens

Reading 6.17 (p. 81) Excerpt from Samuel Beckett, *Waiting for Godot*. Copyright © 1954 by Grove Press, renewed © 1982 by Samuel Beckett, by permission of Grove/Atlantic, Inc.

Reading 6.18 (p. 100) Pablo Neruda, "United Fruit Co." from *Five Decades: Poems 1925–1970*, trs. Ben Belitt. Translation copyright © 1961, 1969, 1972, 1974 by Ben Belitt, by permission of Grove/Atlantic, Inc.

Reading 6.19 (p. 101) Langston Hughes, "Theme for English B" and "Dream Deferred" ("Harlem") from *Collected Poems*. Copyright © 1994 by the Estate of Langston Hughes, by permission of Alfred A. Knopf, Inc.; Gwendolyn Brooks, "The Mother" and "We Real Cool" from *Blacks*, Third World Press, Chicago. Copyright © 1991 by Gwendolyn Brooks, by permission of the author

Reading 6.20 (p. 103) Richard Wright, "The Ethics of Living Jim Crow" from *Uncle Tom's Children*. Copyright © 1937 by Richard Wright, renewed 1965 by Ellen Wright, by permission of HarperCollins Publishers, Inc.

Reading 6.21 (p. 105) Martin Luther King, Jr., "Letter from Birmingham Jail" from *Why We Can't Wait*. Copyright © 1963 by Martin Luther King, Jr., renewed 1991 by Coretta Scott King, by permission of Writers House, Inc., on behalf of The Heirs to the Estate of Martin Luther King, Jr.

Reading 6.22 (p. 107) Excerpts from Malcolm X, *Malcolm X Speaks*. Copyright © 1965, 1989 by Betty Shabazz and Pathfinder Press, by permission of Pathfinder Press

Reading 6.23 (p. 108) Ralph Ellison, "Prologue" from *Invisible Man*. Copyright © 1952 by Ralph Ellison, by permission of Random House, Inc.

Reading 6.24 (p. 109) Alice Walker, "Elethia" from *You Can't Keep a Good Woman Down*. Copyright © 1979 by Alice Walker, by permission of Harcourt Brace & Company

Reading 6.25 (p. 115) Excerpts from Virginia Woolf, *A Room of One's Own*. Copyright © 1929 by Harcourt Brace & Company, renewed 1957 by Leonard Woolf, by permission of Harcourt Brace & Company and The Society of Authors as the literary representative of the Estate of Virginia Woolf

Reading 6.26 (p. 116) Excerpt from Simone de Beauvoir, *The Second Sex*, trs. H. M. Parshley. Copyright © 1952, renewed 1980 by Alfred A. Knopf, Inc., by permission of Alfred A. Knopf, Inc.

Reading 6.27 (p. 118) Anne Sexton, "Self in 1958" from *Live or Die*. Copyright © 1966 by Anne Sexton, by permission of Houghton Mifflin Co.; Sonia Sanchez, "Woman" from *A Blues Book for Blue Black Magical Women*, 1978, by permission of the author; Adrienne Rich, "Translations" from *Diving Into the Wreck: Poems 1971–1972*. Copyright © 1973 by W. W. Norton & Company, Inc., by permission of the author and W. W. Norton & Company, Inc.

Reading 6.28 (p. 129) Excerpts from Octavio Paz, *A Tree Within*, trs. Eliot Weinberger. Copyright © 1984 by Octavio Paz and Eliot Weinberger, by permission of New Directions Publishing Corporation; Seamus Heaney, "Lightenings" from "Part II/Squarings" from *Seeing Things*. Copyright © 1991 by Seamus Heaney, by permission of Farrar, Straus & Giroux, Inc., and Faber & Faber Ltd.

Reading 6.29 (p. 130) Isabel Allende, "Two Words" from *The Stories of Eva Luna*, trs. Margaret Sayers Peden. Copyright © 1989 Isabel Allende, translation copyright © 1991 Macmillan Publishing Company, by permission of Scribner, a division of Simon & Schuster

Reading 6.30 (p. 133) Wislawa Szymborska, "The Terrorist, He Watches" from *People on a Bridge*, trs. Adam Czerniawski, 1996, by permission of Forest Books

Reading 6.31 (p. 135) Chinua Achebe, "Dead Men's Path" from *Girls at War and Other Stories*. Copyright © 1972, 1973 by Chinua Achebe, by permission of Doubleday, a division of Bantam Doubleday Dell Publishing Group, Inc.

Index